Krishna Bista, *Founding Editor*
Morgan State University, USA

Chris R. Glass, *Editor-In-Chief*
Boston College, USA

Vol. **12** No **4** Nov **2022**

JOURNAL OF INTERNATIONAL STUDENTS

A Quarterly Publication on International Education

Access this journal online at http://ojed.org/jis

All 2022 issues feature cover art from international artists who are part of the Public Art Collection curated by the Texas Tech University System. https://ttuspublicart.com/collection/

This journal is a STAR Scholars Network publication, Baltimore, Maryland.

Print ISSN 2162-3104

Online ISSN 2166-3750

Printed in the United States of America

Disclaimer

Journal of International Students

Special Issue | English
**Internationalization for an Uncertain Future:
Emerging Conversations in Critical Internationalization Studies** (2021)
Special Issue Co-Editors:
*Sharon Stein, University of British Columbia, Canada
Dale M. McCartney, University of the Fraser Valley, Canada*

Special Issue | English
Reflection and Reflective Thinking (2020)
Special Issue Co-Editors:
*Georgina Barton, University of Southern Queensland, Australia
Mary Ryan, Macquarie University, Australia*

Special Issue | *Bahasa Indonesia*
International Students and COVID-19 (2020)
Special Issue Co-Editors:
*Handoyo Puji Widodo, King Abdulaziz University, Saudi Arabia
Sandi Ferdiansyah, Institut Agama Islam Negeri, Indonesia and
Lara Fridani, Universitas Negeri Jakarta, Indonesia*

Special Issue | *Chinese*
International Students in China (2020)
Special Issue Co-Editors:
*Mei Tian and Genshu Lu
Xi'an Jiaotong University, China*

Special Issue | English
**Fostering Successful Integration and Engagement
Between Domestic and International Students** (2018)
Special Issue Co-Editors:
*CindyAnn Rose-Redwood and Reuben Rose-Redwood
University of Victoria, Canada*

Special Issue | English
**Role of Student Affairs in International Student
Transition and Success** (2017)
Special Issue Co-Editors:
*Christina W Yao, University of Nebraska-Lincoln, US
Chrystal A. George Mwangi, University of Massachusetts Amherst, US*

Special Issue | English
International Student Success (2016)
Special Issue Editor: *Rahul Choudaha, DrEducation, US*

Emerson is a campus without borders.

Academic Book Series

Call for Book Proposals

The STAR Scholars Book Series seeks to explore new ideas and best practices related to international student mobility, study abroad, exchange programs, student affairs from the US and around the world, and from a wide range of academic fields, including student affairs, international education, and cultural studies. STAR Scholars publishes some titles in collaboration with Routledge (Taylor & Francis), Springer, Palgrave Macmillan, Open Journals in Education (OJED), Journal of International Students, and other university presses. Scholars interested in contributing a book to our current and future book series are invited to submit a brief proposal directly via this _form_. All chapters will go through the standard review process before a decision is made. https://www.ojed.org/index.php/gsm/Series

Series Editors
Dr. Chris R. Glass & Dr. Krishna Bista

For questions and submission, email at Krishna.bista@morgan.edu

---

Recently Published Books

1. *Chinese Students and the Experience of International Doctoral Study in STEM*
2. *Developing Intercultural Competence in Higher Education*
3. *International Student Mobility to and from the Middle East*
4. *Inequalities in Study Abroad and Student Mobility*
5. *The Experiences of International Faculty in Institutions of Higher Education*
6. *International Students at US Community Colleges*
7. *Critical Perspectives on Equity and Social Mobility in Study Abroad*
8. *Online Teaching, Learning and Virtual Experiences in Global Higher Education*
9. *International Student Support and Engagement in Higher Education*
10. *Impact of COVID-19 on Global Student Mobility and Higher Education*
11. *Global Higher Education During COVID-19: Policy, Society, and Technology*
12. *COVID-19 and Higher Education in the Global Context*
13. *Reimagining Mobility in Higher Education*
14. *Cross-Cultural Narratives: Stories and Experiences of International Students*
15. *Reimagining Internationalization and International Initiatives at HBCUs*
16. *Delinking, Relinking, and Linking Writing and Rhetorics*
17. *Global Footprints in Higher Education*

Call for Essays

Everyone has a memorable story of studying or working outside the country of birth. What is your story about studying overseas? What are your cross-cultural experiences from exchange programs or study abroad? Are you a current or former international student? Tell your stories of exploring the words, the world, and the wonders.

Essay Categories

International Student Experience (long-term/degree seeking programs/experiences)
Study Abroad/Exchange Program Experience (short-term/program experience)
Faculty/Staff Experience (International faculty, study abroad mentors, Fulbright scholars)

Languages

You can write your story/essay in any of the following eight languages: Arabic, Chinese, English, French, German, Hindi, Russian, Spanish

Essay Writing Suggestions

Share a story: Focus on moments, encounters, and experiences that shaped your journey as an international student. Tell a story that no one else could tell. Your story can be about friendship, service, freedom, discrimination, injustice, activism, belonging, family, courage, resilience, citizenship, academics, spirituality, parenthood, discovery, inclusion, self-discovery, growth, etc.

Tell your challenges and lessons. Flavor your writing with idioms and figures of speech from your language. Paint the picture. Be concrete about what you have seen in your travels, academic encounters, woes, and wows!

Format Requirements

A story or essay of 1000-1,500 words; Typed in 12-pt size, Times Roman font; double-spaced; 1-inch margins on all sides; includes page numbers. We accept Microsoft Word files only.

More guidelines and sample essays:

https://starscholars.org/lanterns-across-the-sky/

ISSN: 2162-3104 Print/ ISSN: 2166-3750 Online
© *Journal of International Students*
http://ojed.org/jis

Editorial Team

Founder/Executive Editor
Krishna Bista, Morgan State University, USA

Editor-in-Chief
Chris R. Glass, Boston College, USA

Senior Editor
Stephanie K. Kim, Georgetown University, USA

Special Issues Editor
Nelson Brunsting, Wake Forest University

Digital Production Team
Senior Copy Editor*: Joy Bancroft, Emporia State University*
Digital Production Editor, Xi *Lin, East Carolina University*
Editorial Assistant (Digital Production): *Sonali Kathuria, Boston College*

Digital Storytelling Team
Editor, Global Connections, *Györgyi Mihályi, Kent State University*
Director, Social Media: *Sarah Schiffecker, Texas Tech University*
Producer, Global Scholar Stories, *Asuka Ichikawa, Boston College*
Producer, Critical Conversations in International Education, *Mary Ann Bodine Al-Sharif, University of Alabama at Birmingham*

EDITORIAL ADVISORY BOARD (2019-2022)

- Dr. Ly Tran, Associate Professor, *Deakin University, Australia*
- Dr. Lydia Andrade, Professor, *University of the Incarnate Word, USA*
- Dr. Stuart Tannock, Senior Lecturer, *University College London, UK*
- Dr. Lien Pham, *Lecturer, University of Technology Sydney, Australia*
- Dr. Janet Ilieva, Founder/Director, *Education Insight,* UK
- Dr. Yingyi Ma, Associate Professor, *Syracuse University, USA*
- Dr. Nicolai Netz, *German Center for Higher Education Research and Science Studies (DZHW), Germany*

Our editorial team is engaged with universities in 20 countries across the world including Australia, Bangladesh, Canada, China, Finland India, Korea, Laos, Mexico, the Netherlands, New Zealand, Portugal, Saudi Arabia, South Africa, Taiwan, Thailand, Turkey, United Kingdom, United States, and Vietnam.

☆ = 2021 *Distinguished Service Award*
★ = *2021 Editor's Choice Award*
◊ = *2021 Excellence in Peer Review Award*

Section Editors

Section Editor (Editorials): Ly Tran, Deakin University
Section Editor (Book Review): Lisa Unangst, Ohio University
Section Editor (Research-in-Context): Jenna Mittelmeier, The University of Manchester
Section Editor (Cross-Border Reflections): Natalie Cruz, Charleston Southern University

Associate Editors

Robert Coelen, University of Groningen (NL)
Kun Dai, Chinese University of Hong Kong (HK)
Carol Griffiths, Girne American University (TR)
Jasper Kun-Ting Hsieh, The University of New South Wales (AU)
Katie Koo, Texas A&M University – Commerce (US)
Masha Krsmanovic, The University of Southern Mississippi (US)
Shu-Wen Lan, National Pingtung Unviersity of Science and Technology (TW)
Charles Mathies, University of Jyväskylä (FI)
Pii-Tuulia Nikula, Eastern Institute of Technology (NZ)
Mohammad Nurunnabi, Prince Sultan University (SA)
Ateeb Ahmad Parray, BRAC James P. Grant School of Public Health (BD)
Thanh Pham, Monash University (AU)
Luísa Helena Ferreira Pinto Pinto, University of Porto (PT)
CindyAnn Rose-Redwood, University of Victoria (CA)
Laura Soulsby, Randolph-Macon College (US)
Melissa Whatley, North Carolina State University (US) ☆
Handoyo Puji Widodo, King Abdulaziz University (SA)
Cora Lingling Xu, Durham University (UK)

Recent Publications

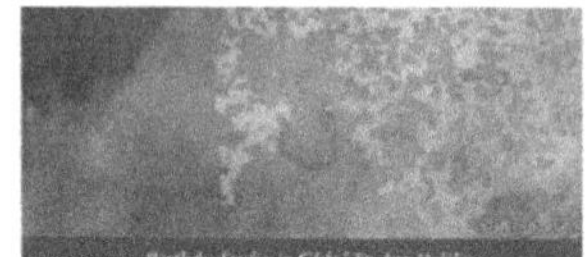

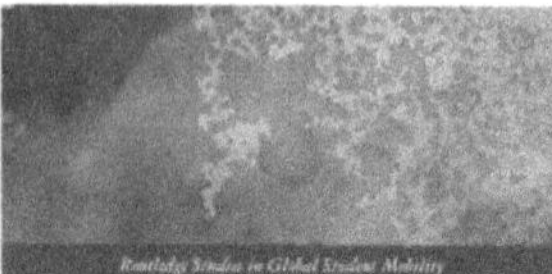

Open Journals in Education (OJED) publishes high quality peer reviewed, open access journals based at research universities. OJED uses the Open Journal System (OJS) platform, where readers can browse by subject, drill down to journal level to find the aims, scope, and editorial board for each individual title, as well as search back issues. OJED journals are required to be indexed in major academic databases to ensure quality and maximize article discoverability and citation. Journals follow best practices on publication ethics outlined in the COPE Code of Conduct. Explore our OJED Journals at www.ojed.org

***

A. Noam Chomsky Global Connections Awards celebrate the power of human connections. The awards recognize distinguished service to the global mission of the STAR Scholars Network. Several individuals with a deep impact on advancing global, social mobility are recognized every year.

For more information, visit https://starscholars.org/global-connections-award/

Indexing

ISSN: 2162-3104 Print/ ISSN: 2166-3750 Online
Journal of International Students
http://ojed.org/jis

SUBJECT: Education- Higher Education/ DEWEY #378

Directory of Open Access Journals, 2011-
EBSCOhost, Education Source, 03/01/2012-
Gale
- o   Academic OneFile, 09/01/2011-
- o   Contemporary Women's Issues, 09/01/2011-
- o   Educator's Reference Complete, 09/01/2011-
- o   Expanded Academic ASAP, 09/01/2011-
- o   InfoTrac Custom, 09/01/2011-

ProQuest
- o   Education Collection, 10/01/2011-
- o   Education Database, 10/01/2011-
- o   Education Database (Alumni Edition), 10/01/2011-
- o   ProQuest Central, 10/01/2011-
- o   ProQuest Central - UK Customers, 10/01/2011-
- o   ProQuest Central (Alumni Edition), 10/01/2011-
- o   ProQuest Central (Corporate), 10/01/2011-
- o   ProQuest Central (US Academic Subscription), 10/01/2011-
- o   ProQuest Central China, 10/01/2011-
- o   ProQuest Central Essentials, 10/01/2011-
- o   ProQuest Central Korea, 10/01/2011-
- o   ProQuest Central Student, 10/01/2011-
- o   ProQuest Research Library, 10/01/2011-
- o   ProQuest Research Library (Corporate), 10/01/2011-
- o   ProQuest Social Sciences Premium Collection, 10/01/2011-
- o   Research Library (Alumni Edition), 10/01/2011-
- o   Social Science Premium Collection, 10/01/2011-

Clarivate Analytics
- o   Web of Science
- o   Emering Sciences Citation Index
- o   Higher Education Abstracts

Source: Ulrichsweb Global Serials Directory

You may access the print and/or digital copies of the Journal of International Students from **686 libraries worldwide** (as of July, 2022).

The Journal of International Students (Print ISSN 2162-3104 & Online ISSN 2166-3750) is a member of the STAR Scholars Network Open Journals in Education (OJED), a OJS 3 platform for high-quality, peer-reviewed academic journals in education.

JIS is a Gold Open Access journal and indexed in major academic databases to maximize article discoverability and citation. JIS follows best practices on publication ethics outlined in the COPE Code of Conduct. Editors work to ensure timely decisions after initial submission, as well as prompt publication online if a manuscript is accepted for publication.

Upon publication articles are immediately and freely available to the public. The final version of articles can immediately be posted to an institutional repository or to the author's own website as long as the article includes a link back to the original article posted on OJED.

None of the OJED journals charge fees to individual authors thanks to the generous support of our institutional sponsors.

For further information

Editorial Office
Journal of International Students
URL: http://ojed.org/jis
E-mail: contact@jistudents.org

ISSN: 2162-3104 Print/ ISSN: 2166-3750 Online
2022 Volume 12, Number 4
© *Journal of International Students*
http://ojed.org/jis

CONTENTS

JOURNAL OF
INTERNATIONAL
STUDENTS
国际学生杂志 "来华留学生" 专刊
SPECIAL ISSUE ON INTERNATIONAL STUDENTS IN CHINA
2020 VOL. 10, NO. S1

JOURNAL OF
INTERNATIONAL
STUDENTS
2020 VOL. 10, NO. S3

JOURNAL OF
INTERNATIONAL
STUDENTS
2020 VOL. 10, NO. 4

JOURNAL OF
INTERNATIONAL
STUDENTS
Special Issue: Reflection and Reflexive Thinking
2020 VOL. 10, NO. S2
Access this journal online at ojed.org/jis

JOURNAL OF
INTERNATIONAL
STUDENTS
2021 VOL. 11, NO. 1
Access this journal online at ojed.org/jis

The *Journal of International Students* is a Gold Open Access publication thanks to the generous institutional sponsorship of Old Dominion University and publication partnership of Emerson College and American Council on Education.

© *Journal of International Students*
Volume 12, Issue 2 (2022), pp. 795-816
ISSN: 2162-3104 (Print), 2166-3750 (Online)
doi: 10.32674/jis.v12i2.3594
ojed.org/jis

OJED
OPEN JOURNALS IN EDUCATION

Engagement of International Students at Irish Higher Education Institutions

Merike Darmody
The Economic and Social Research Institute, Ireland

Sarah Groarke
The Ombudsman for Children's Office, Ireland

Georgiana Mihut
University of Warwick, United Kingdom

ABSTRACT

Existing research paints a mixed picture of how international students fare academically following a transition to a host higher education institution. Most studies that have examined differences between domestic and international students' engagement have treated international students as a homogenous group. Less evidence is available on the experiences of international students from different regional groups. Drawing on Irish Student Engagement Survey data, this article explores the extent to which international students' engagement differs from that of their Irish peers, and whether there are differences across regions of origin. The findings indicate that while international students are highly engaged compared with their Irish counterparts, regional differences persist when the data were disaggregated. The article is of potential interest to policymakers and higher education institutions, offering insights into how the provision of services and supports to international students could be better targeted.

Keywords: international students, regional differences, Republic of Ireland, student survey, student engagement

INTRODUCTION

Across developed countries the rapid growth in international student mobility has become an important feature of the higher education landscape, resulting in an increasingly ethnoculturally diverse student body. Students from Asia form the largest group of international students in Organisation for Economic Cooperation and Development (OECD) countries, followed by students from Europe and Africa (OECD, 2020). In order to accommodate cultural diversity while addressing the academic needs of both domestic and international students, higher education institutions (HEIs) have been urged to adopt teaching practices that consider the academic needs of different groups of students (Crose, 2011). International students are a highly motivated, engaged, and self-selected group (Cho et al., 2020), yet differences in learning approaches and classroom engagement exist between groups of students from different geographic areas (Vazirani et al., 2018). However, most existing studies on the engagement of international students focus on just one national or ethnic group or compare the engagement of domestic students with that of international students as a homogenous group (Fakunle et al., 2016; Irish Survey of Student Engagement [ISSE], 2019; Lee et al., 2013; Yu & Moskal, 2019). The few existing studies that have considered different countries or regions of origin have found differences between national groups across personal, emotional, and social adjustment aspects (Rienties & Tempelaar, 2013) and learning experiences (Ammigan et al., 2021).

In this context, the concept of student engagement, which broadly refers to meaningful student involvement with the learning environment, has acquired prominence as HEIs seek to provide learning experiences to all students that "lead to high quality learning" (Coates, 2006, p. 27). Teaching students from around the world at HEIs poses both didactical as well as pedagogical challenges stemming from differences between education systems that need to be addressed in order to provide students with an engaging learning environment (Faas, 2020). In this regard, better understanding how different groups of (international) students engage with the learning environment is warranted, as positive engagement has been found to contribute significantly to positive student experience and ultimately their academic success (Harper & Quaye, 2015; Wang & BrckaLorenz, 2018). The disaggregation of data on student engagement offers an important means for HEIs to identify challenges that particular groups of international students may face and to inform the development of targeted supports, thereby enhancing international students' engagement in host HEIs. In this way, international students can also be considered by host institutions as a resource to support all students;

support structures designed for these students can be used more broadly to enhance the experiences of all students (Mihut, 2019).

The engagement of international students in higher education is a relatively under researched area in Ireland (O'Connor, 2010), particularly regarding the engagement of international students from different regional groups. One exception is a study by Finn et al. (2021), which demonstrates differences in academic satisfaction among students from diverse regions of origin. Reflecting the student mobility trends across industrialized countries, the number of students traveling to Ireland for third-level education has significantly increased, with the United States of America, United Kingdom, China, India, Malaysia, Canada, and Saudi Arabia among the most common countries of origin (Higher Education Authority [HEA], 2020a). Considering financial challenges faced by many HEIs and global competition for students, Irish HEIs have sought to develop a better understanding about the engagement of international students to ensure that they can provide a high-quality learning experience to the increased number of international students arriving in Ireland.

Recognizing that international students cannot be treated as a homogenous group (Brooks & Waters, 2011), this article builds on existing studies on student engagement and satisfaction with HEIs (Clarke et al., 2018; Farrelly & Murphy, 2018; Finn et al., 2021) by examining differences in the engagement of international students in Ireland using the Irish Survey of Student Engagement (ISSE). The ISSE recommended that further research disaggregate international student data to pinpoint key differences and indicators most influenced by country of permanent address, a suggestion that is taken up by this article.

The study is guided by the following research questions: How do international students compare with their Irish counterparts across different domains of engagement? Does engagement of students differ by region of origin, after controlling for individual and institutional factors?

Conceptual Framework: Student Engagement

There is considerable variation in how "student engagement" is defined. The concept is generally used to describe meaningful student involvement with the learning environment involving several dimensions. Two main conceptual models have emerged: the North American model of engagement (Fredricks et al., 2004), which captures behavioral, emotional, and cognitive dimensions, and the European approach of engagement (Schaufeli et al., 2002), which includes absorption, vigor, and dedication. Both models are strongly associated with students' academic performance, their approach to learning, and disposition toward the learning environment in general (Alrashidi et al., 2016). Students' levels of engagement have been shown to shape their academic outcomes, student retention, satisfaction with their overall experience, and sense of belonging (Ashwin & McVitty, 2015; Harper & Quaye, 2015).

Student surveys have become one of the largest and most frequently used data sources for quality assessment in higher education, providing evidence-based information on institutional performance (Klemenčič & Chirikov, 2015; Williams, 2014). National surveys have been developed in countries including the United States, Australia, the United Kingdom, and Ireland to provide data that measure student engagement, enabling HEIs to benchmark nationally (Hagel et al., 2012; Tight, 2020) and respond to students' evolving needs and expectations (Leiber, 2020). These surveys include a range of student engagement indicators from student learning to the learning environment, highlighting the concept's multi-dimensional character. This has led to some criticism, as it remains unclear whether the engagement is attributable to the student, the institution, or the interaction between them (Wise et al., 2011). Nevertheless, engagement indicators may help understand how domestic and international students evaluate their learning experience in an HEI.

This article conceptualizes student engagement by drawing on a set of nine engagement measures set out in the ISSE. The ISSE defines student engagement as students' involvement in activities and environments that are likely to generate high-quality learning and views student engagement as reflecting two key elements: the time and effort students put into their studies and other educationally beneficial activities; and how HEIs deploy resources and organize curriculum and other learning opportunities to encourage student participation in meaningful activities that are linked to learning (ISSE, 2019).

LITERATURE REVIEW

At the heart of student engagement are students' learning approaches and experiences within the learning environment (Ashwin, 2014; Coates & McCormick, 2014). Wang and BrckaLorenz (2018) argued that effective learning strategies help students to build on their strengths and facilitate comprehension, ultimately resulting in greater engagement. Higher order forms of learning (analyzing, synthesizing, evaluating, and applying) and higher order thinking skills (creating, evaluating, analyzing, applying, understanding, and remembering) have been found to be positively associated with greater engagement (Krathwohl, 2002).

Students also learn by way of reflecting on and making sense of their current or prior experience and then applying the acquired knowledge in the classroom (McCormick, 2013). However, variability in lecturers' attitudes toward reflection has been found to impact student engagement (Vivekananda-Schmidt et al., 2011). Integrative learning refers to students' learned ability to make connections through the curricula and integrate information from various sources and is essential for deeper learning, improvement of learning, and retention (Woodside, 2018). Integrative learning approaches have been linked to high levels of student engagement as they tend to utilize a variety of ways of introducing and revisiting material (Kelley et al., 2010). Collaborative learning, which requires students to interact with peers, has been shown to have a positive relationship with student achievement and satisfaction (Wang & BrckaLorenz, 2018). Finally, in developing quantitative reasoning skills, students learn to interpret, represent, calculate, and communicate quantitative information. All these approaches provide students with the necessary skills to improve their learning and enhance engagement.

The role of interaction with faculty, support staff, and other students cannot be underestimated in enhancing students' experiences at HEIs (O'Brien & Iannone, 2018; Wang & BrckaLorenz, 2018). Students gain additional learning experience through formal and informal discussion of their academic performance, course work, and other topics with their lecturers (Alqurashi, 2020; Wang & BrckaLorenz, 2018). The extent and quality of student–faculty interaction has been found to positively affect various student outcomes, including knowledge of the subject matter, cognitive skills, attitudes and values, educational attainment, and career choice and development (Pascarella & Terenzini, 2005). Some ethnic groups may find it difficult to approach academic staff—especially staff of a different ethnic background—and anticipate negative perceptions of their ethnic group (Schwitzer et al., 1999). International students from Africa, the Middle East, and Southeast Asia have been found to rate the quality of their interactions with academic staff in U.S. HEIs significantly lower than students from North America and Southern Asia (Glass et al., 2013). Students' relationships with faculty members have been found to act as a strong predictor of learning, over and above their background characteristics, particularly for students of color (Lundberg & Schreiner, 2004). As academic staff are often the main contact point for international students, it is important for them to be aware and correct any implicit biases they may hold about students' background (Glass et al., 2015).

Cultural awareness is also important in interaction with peers, as a student's peer group is an important source of personal development and learning (Farrelly & Murphy, 2018; Pascarella & Terenzini, 2005). In some cases, the quality of interaction between different groups of students is hindered due to language barriers (Hanasaab, 2006). Cross-cultural tensions in HEI environments have been identified by Lee and Rice (2007), who found that students from Asia, Latin America, and the Middle East were more likely to report experiencing discrimination than students from Europe, Canada, and New Zealand.

The above studies indicate that both academic and social factors influence student engagement. The engagement of international students should not be seen as the sole responsibility of the student (Kettle, 2017). Different perceptions between international students and academic staff about essential learning skills can lead to unmatched supports by academic staff, and academic staff should familiarize themselves with the challenges these students are experiencing and the learning strategies they are employing (Wang & BrckaLorenz, 2018). International students may be affected by fluency in the language of instruction (Farrelly & Murphy, 2018; Lee et al., 2013), understanding academic vocabulary, finding the speed of the lecture challenging (Ramsay et al., 1999), difficulties with required critical thinking skills, reluctance to participate in collaborative learning modes such as group discussions (Gillett & Baskerville, 2012), as well as different assessment criteria and course work requirements (Farrelly & Murphy, 2018). Ammigan and Jones (2018) noted that while factors such as arrival, living arrangements, learning, and student support matter, the academic dimension was found to be the most important aspect in influencing the overall student experience (Ammigan et al., 2021).

Learning factors and approaches may also differ between domestic and international students. Some research has alluded to higher engagement of international students compared with their native peers (O'Reilly et al., 2015). However, differences exist between regional groups in their learning approaches and satisfaction with their learning environment (Idris et al., 2019). Challenges experienced by students can be addressed by creating supportive environments for all students (Baik et al., 2019), characterized by university-wide and peer support (Farrelly & Murphy, 2018; O'Reilly et al., 2015).

METHOD

In the Republic of Ireland, higher education is provided by universities, institutes of technology, and colleges of education. Entry into Irish HEIs is highly competitive and based on academic merit. Irish HEIs generally require proof of English proficiency for all international students whose first language is not English. In line with international trends and strategic commitments, international student enrolments have grown over time, with international students accounting for 12% of all enrolments in Irish HEIs in 2018–2019 (Groarke & Durst, 2019; HEA, 2020b). Ireland's international education strategy aims to increase the number of international students studying in Ireland and provide a high-quality student experience (Department of Education and Skills, 2016).

Data and Method

We used anonymized data from the 2019 edition of the ISSE. The ISSE collects data on engagement levels based on students' self-reported perceptions of their experiences and has formative links with the U.S. National Survey of Student Engagement (NSSE) and the Australasian Survey of Student Engagement (AUSSE). Limited personal (e.g., age, gender, and domicile) and institutional variables (e.g., mode of study, program type, ISCED level of study) are collected through the survey, reflecting the approach of the AUSSE.

The survey includes first year and final year undergraduate and taught postgraduate students. The survey adopted a census approach and invited all members of the target cohorts to participate. Responses were weighted by sex, stage of study (first year, final year, taught postgraduate), and mode of study (full time or part time/remote) at institutional level to ensure that the profile of respondents matched the profile of the student population. No additional weighting was applied for international students.

The 2019 survey had a response rate of 29%, with 40,558 students taking part in the study (19,557 first year undergraduate students, 13,951 final year undergraduate students, and 7,050 taught postgraduate students). At 4,409 responses, international students accounted for 11% of the survey respondents. National data show that the proportion of such students in the total student population in 2019 was 12% (HEA, 2020b). In order to facilitate grouping of international students by region of origin, only international students who provided the country of their permanent address were included in our analysis ($n = 3,835$). Overall, the proportions of international student responses by region of origin in the ISSE survey are comparable to the proportions of international student respondents to the Eurostudent VI survey for Ireland (collected in 2016) and to figures compiled by Ireland's Central Statistics Office (CSO) for 2017 (CSO, 2021). A direct comparison with data from CSO is not possible due to

Table 1: Student Engagement Measures

Indicator	Components	*M*	*SD*
Higher-order learning	• applying facts, theories, or methods to practical problems or new situations; • analyzing an idea, experience, or line of reasoning in depth by examining its parts; • evaluating a point of view, decision, or information source; • forming an understanding or new idea from various pieces of information	36.520	14.167
Reflective and integrative learning	• combining ideas from different subjects/modules when completing assignments; • connecting learning to problems or issues in society; • including diverse perspectives in discussions or assignments; • examining the strengths and weaknesses of views on a topic or issue; • trying to better understand someone else's views by imagining how an issue looks from their perspective; learning something that changed understanding of an issue or concept; • connecting ideas from subjects/modules to prior experiences and knowledge	30.907	11.067
Quantitative reasoning	• reaching conclusions based on analysis of numerical information; • using numerical information to examine a real-world problem or issue; • evaluating what others have concluded from numerical information	20.235	14.094
Learning strategies	• identifying key information from recommended reading materials; • reviewing notes after class; • summarizing what was learned in class or from course materials	30.970	12.797

		Mean	SD
Collaborative learning	• asking another student to help understand course material; • explaining course material to one or more students; • preparing for exams by discussing or working through course material with other students; • working with other students on projects or assignments	31.007	12.723
Student-faculty interaction	• talking about career plans with academic staff; • working with academic staff on activities other than coursework; • discussing course topics, ideas, or concepts with academic staff outside of class; • discussing performance with academic staff	14.301	12.482
Effective teaching practices	• clearly explained course goals and requirements; • taught in an organised way; • used examples or illustrations to explain difficult points; • provided feedback on a draft or work in progress; • provided prompt and detailed feedback on tests or completed assignments	34.744	13.896
Supportive environment - How much an institution emphasises:	• Providing support to help students succeed academically; • using learning support services; • contact among students from different backgrounds; • providing opportunities to be involved socially; • providing support for overall well-being; • managing non-academic responsibilities; • attending campus activities and events	28.670	14.012
Quality of interactions	• looks at students, academic advisors, academic staff, support services staff, other administrative staff and offices	39.266	13.571

Source: ISSE (2019); mean and standard deviation measures are based on ISSE 2019 data.

differences in how countries are grouped into regions. It is possible that the ISSE data is not fully representative of all regional groups of international students. We used ordinary least square (OLS) regression to analyze the data.

Variables

The definition of "international student" is based on a student's country of permanent address, or "domicile," prior to their entry to their program of study. International students were grouped into regions of domicile, based on the World Bank administrative classification: (a) East Asia and Pacific, (b) Europe and Central Asia, excluding the European Economic Area (EEA) and the United Kingdom, (c) EEA including the United Kingdom, (d) Latin America and the Caribbean, (e) Middle East and North Africa (MENA), (f) North America, (g) South Asia, and (h) Sub-Saharan Africa.

The ISSE includes nine distinct engagement measures, each of which are computed from a series of items. The possible scores for computed measures range from 0 to 60.

RESULTS

The number of international students from different regions of domicile vary in the 2019 ISSE data, ranging from 91 students from Latin America (0.2%) to 889 from South Asia (2.2%). In 2017, Asian students represented the most numerous groups of international students in Ireland (Central Statistics Office [CSO], 2021). As a group, international students were more likely to be enrolled at a university (53%) than Irish students (45%). This is consistent with population level data, but the ISSE survey participants are more skewed toward non-university participants. At the survey population level, 61% of international students were enrolled in a university (ISSE, 2019). However, among respondents, variations emerged between international students by different regions of domicile. A higher proportion of international students from Sub-Saharan Africa (52%) and Latin America and the Caribbean (52%) were enrolled at an institute of technology than Irish students (49%). International students from all regions of domicile were also more likely to be enrolled in an undergraduate program, compared with their Irish counterparts (45% vs. 14%). The rate of enrolment in graduate programs was highest for international students from South Asia (86%) and lowest for international students from the MENA region (27%).

Previous research on the Irish context has shown that international students have higher levels of engagement than domestic students overall and that their level of engagement has increased over time (Finn et al., 2021; ISSE, 2019). This study has shown that these results persist when disaggregating engagement by region of domicile, with high levels of engagement among international students across the range of indicators. As a response to this study's first research question, Figure 1 illustrates the distribution of means for students from all regions of domicile on all engagement indicators. The figure shows that, overall, levels of engagement do vary slightly between domestic and international students and that engagement levels are consistent across regions of origin. However, on the effective teaching practice indicator, international students from North America register the lowest mean, followed by Irish students.

Figure 1: Mean Scores by Region of Domicile on Engagement Indicators (ISSE, 2019)

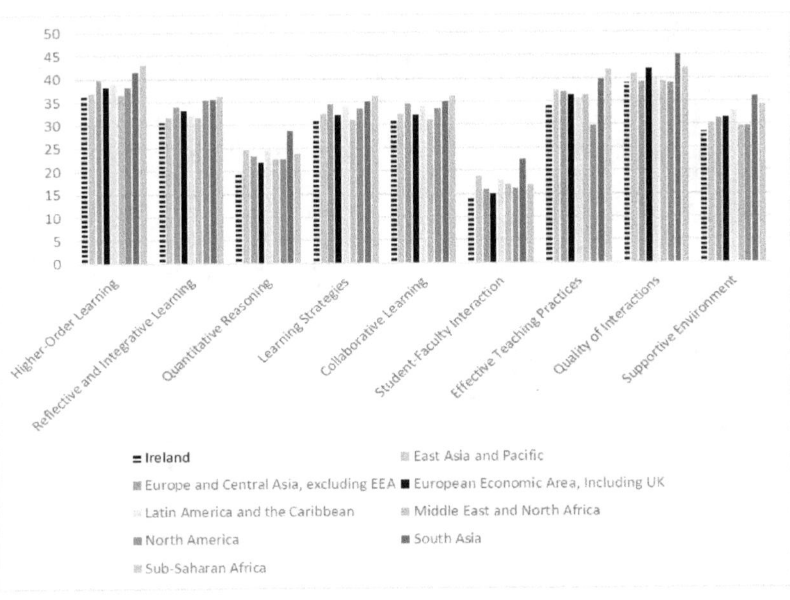

The ISSE collects relatively limited information on the demographic characteristics of respondents. Additional limitations on data analysis and the inclusion of key control variables are due to the use of the anonymized dataset. For example, multilevel analyses are not possible on this dataset. As such, this study is not able to show if variations within HEIs are higher than variation between settings (ISSE, 2019; McCormick, 2013). Race and ethnicity, socioeconomic, and academic performance data are not included

Table 2: OLS Regression Results Across Engagement Indicators

Variable	Higher order learning	Reflective and integrative learning	Quantitative reasoning	Learning strategies	Collaborative learning	Student–faculty interaction	Effective teaching practices	Quality of interactions	Supportive environment
Constant	40.520	34.274	25.804	31.950	31.970	17.394	34.749	40.674 ***	29.374
East Asia and Pacific[a]	0.408	0.388	4.036 ***	1.900 ***	-1.657 ***	3.337 ***	3.195 ***	1.999	1.501 **
Europe and Central Asia, excluding EEA	2.419 **	2.316 ***	3.340 ***	3.025 ***	-1.552 *	2.321 **	2.484 **	.133 ***	2.871 **
EEA, Including UK	1.030	1.417 **	1.614 **	0.941	-1.647 **	0.571	1.732 **	2.863	2.949 ***
Latin America and the Caribbean	1.141	-0.042	3.673 *	2.618	-3.754 **	2.206	1.292	0.648	4.829 **
MENA	-0.138	0.413	2.302 *	0.578	-0.929	2.187 *	2.371 *	0.382	1.242
North America	0.415	3.128 ***	1.895 **	2.072 ***	-.799	1.796 **	-4.132 ***	.153	.360
South Asia	2.067 ***	1.730 ***	5.469 ***	3.112 ***	3.175 ***	5.341 ***	5.115 ***	4.877 ***	7.737 ***
Sub-Saharan Africa	5.642***	4.450 ***	2.937 **	5.117 ***	1.317	1.204	7.234 ***	2.546 **	6.012 ***
Undergraduate (reference graduate)	-4.468 ***	-4.430 ***	-3.106 ***	-2.212 ***	-0.919 ***	-4.104 ***	-1.323 ***	-2.247 ***	1.523 ***
Institute of Technology (reference university)	-2.459 ***	-2.040 ***	-0.597 ***	-1.812 ***	2.268 ***	3.215 ***	1.065 ***	1.118 ***	-2.592 ***
Other higher education type (reference university)	-1.967 ***	-0.669 **	-2.637 ***	-0.839 **	0.686 **	.836 **	-0.970 **	-0.539	-3.315 ***
Part-time or remote (reference full-time)	1.561 ***	0.669 ***	-2.803 ***	2.838 ***	-7.705 ***	-4.260 ***	3.179 ***	1.888 ***	-4.630 ***
Female (reference male)	1.128 ***	1.974 ***	-4.524 ***	1.931 ***	0.328 **	-1.502 ***	-0.490 **	-1.225 ***	0.155
Observations	30,515	40,220	35,197	35,202	39,785	35,145	31,184	28,371	30,932
R^2	0.037	0.058	0.047	0.034	0.060	0.046	0.022	0.018	0.04
Adjusted R^2	0.037	0.057	0.046	0.034	0.059	0.045	0.022	0.018	0.04

Note. *** $p < .001$; ** $p < .01$; * $p > .05$.
[a]Reference for all regions of domicile is Ireland

in the survey. As such, inferential analyses on engagement indicators as outcome variables offer only limited information. However, the data allow for testing of the association between region of domicile and engagement indicators after controlling for the effect of type of course (undergraduate or postgraduate), type of institution (institute of technology, university, and other HEI) mode of study (part time/online or full time), as well as the gender of the respondents. The ordinary OLS regression models (see Table 2) used to answer the second research question of the study explain a small fraction of the variability in engagement indicators, ranging from 2% for effective teaching practice to 6% for collaborative learning. Data on region of domicile was missing for 0.4% of the sample, while no missing data was registered for the control variables included in the analysis. Missing data was higher for the outcome variables included in the study and no data imputations were conducted.

Across models, differences in engagement scores between Irish and international students from different regions of domicile are statistically significant after including the available controls. International students from South Asia were the only group to systematically register statistically significant higher mean scores across all engagement indicators compared with Irish students ($p > .001$). On all but two indicators (collaborative learning and student–faculty interaction) international students from Sub-Saharan Africa had statistically significantly higher mean scores than students from Ireland ($p > .01$). Students from Europe and Central Asia had higher scores than Irish students on all indicators, except for collaborative learning ($p < .05$). Students from Latin America and the Caribbean registered higher scores on the quantitative reasoning and supportive environment indicators, but lower scores on the collaborative learning indicator than Irish students. Students from the MENA region had statistically significantly higher engagement scores than Irish students on the quantitative reasoning, student faculty interaction, and effective teaching practices indicators ($p > .05$). EEA students had statistically significantly higher scores on the following indicators: (a) reflective and integrative learning, (b) quantitative reasoning, (c) effective teaching practices, and (d) supportive environments ($p > .01$), and lower scores on the collaborative learning indicator ($p < .01$). International students from East Asia and Pacific obtained statistically significant higher mean scores on the following indicators: (a) quantitative reasoning, (b) learning strategies, (c) student–faculty interaction, (d) effective teaching practices, and (e) supportive environment. North American international students had statistically significantly higher mean scores compared with Irish students on: (a) reflective and integrative learning, (b) quantitative reasoning, (c) learning strategies, and (d) student–faculty interaction. Students from the North American region also registered statistically significantly lower scores on the effective teaching practices indicator.

Engagement levels remain lower for undergraduate students compared with postgraduate students for all engagement indicators with one exception. Undergraduate students had statistically significantly higher mean scores on the supportive environment indicator. Mean scores were statistically significantly lower at institutes of technology compared with universities for the following indicators: (a) higher order thinking, (b) reflective and integrative learning, (c) quantitative reasoning, (d) learning strategies, and (e) supportive environments. In return, students at institutes of technology were statistically significantly more likely to have higher levels of engagement on the following indicators: (a) collaborative learning, (b) student faculty interaction, (c) effective teaching practices, and (d) quality of interaction. Respondents in part-time and remote programs also reported mixed levels of engagement across indicators compared with their peers in full-time programs. While these students registered statistically significantly higher scores for (a) higher order learning, (b) reflective and integrative learning, (c) learning strategies, (d) effective teaching practices, and (e) quality of interaction, they reported lower engagement on (a) quantitative reasoning, (b) collaborative learning, (c) student–faculty interaction, and (d) supportive environment. Females were statistically significantly more likely than males to report higher scores on the following indicators: (a) higher order learning, (b) reflective and integrative learning, (c) learning strategies, and (d) collaborative learning. On the other hand, males registered statistically significantly higher score on the (a) quantitative reasoning, (b) student–faculty interaction, (c) effective teaching practices, and (d) quality of interaction engagement indicators.

Limitations

This study has some limitations. First, the student survey captures a respondent's perception of experiences and is not an observable fact (Ewell & McCormick, 2020). Second, the small numbers of students from certain regions necessitated the creation of broad country categories. As such, the data precluded a deeper analysis of the heterogeneity that exists within the broader regional categories studied. We acknowledge that students from countries captured by, for example, the Asia categories, may differ in engagement with their host institutions. Third, as previously stated, the lack of demographic data in the ISSE dataset, such as socioeconomic background, ethnicity, linguistic background, and academic achievement, precluded an analysis of the effect of such variables on student engagement.

Given that research in the Australian and U.S. contexts has found an association between student background characteristics and engagement, including socioeconomic status, parents' and students' educational attainment, and language background (Jackling & Natoli, 2011; Radloff & Coates, 2010), the inclusion of some of this demographic information, such as is captured in the NSSE and AUSSE, may have enabled us to produce a more nuanced picture of the engagement of international students in Ireland. Previous research based in the Irish context has shown that, after accounting for region of origin, higher parental education is inversely associated with academic satisfaction (Finn et al., 2021).

DISCUSSION

Internationalization has become a characteristic of contemporary academic life in HEIs across Western societies. Various surveys have endeavoured to explore the engagement of international students in host institutions to enhance student experiences. Despite growing numbers of international students, research on variations in student engagement by regions of origin is sparse. This article responds to this gap by disaggregating data on international students to explore differences in the engagement of international students from different geographic regions.

Consistent with existing research in the Irish context (Clarke et al., 2018; Farrelly & Murphy, 2018; Finn et al., 2021; ISSE, 2019), this study shows that international students in Ireland score higher on most engagement indicators compared with their domestic counterparts. Even when disaggregating engagement by region of domicile, international students are engaging well overall with teaching and learning at Irish HEIs. This is a positive finding concerning international students, considering the importance of the academic dimension in shaping student experiences. This finding may be explained by the selection effect of international students, whereby more motivated students have opted to study abroad, as well as the supports put in place by the Irish HEIs for these students.

Compared with Irish students, one group of international students stands out regarding engagement: the South Asian group tended to show higher levels of engagement across all indicators. This finding may be explained by the high ambitions among this group as indicated in earlier studies (Ramburuth & McCormick, 2001; Zhu & Leung, 2011). However, our findings differ from some previous studies in the U.S. context, which found lower levels of engagement among Asian international students compared with other international students (Zhao et al., 2005). This may be due to between-country differences in student experience that may not be captured by the regional categories used in the analysis. Students from the MENA region had statistically significantly higher engagement scores than Irish students on the quantitative reasoning, student–faculty interaction, and effective teaching practices indicators. The reasons for high engagement of MENA countries, as well as other regions, across these dimensions merits further research.

Disaggregation of data has also shown some variations in the effective teaching practice indicator: North American students scored lower than all other groups in this dimension, possibly reflecting different expectations of these students in this area. Lower academic satisfaction of North American students in Irish HEIs has also been found by a recent study based on Eurostudent survey (Finn et al., 2021). Collaborative learning has been increasingly utilized as a teaching approach in HEIs. After applying control variables, our analysis revealed that for some regions (East Asian and Pacific, European and Central Asia, EEA, Latin America, and the Caribbean), scores in collaborative learning remained lower compared with those of Irish students, possibly indicating more prevalent self-paced learning approach in the education systems in these regions.

We also found that compared to postgraduate students, undergraduates showed lower levels of engagement. As the latter scored higher on supportive environment, this seems to indicate that the support mechanisms put in place by the Irish HEIs may be effective, but that more could be done in other domains of engagement. Findings on type of institution and mode of study offered mixed results and represent a topic that merits further research.

CONCLUSION

This research contributes to studies exploring whether country of domicile explains differences in engagement among Irish and international students. In the context of Ireland's international education policy goals to ensure a high-quality learning experience for international students, this article points to the variation in students' engagement by region of origin and the need for consideration to be given to tailoring of supports to respond to the needs of different groups of international students. Irish HEIs have put in place a range of supports for international students at institutional, faculty, and departmental level, including international offices with international student advisors, induction and academic supports, as well as pastoral care (Clarke et al., 2018). We have shown that different groups of students may need support in specific areas, be it learning approaches or communication with faculty. The picture is likely to be more diverse within HEIs. This makes any blanket recommendations difficult but equally cautions against a "one size fits all" solution to student engagement. Given that learning and student outcomes are linked to engagement, it is important for each institution to determine what is working well in terms of international student engagement in all its dimensions and what needs improvement. In this regard, student engagement surveys offer a good insight into the HEI performance. Further research at the institutional level—including of ISSE data and qualitative studies on student engagement—may assist HEIs to better understand how to improve engagement of international students from different regions.

Though this article primarily focused on examining differences in experiences among the international student population, that domestic students scored lower than international students on most indicators gives rise to questions about Irish student engagement and HEI responses to their needs. Our findings suggest that a "whole institution approach" to supporting the engagement of both international and domestic students may be useful to ensure that the whole student body can benefit from internationalization efforts.

REFERENCES

Alqurashi, E. (2020). What do students engage with the most? A comparative study between high and low achieving students within online learning environments. *Open Learning: The Journal of Open, Distance and e-Learning.* https://doi.org/10.1080/02680513.2020.1758052

Alrashidi, O., Phan, H., & Ngu, B. (2016). Academic engagement: An overview of its definitions, dimensions, and major conceptualisations. *International Education Studies, 9*(12). https://doi.org/10.5539/ies.v9n12p41

Ammigan, R., Dennis, J. L., & Jones, E. (2021). The differential impact of learning experiences on international student satisfaction and institutional recommendation. *Journal of International Students, 11*(4), 299–321. https://doi.org/10.32674/jis.v11i2.2038

Ammigan, R., & Jones, E. (2018). Improving the student experience: Learning from a comparative study of international student satisfaction. *Journal of Studies in International Education, 22*(4), 283–301. https://doi.org/10.1177/1028315318773137

Ashwin, P. (2014). Knowledge, curriculum and student understanding. *Higher Education, 67*, 123–126. https://doi.org/10.1007/s10734-014-9715-3

Ashwin, P., & McVitty, D. (2015). The meanings of student engagement: Implications for policies and practices. In A. Curaj, L. Matei, R. Pricopie, J. Salmi, & P. Scott (Eds.), *The European higher education area: Between critical reflections and future policies* (pp. 343–359). Springer. https://doi.org/10.1007/978-3-319-20877-0_23

Baik, C., Larcombe, W., & Brooker, A. (2019). How universities can enhance student mental wellbeing: The student perspective. *Higher Education Research & Development, 38*(4), 674–687. https://doi.org/10.1080/07294360.2019.1576596

Brooks, R., & Waters, J. (2011). *Student mobilities, migration and the internationalization of higher education.* Palgrave Macmillan.

Central Statistics Office. (2021). *Domiciliary origin of students enrolled in full-time third level institutions* (EDA02). Retrieved June 14, 2021, from https://data.cso.ie/

Cho, H. J., Levesque-Bristol, C., & Yough, M. (2020). International students' self-determined motivation, beliefs about classroom assessment, learning strategies, and academic adjustment in higher education. *Higher Education, 81,* 1215–1235. https://doi.org/10.1007/s10734-020-00608-0

Clarke, M., Yang, L. H., & Harmon, D. (2018). *The internationalisation of Irish higher education.* Higher Education Authority. https://hea.ie/assets/uploads/2018/07/report_internationalisation_of_education_2018.pdf

Coates, H. (2006). The value of student engagement for higher education quality assurance. *Quality in Higher Education, 11*(1), 25–36. https://doi.org/10.1080/13538320500074915

Coates, H., & McCormick, A. C. (2014). Emerging trends and perspectives. In H. Coates & A. McCormick (Eds.), *Engaging university students: International insights from system-wide studies* (pp. 151–158). Springer. https://doi.org/10.1007/978-981-4585-63-7_11

Crose, B. (2011). Internationalization of the higher education classroom: Strategies to facilitate intercultural learning and academic success. *International Journal of Teaching and Learning in Higher Education, 23*(3), 388–395. https://eric.ed.gov/?id=EJ946165

Department of Education and Skills. (2016). *Irish educated, globally connected: An international education strategy for Ireland, 2016–2020.* https://www.gov.ie/en/publication/553ec-irish-educated-globally-connected-an-international-education-strategy-for-ireland-2016-2020/

Ewell, P. T., & McCormick, A. C. (2020). The National Survey of Student Engagement (NSSE) at twenty. *Assessment Update, 32*(2), 1–16. https://doi.org/10.1002/au.30204

Faas, D. (2020). New patterns of migration and higher education in Ireland: What are the implications? In M. Slowey, H. Schuetze, & T. Zubrzycki (Eds.), *Inequality, innovation and reform in higher education* (pp. 71–85). Springer. https://doi.org/10.1007/978-3-030-28227-1_5

Fakunle, L., Allison, P., & Fordyce, K. (2016). Chinese postgraduate students' perspectives on developing critical thinking on an UK education masters. *Journal of Curriculum and Teaching, 5*(1), 27. https://doi.org/10.5430/jct.v5n1p27

Farrelly, T., & Murphy, T. (2018). Hindsight is 20/20 vision: What international students wished they had known before coming to live and learn in Ireland. *Journal of International Students, 8*(4), 1848–1864. https://doi.org/10.32674/jis.v8i4.234

Finn, M., Mihut, G., & Darmody, M. (2021). Academic satisfaction of international students at Irish higher education institutions: The role of region of origin and cultural distance in the context of marketisation. *Journal of Studies in International Education.* https://doi.org/10.1177/10283153211027009

Fredricks, J. A., Blumenfeld, P. C., & Paris, A. H. (2004). School engagement: Potential of the concept, state of the evidence. *Review of Educational Research, 74*(1), 59–109. https://doi.org/10.3102/00346543074001059

Gillett, S., & Baskerville, R. (2012). Student learning preferences: International students in comparative perspective. *International Journal of Learning: Annual Review, 18*(11), 155–176. https://doi.org/10.18848/1447-9494/CGP/v18i11/47814

Glass, C. R., Buus, S., & Braskamp, L. A. (2013). *Uneven experiences: What's missing and what matters for today's international students.* Global Perspective Institute. https://www.gpi.hs.iastate.edu/documents/Report-on-International-Students.pdf

Glass, C., Kociolek, E., Wongtrirat, R., Lynch, R., & Cong, S. (2015). Uneven experiences: The impact of student-faculty interactions on international students' sense of belonging. *Journal of International Students, 5*(4), 353–367. https://doi.org/10.32674/jis.v5i4.400

Groarke, S., & Durst, C. (2019). *Attracting and retaining international higher education students: Ireland.* Economic and Social Research Institute. https://doi.org/10.26504/rs88

Hagel, P., Carr, R., & Delvin, M. (2012). Conceptualising and measuring student engagement through the Australasian Survey of Student Engagement (AUSSE): A critique. *Assessment & Evaluation in Higher Education, 37*(4), 475–486. https://doi.org/10.1080/02602938.2010.545870

Hanasaab, S. (2006). Diversity, international students, and perceived discrimination: Implications for educators and counsellors. *Journal of Studies in International Education, 10*(2), 157–172. https://doi.org/10.1177/1028315305283051

Harper, S. R., & Quaye, S. J. (2015). Making engagement equitable for students in U.S. higher education. In S. J. Quaye & S. R. Harper (Eds.), *Student engagement in higher education: Theoretical perspectives and practical approaches for diverse populations.* Routledge. https://tandfbis.s3.amazonaws.com/rt-media/pdf/9780415895101/Student_Engagement_chpt1_proof.pdf

Higher Education Authority. (2020a). *International enrolments 2014/15–2018/19.* www.hea.ie/statistics/data-for-download-and-visualisations/enrolments/international-enrolments-201415-201819

Higher Education Authority. (2020b). *2018/19 student demographics, all HEA-funded HEIs.* www.hea.ie/statistics/data-for-download-and-visualisations/enrolments/student-demographics-2018-19

Idris, A., Ion, G., & Seery, A. (2019). Peer learning in international higher education: The experience of international students in an Irish university. *Irish Educational Studies, 38*(1), 1–23. https://doi.org/10.1080/03323315.2018.1489299.

Irish Survey of Student Engagement. (2019). *Irish Survey of Student Engagement national report 2019.* https://studentsurvey.ie/sites/default/files/2019-10/StudentSurvey.ie%20National%20Report%202019.pdf

Jackling, B., & Natoli, R. (2011). Student engagement and departure intention: An Australian university perspective. *Journal of Further and Higher Education, 34*(4), 561–579. https://doi.org/10.1080/0309877X.2011.584970

Kelley, J. G., Lesaux, N. K., Kieffer, M. J., & Faller, S. E. (2010). Effective academic vocabulary instruction in the urban middle school. *The Reading Teacher, 64*(1), 5–14. https://doi.org/10.1598/RT.64.1.1

Kettle, M. (2017). *International student engagement in higher education: Transforming practices, pedagogies and participation.* Multilingual Matters.

Klemenčič, M., & Chirikov, I. (2015). How do we know how students experience higher education? On the use of student surveys. In A. Curaj, L. Matei, R. Pricopie, J. Salmi, & P. Scott (Eds.), *The European higher education area* (pp. 361-379). Springer. https://doi.org/10.1007/978-3-319-20877-0_24

Krathwohl, D. R. (2002). A revision of Bloom's taxonomy: An overview. *Theory into Practice, 41*(4), 34–42. https://doi.org/10.1207/s15430421tip4104_2

Lee, B., Farrugia, S. P., & Brown, G. T. L. (2013). Academic difficulties encountered by East Asian international university students in New Zealand. *Higher Education Research and Development, 32*(6), 915–931. https://doi.org/10.1080/07294360.2013.806444

Lee, J. J., & Rice, C. (2007). Welcome to America? International student perceptions of discrimination. *Higher Education, 53*, 381–409. https://doi.org/10.1007/s10734-005-4508-3

Leiber, T. (2020). Student experience and engagement surveys in context: Challenges, recommendations and success factors in international perspective. In P. Pohlenz, L. Mitterauer, & S. Harris-Huemmert (Eds.), *Qualitatssicherung im student life cycle* (pp. 181–196). Waxmann. https://www.waxmann.com/waxmann-buecher/?tx_p2waxmann_pi2%5bbuchnr%5d=4183&tx_p2waxmann_pi2%5b action%5d=show

Lundberg, C. A., & Schreiner, L. A. (2004). Quality and frequency of faculty-student interaction as predictors of learning: An analysis by student race/ethnicity. *Journal of College Student Development, 45*(5), 549–565. https://doi.org./10.1353/csd.2004.0061

McCormick, A. C., Kinzie, J., & Gonyea, R. M. (2013). Student engagement: Bridging research and practice to improve the quality of undergraduate education. In M. B. Paulsen (Ed.), *Higher education: Handbook of theory and research.* Springer. https://doi.org/10.1007/978-94-007-5836-0

McCormick, C. B., Dimmitt, C., & Sullivan, F. R. (2013). Metacognition, learning, and instruction. In I. B. Weiner (Ed.), *Handbook of psychology* (2nd ed., Vol. 7, pp. 69–97). John Wiley & Sons.

Mihut, G. (2019). Outside the comfort zone: How internationalization can be used to support first generation students. In K. Godwin, & H. de Wit (Eds.), *Intelligent internationalization: The shape of things to come* (pp. 160–163). Brill Sense.

O'Brien, B., & Iannone, P. (2018). Students' experiences of teaching at secondary school and university: Sharing responsibility for classroom engagement. *Journal of Further and Higher Education, 42*(7), 922–936. https://doi.org/10.1080/0309877X.2017.1332352

O'Connor, P. (2010). Effective teaching and learning in higher education: A United Kingdom perspective. *The ITB Journal, 11*(1). https://doi.org/10.21427/D7K15Q

O'Reilly, A., Hickey, T., & Ryan, D. (2015). The experiences of American international students in a large Irish university. *Journal of International Students, 5*(1), 86–98. https://doi.org/10.32674/jis.v5i1.445

Organisation for Economic Cooperation and Development. (2020). *Education at a glance 2020: OECD indicators.* https://doi.org/10.1787/69096873-en

Pascarella, E. T., & Terenzini, P. T. (2005). *How college affects students (Volume 2): A third decade of research.* Jossey-Bass.

Radloff, A., & Coates, H. (2010). *Doing more for learning: Enhancing engagement and outcomes: Australasian Survey of Student Engagement: Australasian Student Engagement Report.* Australian Council for Education Research. https://research.acer.edu.au/cgi/viewcontent.cgi?article=1011&context=ausse

Ramburuth, P., & McCormick, J. (2001). Learning diversity in higher education: A comparative study of Asian international and Australian students. *Higher Education, 42,* 333–350. https://doi.org/10.1023/A:1017982716482

Ramsay, S., Barker, M., & Jones, E. (1999). Academic adjustment and learning processes: A comparison of international and local students in first-year university. *Higher Education Research and Development, 18*(1), 129–144. https://doi.org/10.1080/0729436990180110

Rienties, B., & Tempelaar, D. (2013). The role of cultural dimensions of international and Dutch students on academic and social integration and academic performance in the Netherlands. *International Journal of Intercultural Relations, 37*(2), 188–201. https://doi.org/10.1016/j.ijintrel.2012.11.004

Schaufeli, W. B., Salanova, M., González-Romá, V., & Bakker, A. B. (2002). The measurement of engagement and burnout: A two sample confirmatory factor analytic approach. *Journal of Happiness Studies, 3*(1), 71–92. https://doi.org/10.1023/A:1015630930326

Schwitzer, A. M., Griffin, O. T., Ancis, J. R., & Thomas, C. R. (1999). Social adjustment experiences of African American college students. *Journal of Counseling and Development, 77,* 189–197. https://doi.org/10.1002/j.1556-6676.1999.tb02439.x

Tight, M. (2020). Student retention and engagement in higher education. *Journal of Further and Higher Education, 44*(5), 689–704. https://doi.org/10.1080/0309877X.2019.1576860

Vazirani, S., Carmona, C., Vidal, J., Hernaiz-Agreda, N., López-Francés, I., & Benlloch-Sanchis, M. J. (2018). International students integration in classroom: Strategies and support by teachers and local students in higher education. In M. Karasawa, M. Yuki, K. Ishii, Y. Uchida, K. Sato, & W. Friedlmeier (Eds.), *Venture into cross-cultural psychology: Proceedings from the 23rd Congress of the International Association for Cross-Cultural Psychology.* https://scholarworks.gvsu.edu/iaccp_proceedings/2/

Vivekananda-Schmidt, P., Marshall, M., Stark, P., McKendree, J., Sandars, J., & Smithson, S. (2011). Lessons from medical students' perceptions of learning reflective skills: A multi-institutional study. *Medical Teacher, 33*(10), 846–850. https://doi.org/10.3109/0142159x.2011.577120

Wang, R., & BrckaLorenz, A. (2018). International student engagement: an exploration of student and faculty perceptions. *Journal of International Students, 8*(2), 1002–1033. https://doi.org/10.5281/zenodo.1250402

Williams, J. (2014). Student feedback on the experience of higher education. A significant component of institutional research data. In M. E. Menon, D. G. Terkla, & P. Gibbs (Eds.), *Using data to improve higher education* (pp. 67–80). Sense Publishers.

Wise, L., Skues, J., & Williams, B. (2011, December 4-7). *Facebook in higher education promotes social but not academic engagement*. ASCILITE - Australian Society for Computers in Learning in Tertiary Education Annual Conference, Hobart, Tasmania, Australia. https://www.ascilite.org/conferences/hobart11/downloads/papers/Wise-full.pdf

Woodside, J. M. (2018). Real-world rigour: An integrative learning approach for industry and higher education. *Industry and Higher Education, 32*(5), 285–289. https://doi.org/10.1177/0950422218784535

Yu, Y., & Moskal, M. (2019). Missing intercultural engagements in the university experiences of Chinese international students in the UK, *Compare: A Journal of Comparative and International Education,* 49(4), 654–671, https://doi.org/10.1080/03057925.2018.1448259

Zhao, C. M., Kuh, G. D., & Carini, R. M. (2005). A comparison of international student and American student engagement in effective educational practices. *The Journal of Higher Education,* 76(2), 209–231. https://doi.org/10.1080/00221546.2005.11778911

Zhu, Y., & Leung, F. K. S. (2011). Motivation and achievement: Is there an East Asian model? *International Journal of Science and Math Education, 9,* 1189–1212. https://doi.org/10.1007/s10763-010-9255-y

Author Biographies

MERIKE DARMODY is a Research Officer in the Economic and Social Research Institute, Dublin, and an Adjunct Assistant Professor at Trinity College, Dublin. E-mail: Merike.Darmody@esri.ie

SARAH GROARKE was a Policy Officer at the Irish National Contact Point of the European Migration Network, within the Economic and Social Research Institute, Dublin, and currently works at the Ombudsman for Children's Office, Ireland. E-mail:sarahjgroake@gmail.com

GEORGIANA MIHUT is an Assistant Professor in the Department of Education Studies at the University of Warwick United Kingdom. E-mail: georgiana.g.mihut@gmail.com

Article

© *Journal of International Students*
Volume 12, Issue 2 (2022), pp. 817-842
ISSN: 2162-3104 (Print), 2166-3750 (Online)
doi: 10.32674/jis.v12i2.3594
ojed.org/jis

Developing Tailored Messages to Improve Mental Health and Adjustment of Asian International Students

Lan Jin
Purdue University, USA

Lalatendu Acharya
Indiana University – Kokomo, USA

ABSTRACT

The purpose of the study was to develop tailored messages for improving mental health and adjustment of Asian international students (AISs) in the United States. The PEN-3 cultural model was used to contextualize the role of culture in mental health needs of AISs. Applying a mixed method approach, the study developed messages through a multistep participatory process consisting of three focus groups (n = 15 participants), 13 individual interviews, one expert consultation, and an online survey (n = 85 responses). Data analysis led to the development of seven broad themes with seven tailored messages under each theme, including increasing the awareness of mental health and reducing stigma; motivational quotes; available and accessible resources for AISs to improve mental health; seeking help from social network and developing interpersonal skills; adjusting to American culture and college life; coping strategies to reduce stress and improve mental health and adjustment; and safety issues. The implications for culturally responsive programs are discussed.

Keywords: adjustment, Asian international students, coping, intervention development, mental health, tailored messages

INTRODUCTION

Asian international students (AISs) account for approximately 70% of all international students in the United States, the majority of whom come from China (44%), India (24%), and South Korea (6%; Institute of International Education, 2019). Previous studies have illustrated that AISs may encounter unique stressors and adjustment challenges such as sense of confusion and uncertainty in a new cultural environment, language barriers, academic difficulties, social isolation, ethnic discrimination, legal status, and financial problems (Daga et al., 2020; S. Han et al., 2017; Mikal et al., 2015; Ra & Trusty, 2017). These stressors and challenges may increase the likelihood of psychological distress and mental health problems among AISs (Daga et al., 2020; S. Han et al., 2017) and impact their mental health help-seeking behavior (Wong et al., 2014). For example, X. Han et al. (2013) reported that 55% of Chinese international students had depressive symptoms. The different cultural and social context of the United States and its educational environment creates additional challenges. Acharya et al. (2018) found that 46.94% of their college student sample showed depressive symptoms, and international students reported a significantly higher level of depressive symptoms than domestic students.

Previous research showed that AISs experience more difficulties in culturally adjusting to the American environment than their European international peers (Ma et al., 2020). These difficulties are related to the collectivist cultural norms held by several Asian cultures (Triandis, 1995). Collectivist culture emphasizes interdependence, in which members are embedded into cohesive in-groups (Hofstede, 2011). Many AISs typically value family and friends as primary sources of social support in stressful situations and this is a strength, but not having a support system close by and operating in an individualistic cultural environment creates significant challenges. Further, the deep connections with friends and family have an unintended effect of putting them under internal pressure to perform well at school in order to bring honor to the family (Ma et al., 2020). As a result, AISs are less willing to seek outside help for mental health problems than their counterparts who are from individualist cultures that foster independence (Liu et al., 2020). Also, Asian cultures of emotional self-control and humility may result in depressive symptoms and unwillingness to seek help from mental health professionals (Wong et al., 2014). Despite the importance of this problem, there is limited understanding and exploration of culturally sensitive interventions on mental health and adjustment of AISs. To address these limitations, this study aimed to develop culturally tailored messages for improving mental health and adjustment of AISs in the United States.

Messaging as a Strategy To Address AIS Mental Health

Messages are persuasive statements that are created to change behavior in a defined context. These messages could offer factual information or address behaviors in a structured stepwise process or offer workable alternatives (Morrison et al., 2005). In this study, messages are designed and tailored through a participatory process in order to address AIS mental health and help-seeking and other adjustment behaviors. Given the mental health imperative among AISs, supportive messages have been a strategy to assist students with mental health problems. Agyapong et al. (2015) found that supportive messages decreased depressive symptoms, compared with people who only used standard care. Gustafson et al. (2014) discovered that patients with substance abuse who received supportive messages reported fewer drinking days than the control group. Wei et al. (2011) reviewed the efficacy of using supportive messages to promote health behavior and found that 10 out of 16 randomized controlled trial (RCT) studies reported that the intervention group had significantly more improvement than the control group.

Tailoring, as a message strategy, provides specific content to the audiences based on their beliefs, traits, or needs (Kreuter & Wray, 2003). Tailored messages attract more attention, are handled more attentively, cover less unneeded words, and are often seen encouragingly by the message receivers, compared with untailored information (Kreuter & Wray, 2003; Lustria et al., 2013; Marcus et al., 2005; Smeets et al., 2006; Williams-Piehota et al., 2003). When individuals observe information to be relevant to themselves, they are likely to be motivated and persuaded by the messages (Petty & Cacioppo, 1979). Tailored supportive messages have been proven to be effective to improve behavioral outcomes, such as adherence to cancer prevention, mammography screening intentions, and smoking cessation (Jin & Acharya, 2016; Kreuter et al., 2000; Noar et al., 2011; Strecher et al., 1994).

Further, cultural tailoring assumes importance as it may mirror the nuances of language and cultural practices, so that health messages are tailored to the community's spoken language, shared health beliefs, norms, expectations, specific barriers, social practices, and other characteristics (Bramley et al., 2005; Dobson et al., 2017; Nimmon et al., 2012). Cultural tailoring is a focused strategy to improve the outcomes of minority populations by using their cultural practices, philosophies, and preferences as means to facilitate the behavior change (Fisher et al., 2007). Fisher et al. (2007) suggested that increased use of culturally tailored interventions would be likely to eliminate disparities, providing more value and cost-effectivity than untailored interventions. Therefore, this study focused on designing culturally tailored messages for AISs studying in the United States (Griner & Smith, 2006).

Difficulties and Challenges in Adjustment for AISs

AISs have encountered various challenges such as reluctance to seek help, low awareness of mental health and resources, stigmas, and difficulties in cultural adjustment (Daga et al., 2020; Johnson et al., 2018; Ma et al., 2020; Ruzek et al., 2011). Along with low intention to seek help, they are less likely to utilize professional mental health services, exhibit a high rate of premature dropout, and are underserved with psychological counseling (Chen et al., 2020; Liu et al., 2020). This underutilization of mental health services is caused by stigma toward mental illness, mistrust, lack of culturally appropriate service for Asians, limited English proficiency, and lack of culturally tailored messaging, etc. (Daga et al., 2020; Liu et al., 2020).

Another challenge AISs have faced is that they have limited access to their informal support systems in home countries because of geographic distance, time differences, and financial barriers (Ra & Trusty, 2017). Besides, losing face due to social stigma affects their help-seeking behavior regarding mental health (Ma et al., 2020). Ruzek et al. (2011) suggested that AISs with lower adherence to Western cultural values experienced more mental health problems, had lower help-seeking intentions, and underutilized professional mental health services. Their study explored these aspects through the PEN-3 model. AISs are often constructed as a monolith and are also grouped under the larger umbrella of international students. It is important to recognize the cultural and ethnic diversity among them and the complex nature of behaviors they display. However, the Asians as a cultural group also share a number of cultural norms, such as collectivism (e.g., pursuit of common interest), saving face, less self-disclosure than American culture, and value of family honor (Daga et al., 2020; Ma et al., 2020). The goal of this study was to take note of this diversity in AISs and focus the scope to the mental health help-seeking behaviors of AISs and their adjustment to American culture and college life. Therefore, the study put Asian culture at the center of message design and development, with the goal of improving mental health and adjustment of AISs. To facilitate this, we chose the PEN-3 model of health behavior as the theoretical framework, which centralizes culture in health interventions.

Theoretical Framework

The PEN-3 model puts culture at the core of intervention development and implementation (Airhihenbuwa, 1990). It is based on the idea that health behavior is rooted in culture, and that consideration of cultural factors can facilitate the development of successful programs. The model places a health problem within a cultural context in order to guide the intervention development among AISs (Airhihenbuwa, 1995; Airhihenbuwa & Webster, 2004). This model has been widely applied to develop culturally adapted interventions for target populations (Airhihenbuwa et al., 2009; Cowdery et al., 2010; Iwelunmor et al., 2014; Yick & Oomen-Early, 2009). In addition, the PEN-3 model centralizes culture as a frame while identifying health problems, organizing cultural components, and developing the solutions to ensure that the intervention is culturally specific (Airhihenbuwa, 1995).

Previous studies on mental health among minority populations have argued for the need to utilize culturally relevant models in planning for tailored interventions. As outlined in the literature, cultural, structural, and individual factors shape individuals' cultural perceptions about mental illness, beliefs about seeking help, actual help-seeking behavior, who services are targeted to, and what interventions are developed (Iwelunmor et al., 2014; Liu et al., 2020). Given the importance of these cultural forces, the PEN-3 model is a relevant model to guide culturally adapted interventions. The model includes three interrelated and interdependent primary domains, each with three components exploring the concerned culture:

1. Cultural identity, with the components of person, extended family, and neighborhood (PEN), recognizes that health interventions can occur at the person, extended family, and neighborhood levels.
2. Relationships and expectations, with perceptions, enablers, and nurturers (PEN), emphasizes the aspects that affect the person, family, and/or community behaviors.
3. Cultural empowerment, with positive, existential, and negative (PEN) influences, emphasizes the central role of cultural appropriateness in health promotion programs. This domain illustrates the full range of the influences of culture, from positive to negative (Iwelunmor et al., 2014).

The study employed the PEN-3 model, centralizing culture in the core of appropriate intervention, to design the tailored messages to promote mental health among AISs.

METHOD

The study used a mixed method approach to develop the tailored messages through a multistep participatory process consisting of three focus groups (n = 15 participants), 13 individual interviews, one expert consultation, and finally an online survey (n = 85 responses). A mixed methods approach enables the researchers to collect both qualitative and quantitative data thereby capitalizing on the strengths of both methods. True to the mixed methods, this study purposefully integrated both qualitative and quantitative data in collection, analysis, and interpretation stages of designing the messages.

Participants

The participants included 113 undergraduate AISs, recruited through convenience sampling at Purdue University. The eligibility criteria included: (a) ages 18 years and older; (b) full-time undergraduate students; and (c) international students identifying themselves as Asian and holding a F-1 visa. The criteria were assessed through yes/no answers. The participants self-identified as Asian and also noted their country of origin. They also self-identified their gender. As noted earlier, all participants were grouped together as AISs for the purpose of data analysis and message development. Flyers on campus were distributed for recruitment. The study was approved by the Institutional Review Board of Purdue University.

Procedure

In the first step of data collection, we conducted focus groups to understand the preferred content of messages by AISs and the cultural context. After designing tailored messages based on the participants' input, we requested feedback from an Asian therapist from the Counseling and Psychological Center at the university in terms of appropriateness of the messages. Afterward, we conducted individual interviews with further Asian participants to refine the initial messages. Then, we evaluated the degree of helpfulness of the messages through an online survey. Last, we picked 49 tailored messages for use in a subsequent intervention study.

Step 1: Determining Topics of Messages Through Focus Groups

We conducted three focus groups with AISs ($n = 15$ participants) to help create the topics, content, context, and length of tailored messages. We asked participants to complete a demographic survey and then attend a focus group with the researchers. The questions in the focus group included "What topics and contents of messages would you like to receive via email for improving your mental health and adjustment?"; "How long should the messages be, and how often would you like to receive them?"; and "What would motivate you to read these messages"? Each participant received $10 for incentive. The focus groups yielded 50 pages of data, which we thematically analyzed using constant comparative methods (borrowed from grounded theory) within the PEN-3 framework resulting in seven broad themes. The PEN-3 framework provided the larger categories under which we coded the data was (the process of data analysis is described below).

Step 2: Designing Content of Tailored Messages

Within each theme, we designed 10 tailored messages (total 70) guided by the PEN-3 model and literature (see Table 1; Sue et al., 2012; Updegraff et al., 2007). Each message contained a 100- to 200-word text or an image.

Step 3: Receiving Inputs from an Asian Psychotherapist

An experienced Asian psychotherapist from the university counseling and psychological services center examined the 70 messages under the seven broad themes and gave inputs. The psychotherapist was invited for the purpose of ensuring that the designed messages were appropriate and sensitive to Asian cultures, and did no harm to students' emotional well-being. She had extensive experience working with AISs, and was capable of providing feedback on how to make the messages more appropriate for AISs. For example, the psychotherapist suggested adding content about "perfection" into the messages, which were found to commonly cause stress among AISs; removing a few quotes (e.g., "Pain is real. But so is hope" and "My dark days made me strong") that were viewed as unhelpful or discouraging. The researchers further modified the messages based on the psychotherapist's suggestions.

Step 4: Getting Feedback from Individual Interviews to Refine Messages

A sample of 13 AISs reviewed the modified 70 messages and were interviewed for their feedback. The questions for the participants included "What do you think about these messages you just read?" and "How would you suggest to improve these messages to make it appropriate and helpful for Asian international students' mental health and adjustment?" We further refined and tailored these 70 messages from the interview responses. For example, they added information about on-campus resources suggested by the participants (e.g., student organizations, discrimination resources, and wellness resources); included more examples for clarity (e.g., "For example, International Friendship Program connects..."); and changed the wording (e.g., from "simply realize what is happening to you" to "develop understanding of the changes you are experiencing"; from "depression" to "concerns and troubles"). Each participant received $10 as incentive.

Step 5: Testing Helpfulness of Messages in Online Survey

We tested the 70 refined messages through an online survey among AISs ($N = 85$ respondents) on a research participation system, which could be accessed by all undergraduate students. Each AIS respondent was randomly exposed to four themes (40 messages in total, in a random order), and was asked to evaluate the helpfulness of messages in each topic (1 to 5 Likert scale with 1 indicating *extremely unhelpful* to 5 indicating *extremely helpful*; the question was "how helpful is this message to improve your mental health and adjustment?"). The participants received 0.5 course credit on survey completion.

Step 6: Finalizing Tailored Messages

We analyzed the evaluation of helpfulness of messages, ranked them according to their mean score of helpfulness, and picked the most helpful messages. We finalized a total of 49 messages under the seven themes.

Data Analysis

We used a constant comparative method (CCM) borrowed from grounded theory in analyzing the data from the focus groups and developing the messages and themes guided by the PEN-3 framework (Glaser & Strauss, 1967; Strauss & Corbin, 1998). We identified descriptive categories as soon as the focus group data collection had begun, through a process of constant comparison and comparing codes applicable to each category under development (Glaser, 1992).

Table 1

Cultural Identity Dimension of the PEN-3 Model

Dimension	Cultural Identity		
Components	Person	Extended family	Neighborhood
Cultural elements	Asian international students	Family support	Faculty
		Friend support	Cultural organizations

Table 2

Relationships and Expectations Dimension of the PEN-3 Model

Dimension	Relationships and expectations		
Components	Perceptions (Attitudes, views, or knowledge about mental health or seeking help)	Enablers (Factors that are facilitators or barriers to mental health and help-seeking)	Nurturers (Important social network who provides support)
	(Attitudes, views, or knowledge about mental health or seeking help)	(Factors that are facilitators or barriers to mental health and help-seeking)	(Important social network who provides support)
Cultural elements	Stigma attached to mental illness	Social support system	Family
	Need for mental health information	Language barriers	Friends
	Belief that people should rely on self to manage mental health	Available resources	Cultural organizations
	Cultural differences	Cultural differences	
	Interdependence in Asian family		

These categories influenced the development of the following focus groups, so that the emerging concepts might be explored more thoroughly, answering questions that had been raised from the analysis of previous data (Boeije, 2002; Guba & Lincoln, 1994).

We transcribed the recorded focus groups' responses verbatim and analyzed them line by line, using open coding to code as many categories as possible from the data (Strauss & Corbin, 1998). Starting with open coding (e.g., "Stigma attached to mental illness"; "Need for mental health information"), the analysis attempted to identify discrete concepts that could be sorted first (Glaser, 1978). We examined the data sentence by sentence to develop the concepts (Denzin & Lincoln, 2011). Next, we grouped together the discrete concepts that related to the same categories. Subsequently, we used axial coding to formulate relationships within and among the categories. Lastly, we used selective coding to integrate these categories and come up with the central themes (Strauss & Corbin, 1998).

Table 3

Cultural Empowerment Dimension of the PEN-3 Model

Dimension	Cultural Empowerment		
Components	Positive	Existential	Negative
Cultural elements	Available and accessible resources	Knowledge about cultural differences	Stigma
	Social network support	Self-control strategies	Difficulties in adjustment and building social network in the US
	Family support	Campus safety and laws	
	Friends support	Family expectations	

The PEN-3 model guided this process of data analysis. Specifically, we used the PEN-3 model to shape the cultural elements in messages for AISs. During selective coding, we put the codes into the components of the three PEN-3 domains. Afterwards, we created a 3´3 matrix to produce nine cells by crossing the components of the domain of cultural empowerment with the domain of relationships and expectations, based on cultural identity. Then, we developed the central themes and placed them into the appropriate cells within the matrix (see Table 1 to Table 4). We maintained rigor through constant discussions and reflections and coming to an agreement on each point of difference in coding the data.

Further, we showed a sample of the analysis to some participants for their feedback, thus ensuring rigor and quality. The consultation with the Asian psychotherapist also strengthened the process.

RESULTS

Table 5 summarizes the participants' demographic profiles. Over half of the participants identified as females (51.3 %) and 48.7% identified as males. The mean age of the participants was 20 years and they were distributed across 12 countries in Asia with one reporting from the Middle East and seven choosing the "Other" option. Nearly 40% of the participants identified China as their country of origin, 13% India, and 11% South Korea, thus reflecting the actual top three countries from which international students come to study in the United States. The number of years that the participants had studied in the United States ranged from 1 to 7 years (M = 2.57; SD = 1.6). The helpfulness analysis yielded 49 top ranked (most helpful) messages from the 70 messages, unevenly distributed among the seven themes (see Appendix A for sample of the messages). We identified the top 49 helpful messages for a later intervention. The themes of the messages were: increasing mental health awareness and reducing stigma (n = 7); motivational quotes (n = 10); available and accessible resources for AISs to improve mental health and adjustment (n = 6); seeking help from social network and developing interpersonal skills (n = 7); adjusting to American culture and college life (n = 6); coping strategies to improve mental health and adjustment (n = 10); and safety issues (n = 3). The mean score of the helpfulness of the 49 tailored messages was 3.88 out of 5 (ranging from 3.54 to 4.24; 1 indicating *extremely unhelpful* to 5 indicating *extremely helpful*), indicating that the participants perceived the tailored messages as helpful in general.

Emerging Themes on Topics of Messages

The following section describes the seven themes that emerged from the analysis of focus groups guided by the PEN-3 framework, which formed the topics of designed messages.

Increasing Mental Health Awareness and Reducing Stigma

The participants indicated that many AISs were not familiar with mental health issues, or had low awareness of mental illness symptoms. Sometimes the students did not realize that they were at risk of mental illness. For example, Participant (P) 15 described, "You should provide

Table 4. *3′3 Matrix for Designing Tailored Messages for Asian International Students*

Domains	Cultural Empowerment			
		Positive	Existential	Negative
Relationships and expectations	Perceptions	Theme 1: Information to increase awareness of mental health and reduce stigma in Asian students (need for mental health information)	Theme 5: Adjusting to American culture and college life (transition into American college, understand cultural differences, deal with sense of uncertainty, get involved on campus)	Theme 1: Information to increase awareness of mental health and reduce stigma in Asian students (stigma attached to mental illness)
		Theme 2: Motivational quote	Theme 6: Self-control strategies to reduce stress and manage anxiety (physical activities; calmness; keep a stable mind; physical health; entertainment; time-management skills)	
	Enablers	Theme 3: Available and accessible resources for Asian students to improve mental health (mental health services, language skills, communication, academic help, cultural organizations, career consultation)	Theme 7: Campus safety for Asian students	-
	Nurturers	Theme 4: Building relationships with American peers and faculty (social network support is important)	Theme 4: Communication strategies in Asian family for seeking help (expectations of family)	Theme 4: Building relationships with American peers and faculty (hard to make friends with Americans; do not want to bother others)
		Theme 4: Communication strategies in Asian family for seeking help (family is a primary source of support; interdependence)		

Table 5

Demographics (N = 113)

Characteristics	n	%
Sex		
Female	58	51.3
Male	55	48.7
Year in school		
Freshman	36	31.9
Sophomores	27	23.9
Juniors	26	23.0
Seniors	23	21.2
Region of origin		
China	52	46.0
India	17	15.0
South Korea	15	13.3
Taiwan	6	5.3
Indonesia	4	3.5
Malaysia	4	3.5
Singapore	2	1.8
Japan	1	0.9
Philippines	1	0.9
Thailand	1	0.9
Vietnam	1	0.9
United Arab Emirates	1	0.9
Bangladesh	1	0.9
Other	7	6.2
Age (*M, SD*)	20.2	2.13

some information about the symptoms of mental health problems…" P7 stated, "I would like some statistics about what is going on like how many students have depression problem, so that I will feel that I am not the only person who feels depressed." P3 indicated, "The first section can be how to increase awareness of symptoms of depression or risk factors, anxiety— they are increasing awareness about mental health."

Motivational Quotes

The participants pointed out that they would like to read motivational and positive quotes about mental health. The messages in this theme included short motivational statements/quotes and Asian proverbs. For example, P5 mentioned, "I will read if the messages contain motivational statements. I like reading poems—some statements that are short and meaningful; something that I can digest. I like inspiring statements that urge me to overcome the difficulties." Similarly, P19 described,

These are motivational quotes and also relatable for students because at times they will face a lot of difficulty in their personal life or academics. I feel like these are inspirational and reading them reminds me that I can overcome any kind of hardship.

Available and Accessible Resources for AISs to Improve Mental Health and Adjustment

The participants emphasized that they wanted information about accessible and available resources such as mental health services, academic assistance, physical activity groups, the Asian cultural center, student organizations, and international student resources. For example, P14 said, "I think the messages should contain information about what help we can get from which resources, and when they can help me with solving the problems in these areas..." P17 stated, "I hope that international students can take advantage of the programs and resources on campus. I think it would be great if you could list all the resources."

Seeking Help from Social Network and Developing Interpersonal Skills

The participants described that when they encountered emotional or psychological problems, sometimes they were not willing to seek help or did not know how to seek help from family and friends, due to stereotypes or a tendency to solve problems on their own. This theme closely resonated with the first theme of "stigma" as it prevented participants from seeking help regarding their mental health issues. P1 stated,

> I think maybe stereotypes also play a role [in my help-seeking behavior]. Everyone expects Asians to be smart, and that does not apply to me, because I am bad at math. Sometimes I hesitate getting help, because I feel like other people assume that I am intelligent.

P6 noted,

> When there is some problem, most of us try to deal with it on our own and we rarely ask for help. So, I feel like whenever there is a problem, they should definitely go and seek help from maybe their friends, or academic advisor, or anyone.

Additionally, the participants were not sure how to build a good relationship with American peers or how to interact with faculty. The participants offered several suggestions, such as getting involved in a program, making friends with both American and international students, engaging in online interaction, and being active. P25 indicated that "it is hard to cross that barrier if you build it so fast and so strong. So, I would suggest that Asian students make efforts to interact with peers from other cultures from the beginning". P14 said, "You can make friends with the dorm RA or your classmates. Start with a familiar person. You do not have to force yourself to make friends with a stranger."

Difficulty in interacting with instructors/faculty was an additional issue that AISs needed guidance on. Although the participants desired to have a good relationship with the instructors/faculty, they did not know the appropriate approach to interact, saying, "I would like to receive messages about establishing a positive relationship with faculty"; "I am still not sure how to build a good relationship with the American faculty. I would expect to interact with the faculty like friends and to have a stable and long-standing relationship with the faculty."

Adjusting to American Culture and College Life

The participants responded that when they came to the United States, they were struggling with a sense of confusion and unfamiliarity, and did not know how to better adjust to American college and culture. The participants pointed out that attending programs on the campus was a great way to know about the university culture, get along with diverse students, enjoy various activities, and become comfortable with the unfamiliar environment. For example, P19 suggested,

> There is an organization called "UR Global," which is for international students. I attended their activities in my first semester, and then as a volunteer and peer educator. There is also an organization "CRU" in the church. They have an international brunch; whose staff and volunteers are Americans. I learned a lot about culture and getting involved in local activities from them.

P22 mentioned,

> You can also talk about the organizations that celebrate similar things. With Chinese New Year coming up, there is the Chinese association and the Malaysian association to celebrate with food and snacks. There are people out there that celebrate the same things as you do and understand.

American Classroom Norms. The participants perceived that there were great differences between the Asian classroom and the American classroom, which made the process of engaging more difficult for them. For example, P6 narrated,

> It is very different between the US and China. In China, the teacher often calls your name in the class; but in the US, the students always have their hand up, asking or answering questions. They do not care if they are wrong or right. But in China it is different, because before you put your hand up, you have to

think about if your answer is right or not. Sometimes nobody answers, because the students are afraid that they are wrong.

Cultural Differences. Large differences between Asian and American culture were another issue that hindered the progress of cultural adjustment of AISs. For example, P1 stated, "American culture is so different from ours. I am not used to American culture, like they have a lot of parties, they play balls on the roadside, and say hi to you even if you are a stranger." The participants believed that there were many aspects in American culture that are different from Asian culture, while the prior is more open and active and the latter is more introverted.

Coping Strategies To Improve Mental Health and Adjustment

The participants required specific strategies that they can use to improve mental health and adjustment, such as positive thinking, problem-solving skills, time management tips, healthy eating, coping with stress, and physical exercise. P18 stated,

> There was a lecture about mental health, telling you how to transform negative thoughts. Shift your thoughts. I think it is a good skill to have. You can also include some strategies about problem-solving skills. For example, first figure out what causes your distress and look for ways to solve it.

P6 mentioned,

> I would like to receive practical messages that contain specific strategies to reduce stress and eat healthy food. I like to do some exercises, like playing soccer or basketball, to help reduce pressure. Purdue University fitness center offers classes like swimming, dancing, Zumba, yoga, and Pilates - all that kind of stuff.

Safety Issues for AISs

The participants implied that as AISs, they were not familiar with the safety issues in the United States, which caused pressure. For example, one participant emphasized the need of increasing safety awareness and knowledge:

> Safety is another critical issue. Lafayette is a safe place, but there are some aspects you need to be aware of, such as sexual harassment. It is not a topic that is discussed at the incoming student orientation. So, you might offend others unintentionally, or get harassed by others; we need to know how to deal with safety issues.

Therefore, this theme introduced what the students should do to keep safe, and if they have safety problems, where they could go for help. This theme also contains updated information about campus events for Asian students.

Other Features

From the focus groups, the participants also emphasized some desirable features of the messages they liked, such as text that was short, concise, funny, inspiring, specific, or attractive, which was taken into account in developing the messages. For example, P16 described that "I would like to get known the tips to reduce anxiety or manage stress are helpful. More specific they are, the more useful to me. For example, walking, or riding a bike –something you can do easily."

Application of the PEN-3 Model in Developing the Message Content

After determining the topics of messages through focus groups, we designed the tailored messages content using the PEN-3 cultural framework, centralizing culture at the core of the health seeking behavior of the AISs. Application of the PEN-3 model occurred in three steps. In each step, we explored a domain of the model and the cultural inputs incorporated into the message.

Persons, Extended Family, and Neighborhoods

First, we studied the available literature on the mental health and adjustment needs of AISs studying in the United States.

Perceptions, Enablers, and Nurturers

Second, we determined perceptions and enablers (systemic factors) that may restrict or promote mental health and adjustment of AISs, and the degree to which their family and community (nurturers) shaped their cultural values around mental health. We adapted the messages to increase acceptance and potential benefits based on identified perceptions, enabling and nurturing cultural factors. The tailored messages delivered substantial information about mental health and adjustment, improving the awareness of AISs and reducing stigma toward mental illness and help seeking (perceptions). We also developed tailored messages to reflect the specific barriers and protective factors experienced by AISs. These messages featured Asian culture and family contexts including idioms and other cultural elements, such as interdependent relationship with social groups, perseverance, and filial piety (perceptions and enablers). Additionally, the messages contained the information about available local resources for

AIS populations, as well as interpersonal communication strategies with people from diverse cultures (enablers and nurturers).

Positive, Existential, and Negative

Third, we identified cultural norms, practices, and behaviors that play a good role, no role, or harmful role in promoting mental health and adjustment in AISs. We conducted literature review, focus groups, and interviews to address knowledge deficits and benefits of cultural norms regarding mental illnesses. For example, positive components included values emphasizing collectivism in enlisting family and social networks for assistance, values focusing on harmony, and garnering support from other AISs in cultural networks. Existential components were, for example, the Chinese conceptualization of illnesses, which is rooted in the principles of yin-yang and the concept of qi (Taylor & Willies-Jacobo, 2003). Negative components included pressure to maintain harmony, conflict-free relationships, and shame (Yick, et al., 2009). Taking these components into account, we incorporated motivational messages about the benefits of mental health, education on depression, learning about coping skills, and building resilience into the tailored messages.

DISCUSSION

Overall, the tailored messages developed through the participants' inputs reflected Asian cultural norms and AISs' specific needs, which helps AISs address their challenges in the United States (e.g., weak social support, lack of awareness of mental health and available resources, and struggle in asking for help from family and peers). The research enriches prior studies in highlighting the importance of culturally tailored interventions (Dobson et al., 2017; Fisher et al., 2007). The study reinforces that tailored messages attract more attention, are handled more attentively, cover fewer unneeded words, and are often seen encouragingly by the message receivers (Lustria et al., 2013; Marcus et al., 2005; Smeets et al., 2006). Such cultural tailoring functions through raising the personal relevance of messages, which motivates and persuades individuals to change behaviors (Hawkins et al., 2008). Therefore, cultural tailoring may facilitate building of a comfortable and ideal environment in programs that focus on minority populations' needs (Hawkins et al., 2008; Rimer & Kreuter, 2006). The study calls for more culturally tailored interventions that incorporate cultural elements and address needs of underserved groups. Future research could embed the tailored messages into interventions, such as virtual training programs, and investigate the effectiveness of such tailoring in promoting mental health and adjustment of AISs or beyond.

IMPLICATIONS

Tailoring increases the persuasive effectiveness of a message (Kreuter et al., 2000). This study indicated that cultural tailoring could be a practical avenue for advancing culturally responsive interventions. For example, the messages could be used in items such as bookmarks and distributed in incoming student orientation, and pamphlets could be made using the messages as content, designed with images. Apart from that, the tailored messages have the potential to be applied in culturally adapted interventions with other treatments among the AIS population, and improve mental health and adjustment effectively.

The study offered recommendations from the PEN-3 perspective to develop culturally appropriate interventions among AISs. Harnessing Asian value systems (e.g., emphasis on collectivism and social support, saving face, and emotional management) was essential to the development of culturally sensitive interventions (Wong et al., 2014). For example, interventions that promote AISs' interpersonal skills with diverse people can help them build a stronger social support network in the United States. Overall, using the PEN-3 cultural model as the theoretical framework enabled us to identify the intervention entry point as well as promote the perceptions, enablers, or nurturers that are positive, acknowledge those that are existential, and notice the negative. In other words, effective culturally adapted intervention for AISs is as much about stimulating these positive values as it is acknowledging negative values.

Each of the three PEN-3 model dimensions can be used to direct mental health promotion and tailored interventions among AISs. Discussed here are some suggestions for application of these three dimensions in culturally sensitive programs. First, as many Asian communities are collectivist and get their cultural identity from their extended family, neighborhood, and community, those elements should be at the forefront of intervention planning and implementation. Collaborating with members of the community (e.g., peers, faculty, resident assistant, and physicians, etc.) during all stages of the culturally responsive intervention is essential—for example, from designing the tailored messages based on local context to disseminating and utilizing the messages during interactions with AISs. Second, empowering AISs to communicate with families, peers, and other community members (e.g., instructors, faculty, and psychological counselors) can motivate AISs to seek mental health support. For example, improving AISs' understanding of differences in interpersonal relationships and communication styles between the American culture and their own culture may help them effectively interact with people in the university. In addition, tailored messages can include communication strategies used in Asian families for seeking help, such as high-context communication that focuses on underlying context and tone, or use of different means of communication (e.g., written communication). Third, identifying positive cultural norms, such as collectivistic values, family and peer support, and/or traditional festivals hosted by student organizations, can strengthen the cultural relevance of tailored messages. For example, the study suggests that culturally sensitive programs emphasize the message that AIS should view their family, friends, and faculty as a source of support and seek help when facing psychological stress, rather than concealing the problems to save face; AISs should seek proximity to family support emotionally (e.g., "my parents always trust me") or physically (e.g., video chatting) to overcome the challenge of geographic distance and promote adjustment into U.S. college (S. Han et al., 2017).

Limitations and Strengths

The study has several limitations. First, the research did not measure the mental health status of the participants. Therefore, the results may not be generalized to student populations who have major mental health problems. Despite this, the focus of the study is to develop tailored messages that meet needs of AISs and help build their resilience in general, regardless of their current mental health status. Second, a further investigation on the impact of the designed messages would provide an insight on whether these messages can promote the mental health of the participants significantly. Third, the study examined AISs as a broad group to maintain statistical power. Further research on within-group differences in AISs who are composed of diverse cultural backgrounds might reveal differential needs on message tailoring and reactions to the messages.

However, the study has a number of strengths. The research applied a mixed method approach to collect data and develop the messages, including focus groups, individual interviews, and a survey. The mixed methods approach allowed us to acquire in-depth data guiding the design and development of helpful and appropriate messages for AISs. In addition, this study adds to the literature on developing culturally competent programs for the AIS population in the United States (Johnson et al., 2018). The study used the PEN-3 model to centralize culture, integrate culturally relevant factors in the design of culturally tailored messages, and promote mental health and adjustment of AISs through a cultural lens. Research investigating the application of the PEN-3 model on mental health among AISs is missing from the field of culturally sensitive programs, and this research fills that theoretical gap. The results of the study have great potential to be used in practice in international student programming, such as by university administrators, counselors, physicians, staff, faculty, mentors, and peers.

CONCLUSION

In summary, the study developed tailored messages for improving AISs' mental health and adjustment through the PEN-3 cultural framework. We tailored the messages to AISs' difficulties and concerns, including challenges with adjusting to American culture, unwillingness to seek help, social interaction difficulties, and inadequate awareness of mental health and available resources. These messages reflected Asian cultural norms related to mental health, such as collectivism, interdependence, the stigma attached to mental illness and help-seeking, the value of self-management, etc. The study underlined the importance of cultural tailoring as a strategy for intervention in higher education, which may facilitate building an inclusive climate on campus (Hawkins et al., 2008; Rimer & Kreuter, 2006). Future studies could evaluate the effects of tailored messages compared with untailored messages. In addition, future research may test the effectiveness of tailored messages delivered in different formats (e.g., text, image, and video).

REFERENCES

Acharya, L., Jin, L., & Collins, W. (2018). College life is stressful today–Emerging stressors and depressive symptoms in college students. *Journal of American College Health, 66*(7), 655–664. https://doi.org/10.1080/07448481.2018.1451869

Agyapong, V. I., Mrklas, K., Suen, V. Y., Rose, M. S., Jahn, M., Gladue, I., Kozak, J., Leslie, M., Dursun, S., Ohinmaa, A., & Greenshaw, A. (2015). Supportive text messages to reduce mood symptoms and problem drinking in patients with primary depression or alcohol use disorder: protocol for an implementation research study. *JMIR Research Protocols, 4*(2), e55. https://doi.org/10.2196/resprot.4371

Airhihenbuwa, C. O. (1990). A conceptual model for culturally appropriate health education programs in developing countries. *International Quarterly of Community Health Education, 11*(1), 53–62. https://doi.org/10.2190/LPKH-PMPJ-DBW9-FP6X

Airhihenbuwa, C. O. (1995). *Health and culture: Beyond the Western paradigm.* SAGE.

Airhihenbuwa, C., Okoror, T., Shefer, T., Brown, D., Iwelunmor, J., Smith, E., Adam, M., Simbayi, L., Zungu, N., Dlakulu, R., & Shisana, O. (2009).

Stigma, culture, and HIV and AIDS in the Western Cape, South Africa: An application of the PEN-3 cultural model for community-based research. *Journal of Black Psychology, 35*(4), 407–432. https://doi.org/10.1177/0095798408329941

Boeije, H. (2002). A purposeful approach to the constant comparative method in the analysis of qualitative interviews. *Quality and Quantity, 36*(4), 391–409. https://doi.org/10.1023/A:1020909529486

Bramley, D. M., Riddell, T., Whittaker, R., Corbett, T., Lin, R., Wills, M. J., Jones, M., & Rodgers, A. (2005). Smoking cessation using mobile phone text messaging is as effective in Maori as non-Maori. *The New Zealand Medical Journal, 118*(1216), U1494.

Chen, S. X., Mak, W. W. S., & Lam, B. C. P. (2020). Is it cultural context or cultural value? Unpackaging cultural influences on stigma toward mental illness and barrier to help-seeking. *Social Psychological and Personality Science, 11*(7), 1022–1031. https://doi.org/10.1177/1948550619897482

Cowdery, J. E., Parker, S., & Thompson, A. (2010). Application of the PEN-3 model in a diabetes prevention intervention. *Journal of Health Disparities Research and Practice, 4*(1), 3. Available at: https://digitalscholarship.unlv.edu/jhdrp/vol4/iss1/3

Daga, S. S., Lin, K. L., & Raval, V. V. (2020). Asian international students' construals of well-being and distress. *International Perspectives in Psychology: Research, Practice, Consultation, 9*(4), 193–211. https://doi.org/10.1037/ipp0000145

Denzin, N. K., & Lincoln, Y. S. (2011). *The SAGE handbook of qualitative research*. SAGE.

Dobson, R., Whittaker, R., Bartley, H., Connor, A., Chen, R., Ross, M., & McCool, J. (2017). Development of a culturally tailored text message maternal health program: TextMATCH. *JMIR mHealth and uHealth, 5*(4), e49. https://doi.org/10.2196/mhealth.7205

Fisher, T. L., Burnet, D. L., Huang, E. S., Chin, M. H., & Cagney, K. A. (2007). Cultural leverage: interventions using culture to narrow racial disparities in health care. *Medical Care Research and Review: MCRR, 64*(5 Suppl), 243S–282S. https://doi.org/10.1177/1077558707305414

Glaser, B. (1978). *Theoretical sensitivity*. Sociology Press.

Glaser, B. (1992). *Emergence v forcing basics of grounded theory analysis*. Sociology Press.

Glaser, B., Strauss, A. (1967). *The discovery of grounded theory*. Aldine.

Griner, D., & Smith, T. B. (2006). Culturally adapted mental health intervention: A meta-analytic review. *Psychotherapy: Theory, Research, Practice, Training, 43*(4), 531–548. https://doi.org/10.1037/0033-3204.43.4.531

Guba, E. G., & Lincoln, Y. S. (1994). Competing paradigms in qualitative research. In N. K. Denzin & Y. S. Lincoln (Eds.), *Handbook of qualitative research* (pp. 105–117). SAGE.

Gustafson, D. H., McTavish, F. M., Chih, M. Y., Atwood, A. K., Johnson, R. A., Boyle, M. G., Levy, M. S., Driscoll, H., Chisholm, S. M., Dillenburg, L.,

Isham, A., & Shah, D. (2014). A smartphone application to support recovery from alcoholism: A randomized clinical trial. *JAMA Psychiatry, 71*(5), 566–572. https://doi.org/10.1001/jamapsychiatry.2013.4642

Han, S., Pistole, M. C., & Caldwell, J. M. (2017). Acculturative stress, parental and professor attachment, and college adjustment in Asian international students. *Journal of Multicultural Counseling and Development, 45*, 111–126. https://doi.org/10.1002/jmcd.12068

Han, X., Han, X., Luo, Q., Jacobs, S., & Jean-Baptiste, M. (2013). Report of a mental health survey among Chinese international students at Yale University. *Journal of American College Health, 61*(1), 1–8. https://doi.org/10.1080/07448481.2012.738267

Hawkins, R. P., Kreuter, M., Resnicow, K., Fishbein, M., & Dijkstra, A. (2008). Understanding tailoring in communicating about health. *Health Education Research, 23*(3), 454–466. https://doi.org/10.1093/her/cyn004

Hofstede, G. (2011). Dimensionalizing cultures: The Hofstede model in context. *Online Readings in Psychology and Culture, 2*(1). https://doi.org/10.9707/2307-0919.1014

Institute of International Education. (2019). Research & insights: Open doors. Retrieved April 10, 2021, from https://www.iie.org/Research-and-Insights/Open-DoorsIwelunmor, J., Newsome, V., & Airhihenbuwa, C. O. (2014). Framing the impact of culture on health: a systematic review of the PEN-3 cultural model and its application in public health research and interventions. *Ethnicity & Health, 19*(1), 20-46. https://doi.org/10.1080/13557858.2013.857768

Jin, L., & Acharya, L. (2016). Cultural beliefs underlying medication adherence in people of Chinese descent in the United States. *Health Communication, 31*(5), 513-521. https://doi.org/10.1080/10410236.2014.974121

Johnson, L. R., Seifen-Adkins, T., Singh Sandhu, D., Arbles, N., & Makino, H. (2018). Developing culturally responsive programs to promote international student adjustment: a participatory approach. *Journal of International Students, 8*(4), 1865–1878. https://doi.org/10.32674/jis.v8i4.235

Kreuter, M. W., Oswald, D. L., Bull, F. C., & Clark, E. M. (2000). Are tailored health education materials always more effective than non-tailored materials? *Health Education Research, 15*(3), 305–315. https://doi.org/10.1093/her/15.3.305

Kreuter, M. W., & Wray, R. J. (2003). Tailored and targeted health communication: Strategies for enhancing information relevance. *American Journal of Health Behavior, 27*(Suppl 3), S227–S232. https://doi.org/10.5993/ajhb.27.1.s3.6

Liu, H., Wong, Y. J., Mitts, N. G., Li, P. J., & Cheng, J. (2020). A phenomenological study of East Asian international students' experience of counseling. *International Journal for the Advancement of Counselling, 42*(3), 269–291. https://doi.org/10.1007/s10447-020-09399-6

Lustria, M. L. A., Noar, S. M., Cortese, J., Van Stee, S. K., Glueckauf, R. L., & Lee, J. (2013). A meta-analysis of web-delivered tailored health behavior change interventions. *Journal of Health Communication, 18*(9), 1039–1069. https://doi.org/10.1080/10810730.2013.768727

Ma, K., Pitner, R., Sakamoto, I., & Park, H. Y. (2020). Challenges in acculturation among international students from Asian collectivist cultures. *Higher Education Studies, 10*(3), 34–43.

Marcus, A. C., Mason, M., Wolfe, P., Rimer, B. K., Lipkus, I., Strecher, V., Warneke, R., Morra, M. E., Allen, A. R., Davis, S. W., Gaier, A., Graves, C., Julesberg, K., Nguyen, L., Perocchia, R., Speyer, J. B., Wagner, D., Thomsen, C., & Bright, M. A. (2005). The efficacy of tailored print materials in promoting colorectal cancer screening: Results from a randomized trial involving callers to the National Cancer Institute's Cancer Information Service. *Journal of Health Communication, 10*(Suppl 1), 83–104. https://doi.org/10.1080/10810730500257754

Mikal, J. P., Yang, J., & Lewis, A. (2015). Surfing USA: How internet use prior to and during study abroad affects Chinese students' stress, integration, and cultural learning while in the United States. *Journal of Studies in International Education, 19*(3), 203–224. https://doi.org/10.1177/1028315314536990

Morrison, F. P., Kukafka, R., & Johnson, S. B. (2005). Analyzing the structure and content of public health messages. *AMIA Annual Symposium Proceedings, 2005,* 540–544.

Nimmon, L., Poureslami, I., & FitzGerald, J. M. (2012). What counts as cultural competency in telehealth interventions? A call for new directions. *Journal of Telemedicine and Telecare, 18*(7), 425–426. https://doi.org/10.1258/jtt.2012.120517

Noar, S. M., Grant Harrington, N., Van Stee, S. K., & Shemanski Aldrich, R. (2011). Tailored health communication to change lifestyle behaviors. *American Journal of Lifestyle Medicine, 5*(2), 112–122. https://doi.org/10.1177/1559827610387255

Petty, R. E., & Cacioppo, J. T. (1979). Issue involvement can increase or decrease persuasion by enhancing message-relevant cognitive responses. *Journal of Personality and Social Psychology, 37*(10), 1915–1926. https://doi.org/10.1037/0022-3514.37.10.1915

Ra, Y. A., & Trusty, J. (2017). Impact of social support and coping on acculturation and acculturative stress of East Asian international students. *Journal of Multicultural Counseling and Development, 45,* 276–291. https://doi.org/10.1002/jmcd.12078

Rimer, B. K., & Kreuter, M. W. (2006). Advancing tailored health communication: A persuasion and message effects perspective. *Journal of Communication, 56,* S184–S201. https://doi.org/10.1111/j.1460-2466.2006.00289.x

Ruzek, N. A., Nguyen, D. Q., & Herzog, D. C. (2011). Acculturation, enculturation, psychological distress and help-seeking preferences among

Asian American college students. *Asian American Journal of Psychology*, *2*(3), 181–196. https://doi.org/10.1037/a0024302

Smeets, T., Brug, J., & de Vries, H. (2006). Effects of tailoring health messages on physical activity. *Health Education Research*, *23*(3), 402–413. https://doi.org/10.1093/her/cyl101

Strauss, A., & Corbin, J. (1998). *Basics of qualitative research: Grounded theory. procedures and technique* (2nd ed.). SAGE.

Strecher, V. J., Kreuter, M., Den Boer, D.-J., Kobrin, S., Hospers, H. J., & Skinner, C. S. (1994). The effects of computer-tailored smoking cessation messages in family practice settings. *Journal of Family Practice*, *39*(3), 262–270.

Sue, S., Yan Cheng, J. K., Saad, C. S., & Chu, J. P. (2012). Asian American mental health: A call to action. *The American Psychologist*, *67*(7), 532–544. https://doi.org/10.1037/a0028900

Taylor, L., & Willies-Jacobo, L. J. (2003). The culturally competent pediatrician: Respecting ethnicity in your practice. *Contemporary Pediatrics*, *20*(6), 83. https://link.gale.com/apps/doc/A104032011/AONE?u=anon~79606c9a&sid=googleScholar&xid=1b5a791f

Triandis, H. C. (1995). *Individualism & collectivism*. Boulder, CO: Westview Press

Updegraff, J. A., Sherman, D. K., Luyster, F. S., & Mann, T. L. (2007). The effects of message quality and congruency on perceptions of tailored health communications. *Journal of Experimental Social Psychology*, *43*(2), 249–257. https://doi.org/10.1016/j.jesp.2006.01.007

Wei, J., Hollin, I., & Kachnowski, S. (2011). A review of the use of mobile phone text messaging in clinical and healthy behaviour interventions. *Journal of Telemedicine and Telecare*, *17*(1), 41–48. https://doi.org/10.1258/jtt.2010.100322

Williams-Piehota, P., Schneider, T. R., Pizarro, J., Mowad, L., & Salovey, P. (2003). Matching health messages to information-processing styles: Need for cognition and mammography utilization. *Health Communication*, *15*(4), 375–392. https://doi.org/10.1207/S15327027HC1504_01

Wong, Y. J., Wang, K. T., & Maffini, C. S. (2014). Asian international students' mental health related outcomes: A person context cultural framework. *The Counseling Psychologist*, *42*, 278–305. http://dx.doi.org/10.1177/0011000013482592

Yick, A. G., & Oomen-Early, J. (2009). Using the PEN-3 model to plan culturally competent domestic violence intervention and prevention services in Chinese American and immigrant communities. *Health Education, 109* (2), 125-139. https://doi.org/10.1108/09654280910936585

Author Biographics

LAN JIN, PhD, is an intercultural research specialist in the Center for Intercultural Learning, Mentorship, Assessment and Research (CILMAR) at Purdue University. Her major research interests lie in the area of intercultural competence development, program design and evaluation, and mental health of international students. Email: jin124@purdue.edu

LALATENDU ACHARYA, PhD, is an assistant professor in the Department of Allied Health Science at Indiana University Kokomo. His research examines the different pathways to influence health behavior and address disparities through participatory health communication, health promotion and marketing interventions. Under this thematic area, he works on addressing health behavioral issues and disparity outcomes in the fields of mental health and environmental health, especially in adolescents, college students, and vulnerable communities. Email: lacharya@iu.edu

Article

© *Journal of International Students*
Volume 12, Issue 4 (2022), pp. 843-866
ISSN: 2162-3104 (Print), 2166-3750 (Online)
doi: 10.32674/jis.v12i2.3594
ojed.org/jis

Intracultural and Intercultural Contact Orientation of International Students in Japan: Uncertainty Management by Cultural Identification

Norihito Taniguchi
Jiro Takai
Nagoya University, Japan

Dariusz Skowronski
Temple University, Japan

ABSTRACT

The lack of exchange between international students and host nationals in Japan has long been a pressing issue, yet very little progress has been made to rectify this situation. In this study, we examined this issue by focusing on how international students in Japan perceive cultural contact with their host and home culture members during their sojourn. The study applied a qualitative approach based on grounded theory, collecting data through semi-structured interviews with 41 international students from China, the United Kingdom, and the United States. According to the social identity and anxiety/uncertainty management approach, we interpreted the findings on how international students manage uncertainty in the Japanese environment by identifying with the host and their own home cultures for their psychological well-being, which we distinguished as intercultural or intracultural contact orientation. International students demonstrated an intracultural rather than intercultural contact orientation due to the host nationals reacting to them as "foreigners."

Keywords: adaptation, adjustment, cultural contact, cultural identification, international students, psychological well-being, Japan

In 2008, the Japanese government declared a plan to host 300,000 international students by 2020 to fortify its labor force by retaining them after graduation, while simultaneously internationalizing its own college students by increasing their presence on campuses and the cross-cultural interaction thereof (Ashizawa, 2013). By 2019, the number had reached 312,214 (228,403 in higher education institutions), a 4-fold increase from 1999 (Japan Student Services Organization, 2019). A recent survey showed that 92% of privately financed international students were satisfied with their study abroad. However, of these, only about 40% reported that they actually "made Japanese friends" (Japan Student Services Organization, 2018). Contrary to the government's aims, the increase in the number of international students has not necessarily led to increased relationship building with Japanese cohorts.

This lack of cross-cultural exchange has been documented by academic research (e.g., Kagami, 2006; Murphy-Shigematsu, 2002a, 2002b; Takai, 1995). While various factors affect insufficient engagement on both sides, the literature on this matter makes reference to multiple psychological barriers for international students in Japan. For example, Western students (typically Caucasian) are treated as outsiders, and some complain that they are never allowed to forget that they are foreigners; it makes them aware of being perceived as "different" by the Japanese (Murphy-Shigematsu, 2002a). In other studies, Chinese students encounter more psychological difficulties than Western students due to their ambivalent acculturation attitudes toward Japanese culture (Yin et al., 2021). Korean students also feel prejudice and discrimination by the Japanese, most likely due to Japan's strong sense of group consciousness, which creates a psychological barrier for them to accept Koreans into their peer membership (Murphy-Shigematsu, 2002b). Regardless of international students' nationalities, they face these psychological struggles in their relationship with their hosts, preferring to stay within their own groups.

Meanwhile, such psychological distress might be buffered by receiving social support from compatriots and other foreign nationals in Japan, and thus their social network formation is not limited to the hosts. The psychological well-being (e.g., sense of well-being and self-esteem) of international students in the host country, namely, psychological adjustment, is strongly affected by personality, life changes, and social support (Ward & Kennedy, 1994). Notably, social support from compatriots and co-internationals strongly affects their psychological state in allowing them to maintain their own culture, while helping to cope with stress (Bochner et al., 1977). International students in Japan mainly receive emotional support (e.g., mental stability) from their compatriots, academic support (e.g., Japanese language and culture) from the Japanese, and recreational support (e.g., off-campus activities) from other foreign nationals (Takai, 1995). Recent research suggests that international students need to learn the social skills of Japanese people to actively receive such support (Tanaka & Okunishi, 2016). Naturally, the more they engage with people, the more they receive social support, leading to their psychological well-being. Thus, social network formation is the key to the international student's mental health, and addressing the issues of social engagement, or the lack thereof, is important.

In the psychological well-being literature, many researchers have confirmed that group identification enhances individuals' psychological well-being (e.g., Haslam, 2004; Jetten et al., 2010; Sani et al., 2015; Wakefield et al., 2017). The concept of group identification, which is our sense of belonging to the group, coupled with our sense of commonality with its members (Sani et al., 2015), derives from the social identity paradigm of social psychology (Haslam, 2004). Social identity theory (Tajfel & Turner, 1986) deals with how individuals perceive themselves to be members of a particular social group. Those who share common group membership constitute the ingroup, while those of other groups are the outgroup. In line with this perspective, group identification can buffer the individual from the everyday stress of life by providing a sense of belonging and security, increasing the likelihood of the individual perceiving the availability of useful support from fellow ingroup members (Jetten et al., 2010). Also, stronger identification with each cultural group (or multiple group membership) predicts better psychological well-being in the cross-cultural community (Wakefield et al., 2017). Likewise, in the case of international students who experience identity shift, they can attain psychological well-being by identifying with the host cultural group, while concurrently identifying with their cultural group of origin (cultural identification; de la Sablonnière et al., 2016). Recent literature has found that individuals do not identify with a cultural group that adds negative value to their social identity; instead, if the new cultural group has a positive value, they are likely to want to participate in it, and subsequently increase identification with that group (Cardenas & de la Sablonnière, 2020).

Furthermore, this cultural identification, which serves as norms or guides for how they should think, feel, and behave, allows them to reduce or manage uncertainty effectively in intercultural situations, where their traditional norms may be ineffective (Hogg & Belavadi, 2017). Individuals experience greater uncertainty when communicating with persons from different cultures (Gudykunst, 2005). Additionally, intercultural situations pose more anxiety than intracultural (Gudykunst & Nishida, 2001); thus, hosts may be compelled to avoid encounters with international students (Neuliep, 2012). Likewise, if international students feel intergroup anxiety, and lack self-confidence in communicating with the hosts, they would have difficulty engaging with them (Florack et al., 2014). If both international students and their hosts have a high level of anxiety (and uncertainty), they are less likely to interact (Logan et al., 2014). From the above, it would seem to reason that the anxiety/uncertainty management approach (Gudykunst, 2005), as well as the social identity approach, are crucial for investigating the engagement between international students and their hosts.

Taken together, the literature suggests that investigating the psychological well-being of international students and their engagement with both hosts and nonhosts is crucial for addressing issues pertaining to their mutual engagement or lack thereof. The utility of examining these issues through the social identity and anxiety/uncertainty management approaches is also evident. Accordingly, this study aims to clarify how international students perceive their interaction with the host and home culture members, especially the factors promoting or hindering this engagement.

In this study, "international students" are defined as a student from a foreign country who is granted the status of residence as "university student" (student visa) and who is receiving education at a university in Japan (Japan Student Services Organization, 2019). "Host culture" refers to Japanese culture. "Hosts" or "host culture members" refers to Japanese who engage or communicate with international students, including fellow students (classmates or peers), nonstudent adults at their workplace, and host families. By contrast, "home culture" pertains to that of the international student's home country. "Home culture members" refers to, in general, friends/relatives in their home country or compatriots in Japan.

METHOD

We employed qualitative research to explore international students' cultural contact perceptions in Japan using grounded theory (Charmaz, 2014). Grounded theory aims to generate a theory pertaining to a certain process from data provided by participants post hoc (Creswell & Poth, 2016). For our purposes, the grounded theory was suitable, given the paucity of research on the topic, and the exploratory nature of our research aims to explore international students' cultural contact perception.

In addition, this study addressed the lack of cross-cultural exchange between international students and the hosts; it required quality assurance of international students' narratives, not their prejudices. According to the

Contact Hypothesis (Allport, 1954), quantitative and qualitative contacts are essential to reduce prejudice between international students and host and home culture members. To prevent such prejudice, we set three conditions for participation in this study. First, this study focused on international students from three countries: China, England, and the United States. The reasons to enumerate three countries are because first, those countries are prime study abroad destinations of Japanese students; about 62.1% of Japanese students choose China, the United Kingdom, and the United States (Organisation for Economic Cooperation and Development, 2017), and second, those are the leading countries in Asia and Western countries where Japan hosts international students (Japan Student Services Organization, 2019). Next, we set two additional conditions for participation: (a) enrollment in Japanese higher education institutions for over one semester, and (b) engaging in active contact with the Japanese or compatriots/fellow internationals for more than two or three times a week. By setting these conditions, we assured the quality of international students' narratives. After completing the research design, this study was approved by the Nagoya University Institutional Review Board on May 22, 2019 (ID:1286).

Participants and Recruitment Process

We recruited international students by email from June 2019 to February 2020 through several faculty at large public universities with a sizable international student population in Tokyo and Nagoya, Japan. We gathered a total of 53 participants during the above period and selected 41 participants who met all three participation conditions of this study. Table 1 presents the demographic information of participants. The first author conducted semistructured interviews with 41 participants for 60–90 minutes in English. In line with the study's aim and relevant literature review, the contents of the interviews were: (a) demographic information; (b) differences in communication; (c) host/home cultural identity; (d) motivation/stress; (e) behavioral changes; (f) culture shock; and (g) positive/negative experiences through interaction.

Data Collection and Analysis

Guided by grounded theory (Charmaz, 2014), we used theoretical sampling to collect and analyze data. Theoretical sampling is an iterative sampling process in which data from prior interviews identifies whom to interview, the addition of participants, and subsequent adoption of new concepts. All interviews were recorded with the consent of the participant, and the data were later transcribed. We analyzed transcripts in three steps: initial coding, focused coding, and theoretical coding. The first author coded the interview data line by line, then coded these into broader categories, and finally sorted out the tentative major and subcategories.

Table 1

Demographic Information of Participants (N =41)

Student profile	n	%
Gender		
Male	11	27
Female	30	73
Age range		
18–20 years	12	29
21–30 years	29	71
Country		
China	8	19
United Kingdom	9	22
United States	24	59
Academic status		
Undergraduate	17	41
1-year exchange	15	37
Master	3	7
Pre-master	2	5
Pre-doctor	1	3
G30 (Full-degree program taught in English)	3	7
Japanese language proficiency		
High	17	42
Intermediate	12	29
Low	12	29
Period in Japan		
Less than 1 year	28	68
1 to under 2 years	7	17
2 to under 3 years	4	10
More than 3 years	2	5

After the tentative conceptual categories were determined, they were checked for relevance with data, codes, and analytical memos, and fitted into a tentative conceptual model that reflected this study's phenomena of interest. Then, the first author repeatedly checked the tentative model with the second author and subsequently with the participants to confirm whether it reflected and described their worldviews. If not, we interviewed additional participants and refined the categories. We stopped the interviews when no further data were observed to provide new insights and when the concept was adequately established (theoretical saturation; Charmaz, 2014, p. 214). Such iterative data collection and analysis process controlled authors' biases, reflecting participants' worldviews, and shaping a solid foundation for a robust theoretical model of cultural contact (Creswell & Poth, 2016). Overall, two major categories, each containing four subcategories, emerged from the analysis in this study, which will be provided below.

Table 2

Major Categories and Subcategories

Major categories	Subcategories
1. Intercultural contact orientation	1.1: Identifying with host cultural identity as primary and home cultural identity as secondary
	1.2: Motivation to learn host cultural norms / self-imposed stress
	1.3: Imitating host cultural behavior
	1.4: Engaging with hosts
2. Intracultural contact orientation	2.1: Identifying with home culture identity as primary and host cultural identity as secondary
	2.2: Motivation to maintain home cultural norms / stress imposed by hosts
	2.3: Maintaining home cultural behavior
	2.4: Clashing with host cultural norms

RESULTS

From the responses of the 41 international students, two major categories emerged regarding their cultural contact. The first category was named "intercultural contact orientation." This refers to engagement with people from different cultures. The second category was labeled "intracultural contact orientation." This pertains to engagement with people from the same or similar cultures. The two major categories are not mutually exclusive. For instance, some may communicate both with the Japanese and the international students equally, whereas others have more or less communication with either group. The two major categories were further divided into four subcategories respectively, as indicated in Table 2. Quotations from research participants are shared to exemplify each category.

Intercultural Contact Orientation

The first major category drawn from the data was intercultural contact orientation. International students with this orientation basically want to assimilate into Japanese culture and be like the Japanese. They tend to engage with the hosts such as Japanese students and Japanese adults at work rather than engaging with other international students. From this perspective, four subcategories explained the properties of the contact orientation in detail.

Identifying with Host Cultural Identity as Primary and Home Cultural Identity as Secondary

Adjustment to Japanese society involves making decisions about how much of the host culture to take on and how much of one's home culture to retain. Many participants saw themselves as actively changing to fit in with Japanese culture, while maintaining the identity, language, and traditions of the home culture was also an integral part of international students' lives while in Japan. In this context, this code emerged during data analysis as the most typical and basic perception of participants through engagement with Japanese students: "I would try (to be) 100% Japanese. I want to assimilate as much as I can. [But] it completely depends on whom I talk to and interact with" (U.S. student).

Notably, several participants felt being accepted by the Japanese, feeling safe and comfortable in their new environment. This accepted experience, in turn, stirred participants to accept the Japanese culture. Consequently, the emphasis on identification with host cultural identity (Japanese) emerged in this study: "Because you are accepted for who you are (by the Japanese), you should accept how they (the Japanese) do things. A lot of my friends or Japanese accepted me for who I am" (U.K. student).

In particular, those who were half-Japanese, regardless of their origins, perceived that their Asian appearance faded their awareness of racial differences, which facilitated them to identify as Japanese culture members: "I honestly forgot (my race) here because it does not really matter. People see me (the Japanese) because I act like Japanese" (U.S. student).

Not to be seen as foreigners by the Japanese was indispensable for participants to be able to recognize themselves as members of Japanese social circles.

Motivation to Learn Host Cultural Norms / Self-Imposed Stress

Many participants who made decisions about taking on Japanese culture often expressed a desire to learn the cultural norms by engaging with many Japanese. Intercultural communication with the Japanese enabled participants to obtain actual cultural information and internalize it: "I would like to interact with more Japanese students just because they are heavily into the[ir] studies (diligence)... I am personally motivated" (U.S. student).

However, some participants who wanted to understand Japanese cultural norms deeply were confused by the indirect communication style of the hosts, causing much ambiguity and unfamiliarity: "It is very hard to gauge how Japanese people feel about you. You always worry about how they might feel about you" (U.S. student).

Those participants with a strong motivation to learn Japanese cultural norms put pressure on themselves to be like the Japanese; some participants changed their direct communication styles to be more indirect to suit their hosts.

Imitating Host Cultural Behavior

Many participants perceived that imitating Japanese cultural behaviors was the most appropriate way to internalize the host culture. Those students first focused on differences in behaviors between the Japanese and their own cultures, and then observed meanings and ways of the behaviors, and finally modeled the behaviors: "I just observe everyone and what is the norm...I tried to change by using more Japanese. I would try to imitate a conversation with people I don't know" (U.S. student).

As a result of imitating Japanese cultural behaviors, those students felt inclusiveness of the Japanese community while some students even felt like an inhabitant with prolonged residence: "I tried to assimilate and felt more included. I become more comfortable and have a sense of community like the style of dress, cultural behavior like bowing" (U.S. student).

Such emotional change induced participants to internalize Japanese cultural norms further. The more they internalized these norms, the more they thought, felt, and behaved like the Japanese.

Engaging with Hosts

While many participants imitated Japanese thoughts, feelings, and behaviors, successful experiences of building relationships with the Japanese led participants to assimilate into their culture more easily. The most common relationships were friendships with Japanese students, while others had romantic relationships or marriage relationships with them: "I hang out with [Japanese friends]. Around this time, I wanted to establish a strong relationship with others (the Japanese). I had more self-confidence and social" (U.S. student).

The intimate relationships with the Japanese gradually broke participants' stereotypes against them, making them feel part of their community. The experiences, then, triggered changes of participants' thoughts, feelings, and behaviors of the home culture into those of the host culture: "I start[ed] living [in], interacting [with], going to places where the Japanese go, not tourists. I changed the perspective from that of a tourist to that of an inhabitant" (U.K. student). Such deep engagement with the Japanese prompted participants' identification as members of the Japanese social circle.

As discussed, participants who identified with host cultural identity were motivated to learn host cultural norms and imitate its behaviors. Those participants often established relationships with the Japanese, which further allowed them to identify themselves as host culture members. In this way, participants gradually assimilated into the host culture. This cyclical process refers to the process of intercultural contact.

Intracultural Contact Orientation

The second major category drawn from the data was intracultural contact orientation. International students with this orientation generally maintain their own culture and consider Japanese culture separate. They typically spend time with international students or other foreign people living in Japan from the same or similar cultures, rather than engaging with the Japanese students. From this view, four subcategories closely described the components of the contact orientation.

Identifying with Home Cultural Identity as Primary and Host Cultural Identity as Secondary

Commonly, any study abroad aims to adjust to the host culture and learn it. However, a majority of participants in this study recognized that their cultural values and personalities were incompatible with the Japanese cultural norms: "I have never wanted to adapt to Japanese culture...I already have all of the cultures that I want...I do not really think it fits with my personality" (U.S. student).

Notably, those participants, in particular Caucasians, repeatedly sensed the Japanese seeing them as foreigners, which hindered their involvement in Japanese culture, resulting in the strengthening of their home cultural maintenance: "I was automatically called Ryuugakusei (international student). The fact that I was identified (as an) international student, makes me (feel) like...(I) am temporally here" (U.K. student).

Participants with multicultural backgrounds or strong ethnic identities were fully aware of being treated as foreigners by the Japanese. As those participants originally had strong bonds to their own culture, they had no intention of assimilating into Japanese culture: "I feel like China is very big and propaganda. The nationalism is very big concept and deeply rooted in the Chinese mindset. Wherever I am, I am still Chinese" (U.S. student).

These narratives suggested that their home cultural identities were deeply rooted in their heart, and the "foreigner treatment" by the Japanese is a crucial psychological barrier toward mutual interaction between participants and the Japanese.

Motivation to Maintain Home Cultural Norms / Stress Imposed by Hosts

Participants who realized the incompatibility between their own culture and Japanese culture often maintained their own cultural norms, engaging with those from the same/similar cultures, and recalling their own cultural standards of the home country: "[I have mainly] Chinese friends. It's easy and fast to get to know each other...Japanese people are slowly and slowly [taking] down the wall" (U.S. student).

Some participants who maintain their own cultural norms felt stress from the Japanese, likely because their home cultural norms rarely worked well in Japan: "It is stressful for me. Usually, the Japanese are really in their friends' group and walk together. It is hard to get into a relationship" (U.S. student).

Those participants were stressed from the contrast in their interpersonal communication style between the Japanese, such as low context versus high context (Hall, 1989).

Maintaining Home Cultural Behavior

Most participants made considerable effort to follow the Japanese mannerisms, whereas many participants maintained their own cultural norms and behaviors simultaneously. The latter participants often continued engaging with their family and friends back home, so they can be themselves, behaving naturally as if they were in their own country: "I keep in contact with family and friends to maintain my [American] cultural identity. [I] keep normal school schedules as same as I would have in the United States" (U.S. student).

Furthermore, those participants often rejected losing their own culture, as well as imitating Japanese cultural behaviors (e.g., wearing clothing like a Japanese): "I don't want to lose everything I had... Here woman's fashion is such that everybody looks the same... I still want to be myself and an individual person" (U.S. student).

Maintaining their home cultural behaviors made participants feel more distance toward Japanese culture. The more they maintained their own culture, the more they thought, felt, and behaved like they were in their own country despite being in Japan.

Clashing with Host Cultural Norms

Participants who maintained their own cultural thoughts, feelings, and behaviors were forced to confront Japanese cultural norms through engagement with the Japanese. Those participants often experienced clashes between their own values and those of the hosts. The most common clashes were related to traditions of work and gender in Japanese society: "In Japan, women retire from working very early...In the work situation, it is not good to be different and disagree with people and there is also a hierarchy" (U.S. student).

In particular, some participants from China faced stereotyping of foreigners by the Japanese. Although negative portrayals of Chinese tourists in media might have also been an impetus, Chinese participants struggled with a preset unfavorable impression of the Chinese held by Japanese: "One day, when I left work, the manager told me, 'I don't feel you are like Chinese (You are really Japanese).' I [was] surprised. I felt very subtle [discrimination]" (Chinese student).

As stated, participants who identified with home cultural identity as primary maintained their home cultural norms and behavior. They often clashed with host cultural norms and finally identified themselves as their own culture members again, having given up trying to adjust to the host culture. In this way, participants gradually separated from the host culture. This cyclical process is typical of intracultural contact, as contrasted with intercultural contact.

Summary of Results

To summarize, participants in our study perceived intercultural contact as a process of assimilation to the host culture and intracultural contact as a process of separation from it. It should be noted that being thought of as a foreigner by the hosts is crucial in whether participants assume identification with the host or home cultural identity as primary. In short, while participants engaged with the Japanese more when they did not feel being perceived as a foreigner by them, but on the contrary, they engaged with their compatriots more if they did feel so.

DISCUSSION

The data analysis derived two cultural contact orientations: intercultural and intracultural. As described in the introduction, we interpreted our findings through the social identity and anxiety/uncertainty management approaches. These approaches allowed us to propose a theoretical model of "uncertainty management by cultural identification."

Interpretation by Social Identity Approach

First, we interpreted our findings by the social identity approach (Tajfel & Turner, 1986). This approach emphasizes the importance of one's identity, in this case, that of a constituent of the home culture and the host culture. International students, by virtue of their entry into a foreign environment, are compelled to have their "foreignness" accentuated. The intergroup nature of their contact with the hosts is highly salient, and they have a clear sense of ingroup (fellow international students, compatriots) versus the outgroup (hosts). However, as their sojourn progresses, they may come to accept the host culture and feel part of this group as their ingroup. Successful adjustment, then, entails cognitively categorizing oneself as a member of both the home and host cultures, i.e., ingroup identity in both groups. This integration of two identities allows one to have positive affect toward both groups; hence, ingroup favoritism is unlikely to occur. On the other hand, a strong identity toward one group induces the perception of competition between groups and downward comparison toward the outgroup results, giving the ingroup a feeling of superiority.

In the case of international students, the natural outgroup is the hosts, which could lead to shunning the hosts and attraction toward compatriots. The properties of "intracultural contact orientation" in our findings can be explained in that tightly knit ethnic or cultural groups tend to be exclusive toward other groups, and this exclusion gives them a sense of collective self-esteem. The need to feel a sense of pride for themselves compels them to feel good about their own group, while simultaneously feeling aversiveness toward the host outgroup.

On the contrary, the properties of "intercultural contact orientation" can be described in the following. Once international students feel accepted by the host cultural group, they are not only comfortable with host norms and customs but abiding by these become natural. Internalizing the host culture makes them feel part of the host group; hence the hosts are perceived as their ingroup, just as their compatriots are. As discussed, while international students can cognitively emphasize either the host/home cultural identity, they can also identify themselves as host and home culture members. These variations in assumed identity are what we hereon refer to as host/home cultural identification.

This host/home/both cultural identification is consistent with what had been discussed in prior literature, which purports that individuals positively appraise either host/home or both cultures, participating in the identified cultural group(s), thus increasing their identification with either or both cultures (Cardenas & de la Sablonnière, 2020). The stronger identification with either host/home or both cultural groups would buffer daily stress of life (Jetten et al., 2010), leading to better psychological well-being (Wakefield et al., 2017).

Interpretation by Anxiety/Uncertainty Management Approach

The anxiety/uncertainty management approach (Gudykunst, 2005) also provides a suitable perspective for interpreting our results. This approach posits that international students feel uncertainty/anxiety in intercultural situations and, to manage them, they are motivated to engage with host/home culture members.

The properties of "intercultural contact orientation" can be interpreted by this approach that once international students identify themselves as host culture members, they are motivated to learn host norms, and they feel compelled to engage with the hosts owing to being a part of the host community (Turner, 1988). As the host interactions increase and international students' anxiety toward the hosts decreases (Logan et al., 2014), they can imitate the host cultural behavior, hence internalizing the host culture within their cognitive-behavioral patterns. Such imitation facilitates them to develop social skills in the host culture (Oguri & Gudykunst, 2002), increasing their confidence in predicting the hosts' behaviors, which Gudykunst (2005) refered to as "attributional confidence," resulting in deriving higher satisfaction with their relationship with the hosts (Florack et al., 2014). As the more host relationships become intimate, their interactions become more personalized, more synchronized, and less apprehensive (Gudykunst et al., 1987; Neuliep, 2012). Consequently, international students increasingly perceive the hosts as their ingroup, and consequently feel more a part of the host community.

By contrast, pertaining to "intracultural contact orientation," if international students identify themselves with their home culture more, they may feel aversiveness toward the hosts. Perceiving the hosts as an external entity makes them feel higher anxiety toward the hosts, and subsequently, they may avoid interaction with them (Logan et al., 2014). In order to reduce this amplified anxiety caused by the hosts, international students are motivated to engage with compatriots to feel comfort in the company of their own kind, hence reaffirming their home cultural norms (Turner, 1988). The more international students engage with home culture members, the more they find similar/shared norms, allowing them to forget about the threats and anxiety imposed by the host culture (Florack et al., 2014). Subsequently, international students maintain their behavior as if they were in their own country. However, such rigid maintenance of home behaviors often leads to clashes with the host culture, having detrimental effects on their relationships with hosts, which heightens their anxiety (Neuliep, 2012; Stephan & Stephan, 2000). Consequently, international students perceive the hosts as an outgroup, as a means to protect themselves from stress, and their home cultural enclave provides a defensive function.

Proposing a Theoretical Model of Uncertainty Management by Cultural Identification

We propose a grounded theory model of uncertainty management by cultural identification by integrating interview data and these theoretical accounts. Taken together, social identity approach explains that international students cognitively categorize themselves as host/home culture members. Anxiety/uncertainty management approach describes uncertainty management as the motivation of cultural contact and highlights interpersonal communication factors that influence uncertainty management, such as motivation to interact, behavioral adaptability, and relationship development. We name the integration of these theoretical accounts "uncertainty management by cultural identification."

Uncertainty management by cultural identification implies that individuals are motivated to manage uncertainty by identifying as one or more cultural group members in intercultural situations for individuals' psychological well-being. This model's basic ideas are provided below. Cognitively, individuals identify with particular culture group members; hence, they fit themselves in with the relevant referent groups. Affectively, identification with a particular group and its subsequent management can evoke both positive and negative emotions. Behaviorally, identification and evoked emotions guide one's behavior in alignment toward the norms of the specific group they identify with. Interactions with others invoke particular identifications, which subsequently affect cognitive, affective, and behavioral patterns. Cultural contact, then, initiates this cyclical identification process. We propose two identifications: intercultural and intracultural, which we refer to as contact orientation (see Figure 1).

Intercultural Contact Orientation

As had been described earlier, intercultural contact orientation refers to when individuals cognitively identify with host culture group members and feel that they fit in with the host cultural group. On the affective level, they are apt to seek acceptance from the hosts, and they are highly motivated to learn host cultural norms to gain their approval. On the contrary, they may feel pressure and difficulty in trying to become just like the hosts. On the behavioral level, identification with and emotional attachment to the host culture will guide one's behavior in alignment with the host norms, i.e., internalizing host cultural behaviors. Through increased interaction with the hosts, they mimic the host behaviors, attaining essential social skills and knowledge of interpersonal rituals and customs, which allows them the confidence to expand their involvement with more host members. This high level of engagement with the hosts instills identification with the host culture. Intercultural contact, then, initiates this cyclical identification process involving cognitive, affective, and behavioral components.

In our case, the Japanese culture, international students with an intercultural contact orientation are likely to engage actively with Japanese hosts, consider themselves as part of their group, sharing their ingroup, and at times consider themselves as bona fide Japanese culture members. They are eager to learn Japanese cultural norms (e.g., bowing) and

Figure 1

Inter-cultural Contact Orientation

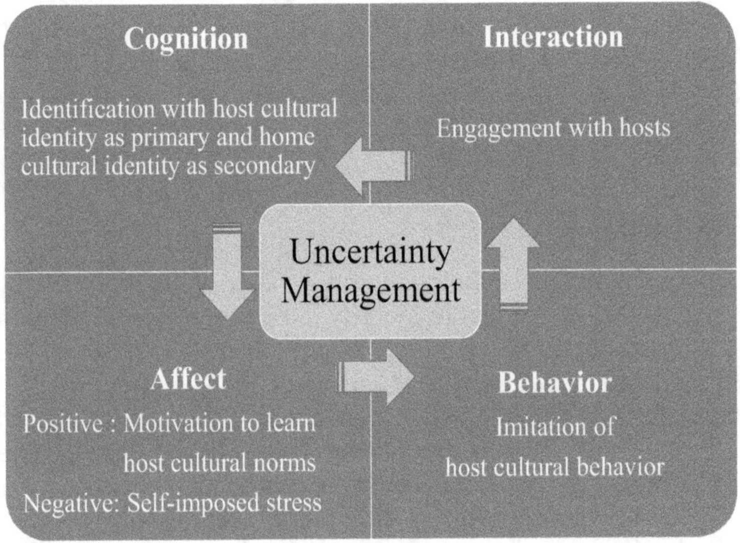

Intra-cultural Contact Orientation

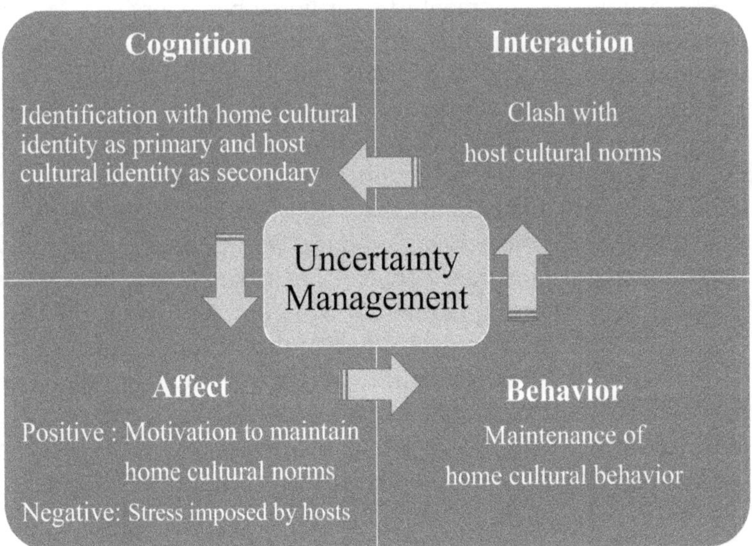

consciously mimic Japanese behavior patterns. Consequently, the Japanese hosts feel comfortable relating with such students, which facilitates the expansion of their host interpersonal network. Being completely immersed in Japanese social circles, students come to see themselves as "one of the hosts" and assume a Japanese cultural identity more significant than their home cultural identity. Our study found the typical students with an intercultural contact orientation to be half-Japanese, or those who are foreign nationals born and raised in Japan, along with those interested in working in Japan and those with a Japanese spouse.

Intracultural Contact Orientation

As previously explained, intracultural contact orientation refers to when individuals feel compelled to identify more strongly with the home culture as a reaction to the cultural, environmental transition. Their cognitive orientation, therefore, that of self-perception as a member of the home culture, and with that, their stance toward cultural adjustment is that of cultural maintenance. On the affective level, they derive positive affect from home cultural norms, while feeling stress from the host culture. Behaviorally speaking, they stick to their home cultural norms, without attempting to learn the host behavioral customs and rules. Because of this, their interactions with the hosts are likely to accompany interpersonal clashes. Such discord of values invokes a strong home cultural identification, leading to retainment of their home behaviors.

In our case, international students with an intracultural contact orientation engage more with compatriots and other nationals aside from the hosts. While they may engage in contact with the Japanese, they consider their own home cultural identity as primary and perceive the interaction as being intergroup. They observe their home cultural norms (e.g., greetings) rather than emulating the host norms and behave as though they are in their home country. By interacting with people in Japan, they become aware of the discrepancy between Japanese society's norms and their own culture, which prompts them to be defensive toward their own culture, feeling that the hosts present a certain extent of the threat to their being. Subsequently, they prefer to form their own subcommunities to protect their values. Some examples of such students include third culture people, those from multicultural backgrounds, those with a strong ethnic identity, and those who consider themselves loyal patriots of their home country.

Summary of Uncertainty Management by Cultural Identification

To summarize, uncertainty management by cultural identification provides two contact orientations: intercultural and intracultural contact orientation. In the continuum between the two orientations, individual international students can be situated regarding their personal cultural contact orientation in intercultural situations for attaining psychological well-being; some communicate both with the Japanese and the international students equally, whereas others have more or less communication with either group. Figure 2 describes the intracultural–intercultural continuum of contact.

Figure 2

Intracultural–Intercultural Continuum of Contact

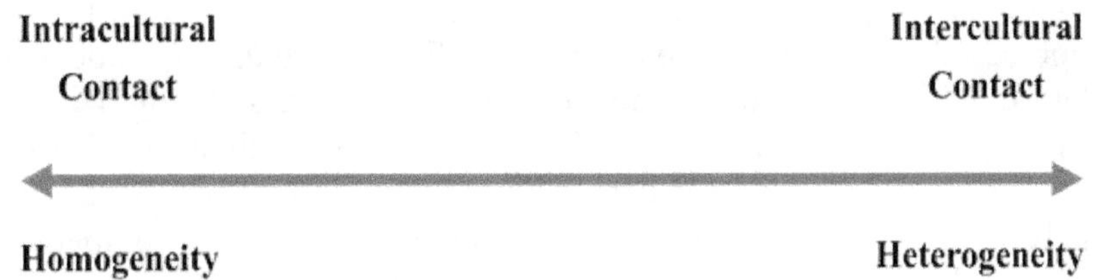

Intracultural Contact Orientation and "Foreignness" in Japanese Higher Education Institutions

From our findings, we conclude that a majority of international students demonstrate an intracultural rather than intercultural contact orientation due to the perceived feeling of "foreignness" from hosts. The sense of "foreignness" perceived from the Japanese is consistent with previous literature suggesting the psychological barriers felt by international students in Japan (Murphy-Shigematsu, 2002a, 2002b; Yin et al., 2021).

One possible explanation for this phenomenon may result from institutional practices of hosting international students in Japanese higher education institutions. The ratio of international students to all students enrolled in Japanese higher education in 2019 was 7.8% (Japan Student Services Organization, 2019). Due to a relatively culturally homogeneous student body, the Japanese higher education institutions have traditionally treated international students separately from Japanese students in their academics and lives (Ebuchi, 1997; Takai, 1995). This separatism has been a dominant impetus for policy among Japanese higher education institutions even today. For example, since 2008, major universities had begun offering English language degree programs under the auspices of the Global 30 (G30) initiative of the Japanese government (Kuroda et al., 2019). The curriculum of the G30 program is offered separately from that of Japanese students, and G30 students have little or no opportunity to take courses with Japanese students. Consequently, they form friendships amongst their international classmates, and little mingling between the host students can be afforded. This is consistent with the findings of Kagami (2006), who suggested that institutionalized impediments from within the university, such as vital announcements being made only in Japanese, and separate classes being held for international students and Japanese students, exacerbate their feeling of isolation. Such institutionalized separation between hosts and internationals results in the formation of monocultural communities on campus, with little mixing. The increased number of compatriots and fellow international students on modern-day Japanese university campuses provides them with an adequate pool of potential, "easy" targets to build their local social network. In fact, Takai (1995) demonstrated that international students in Japan rely on social support in the following order: first, their compatriots, second, the Japanese, and last, other nationals. Readily available access to fellow international students leads them to favor contact with compatriots and other nationals, resulting in them adhering to their home cultural identity.

Universities and their faculty in Japan should integrate international students and Japanese students into one student body in both academic and daily lives. This integrationism should be the central principle to host international students in Japanese higher education institutions (Ebuchi, 1997; Takai, 1995). Although separatism is still the dominant principle, some universities and their faculty have embodied cultural integration, by offering an increased number of courses offered in English for co-learning and building residences to house both international students and Japanese students together. These institutional efforts have been effective in ameliorating international students' academic and living conditions. For international students, being treated as individuals daily in one student body may eliminate the perceived feeling of "foreignness." Self-initiated relationships, in which partners do not perceive themselves as host or sojourner, go beyond cultural barriers and leads to positive contact based on Allport's (1954) contact hypothesis. Such positive contact is indispensable for the constructive coexistence of international students and Japanese students in Japanese society.

CONCLUSION

The purpose of this study was to understand how international students recognize engagement with their host and home culture members. Our findings revealed that international students in Japan demonstrate an intracultural rather than intercultural contact orientation due to the perceived feeling of "foreignness" from hosts. The previous literature presupposed that international students are determined to adjust to the host country; in fact, our present study demonstrated that they decide by themselves to what extent they will adjust to the host culture and engage with the hosts. In short, we demonstrated the importance of reconsidering the meaning of adjustment from the perspective of the international students.

Although our findings from this study add to the existing literature on cultural contact studies, some limitations deserve mention. First, international students are not compelled to experience uncertainty in intercultural contact if the norms are similar between host and home cultures. Future studies, thus, should investigate this proximity in the cultural distance (Triandis, 1995) by adding a large number of countries and gathering a statistically sufficient number of samples. Second, pertaining to individual-level cultural distance, such as the degrees of host/home cultural identification, degrees of understanding and appreciation for host/home culture, and the readiness for cultural contact, should be included and examined in cultural contact experience.

REFERENCES

Allport, G. W. (1954). *The nature of prejudice*. Addison-Wesley.

Ashizawa, S. (2013). Nihon no gakuseikokusaikouryuseisaku [International student exchange policy in Japan]. In M. Yokota & A. Kobayashi (Eds.), *Internationalization of Japanese university and the international mindset of Japanese students* (pp. 13–38). Gakubunsha.

Bochner, S., McLeod, B. M., & Lin, A. (1977). Friendship patterns of overseas students: A functional model. *International Journal of Psychology, 12*(4), 277–294. https://doi.org/10.1080/00207597708247396

Cardenas, D., & de la Sablonnière, R. (2020). Participating in a new group and the identification processes: The quest for a positive social identity. *British Journal of Social Psychology, 59*(1), 189–208. https://doi.org/10.1111/bjso.12340

Charmaz, K. (2014). *Constructing grounded theory* (2nd. ed.). SAGE.

Creswell, J. W., & Poth, C. N. (2016). *Qualitative inquiry and research design: Choosing among five approaches*. SAGE.

de la Sablonnière, R., Amiot, C. E., Cárdenas, D., Sadykova, N., Gorborukova, G. L., & Huberdeau, M.-E. (2016). Testing the subtractive pattern of cultural identification. *European Journal of Social Psychology, 46*(4), 441–454. https://doi.org/10.1002/ejsp.2178

Ebuchi, K. (1997). *Study of the internationalization of universities.* Tamagawa Daigaku Shuppanbu.

Florack, A., Rohmann, A., Palcu, J., & Mazziotta, A. (2014). How initial cross-group friendships prepare for intercultural communication: The importance of anxiety reduction and self-confidence in communication. *International Journal of Intercultural Relations, 43*, 278–288. https://doi.org/10.1016/j.ijintrel.2014.09.004

Gudykunst, W. B. (2005). *Theorizing about intercultural communication.* SAGE.

Gudykunst, W. B., & Nishida, T. (2001). Anxiety, uncertainty, and perceived effectiveness of communication across relationships and cultures. *International Journal of Intercultural Relations, 25*(1), 55–71. https://doi.org/10.1016/S0147-1767(00)00042-0

Gudykunst, W. B., Nishida, T., & Chua, E. (1987). Perceptions of social penetration in Japanese-North American Dyads. *International Journal of Intercultural Relations, 11*(2), 171–189. https://doi.org/10.1016/0147-1767(87)90017-4

Hall, E. T. (1989). *Beyond culture.* Anchor.

Haslam, S. A. (2004). *Psychology in organizations.* SAGE.

Hogg, M. A., & Belavadi, S. (2017). Uncertainty management theories. In *Oxford Research Encyclopedia of Communication.* https://doi.org/10.1093/acrefore/9780190228613.013.495

Japan Student Services Organization. (2018). *Lifestyle survey of privately financed international students.* Retrieved September 1, 2021, from https://www.studyinjapan.go.jp/ja/_mt/2020/08/seikatsu2017.pdf

Japan Student Services Organization. (2019). *International students in Japan 2019.* Retrieved September 1, 2021, from https://www.studyinjapan.go.jp/ja/_mt/2020/08/date2019z.pdf

Jetten, J., Haslam, S. A., Iyer, A., & Haslam, C. (2010). Turning to others in times of change. In S. Stürmer & M. Snyder (Eds.), *The psychology of prosocial behavior* (pp. 139–156). https://doi.org/10.1002/9781444307948.ch7

Kagami, T. (2006). How do educational interventions effect attitudes of multicultural understanding? A case study of a simulation game and cooperative group work. *Intercultural/Trans-cultural Education, 24*, 76–91. https://ci.nii.ac.jp/naid/40007379837/

Kuroda, K., Sugimura, M., Kitamura, Y., & Asada, S. (2019). *Internationalization of higher education and student mobility in Japan and Asia.* Retrieved September 1, 2021, from https://www.jica.go.jp/jica-ri/publication/other/l75nbg000010mg5u-att/Background_Kuroda.pdf

Logan, S., Steel, Z., & Hunt, C. (2014). Investigating the effect of anxiety, uncertainty and ethnocentrism on willingness to interact in an intercultural communication. *Journal of Cross-Cultural Psychology, 46*(1), 39–52. https://doi.org/10.1177/0022022114555762

Murphy-Shigematsu, S. (2002a). Psychological barriers for international students in Japan. *International Journal for the Advancement of Counselling, 24*(1), 19–30. https://doi.org/10.1023/A:1015076202649

Murphy-Shigematsu, S. (2002b). Psychological struggles of Korean international students in Japan. *International Education Journal, 3*, 75–84.

Neuliep, J. W. (2012). The relationship among intercultural communication apprehension, ethnocentrism, uncertainty reduction, and communication satisfaction during initial intercultural interaction: An extension of anxiety and uncertainty management (AUM) theory. *Journal of Intercultural Communication Research, 41*(1), 1–16. https://doi.org/10.1080/17475759.2011.623239

Organisation for Economic Cooperation and Development. (2017). *Education at a glance 2017*. https://doi.org/10.1787/19991487

Oguri, M., & Gudykunst, W. B. (2002). The influence of self construals and communication styles on sojourners' psychological and sociocultural adjustment. *International Journal of Intercultural Relations, 26*(5), 577–593. https://doi.org/10.1016/s0147-1767(02)00034-2

Sani, F., Madhok, V., Norbury, M., Dugard, P., & Wakefield, J. R. H. (2015). Greater number of group identifications is associated with healthier behaviour: Evidence from a Scottish community sample. *British Journal of Health Psychology, 20*(3), 466–481. https://doi.org/10.1111/bjhp.12119

Stephan, W. G., & Stephan, C. W. (2000). An integrated threat theory of prejudice. In *Reducing prejudice and discrimination.* (pp. 23–45). Lawrence Erlbaum Associates.

Tajfel, H., & Turner, J. C. (1986). An integrative theory of intergroup conflict. In M. A. Hogg & D. Abrams (Eds.), *Intergroup relations: Essential readings* (pp. 94–109). Psychology Press.

Takai, J. (1995). Social provisions and the ajustment of international students to Japanese culture. *Intercultural/Trans-cultural Education, 8*, 106–116. https://ci.nii.ac.jp/naid/10025814102/

Tanaka, T., & Okunishi, Y. (2016). Social skills use of international students in Japan. *Japanese Psychological Research, 58*(1), 54–70. https://doi.org/10.1111/jpr.12097

Triandis. (1995). *Individualism & collectivism*. Westview Press.

Turner, J. H. (1988). *A theory of social interaction*. Stanford University Press.

Wakefield, J. R. H., Sani, F., Madhok, V., Norbury, M., Dugard, P., Gabbanelli, C., Arnetoli, M., Beconcini, G., Botindari, L., Grifoni, F., Paoli, P., & Poggesi, F. (2017). The relationship between group identification and satisfaction with life in a cross-cultural community sample. *Journal of Happiness Studies, 18*(3), 785–807. https://doi.org/10.1007/s10902-016-9735-z

Ward, C., & Kennedy, A. (1994). Acculturation strategies, psychological adjustment, and sociocultural competence during cross-cultural transitions. *International Journal of Intercultural Relations, 18*(3), 329-343. https:// doi.org/10.1016/0147-1767(94)90036-1

Yin, M. X., Aoki, K., Liao, K. Y. H., & Xu, H. (2021). An exploration on the attachment, acculturation, and psychosocial adjustment of Chinese international students in Japan. *Journal of International Students, 11*(1), 176–194. https://doi.org/10.32674/jis.v11i1.1454

Author Bios

NORIHITO TANIGUCHI, JD, is a PhD candidate in the Graduate School of Education and Human Development at Nagoya University in Japan. His major research interests lie in the area of cross-cultural adjustment, acculturation, and intercultural competence. Email: taniguchi.norihito@i.mbox.nagoya-u.ac.jp

JIRO TAKAI, PhD, is a Professor in the Graduate School of Education and Human Development at Nagoya University in Japan. His major research interests lie in the area of interpersonal competence, self in social interaction, interpersonal conflict strategies, and cross-cultural adjustment. Email: jtakai@cc.nagoya-u.ac.jp

DARIUSZ SKOWRONSKI, PhD, is an Associate Professor, psychological studies, Temple University in Japan. His major research interests lie in the area of clinical and counseling psychology, psychotherapy, online counseling, behavioral psychology and neuroscience. Email: dariusz.skowronski@tuj.temple.edu

© *Journal of International Students*
Volume 12, Issue 4 (2022), pp. 867-888
ISSN: 2162-3104 (Print), 2166-3750 (Online)
DOI: https://doi.org/10.32674/jis.v12i4.4076
ojed.org/jis

OJED
OPEN JOURNALS IN EDUCATION

Sociocultural Adaptation Among University Students in Hungary: The Case of International Students From Post-Soviet Countries

Aigerim Yerken
Róbert Urbán
Lan Anh Nguyen Luu
Eötvös Loránd University, Hungary

ABSTRACT

With the number of international students increasing worldwide, the sociocultural adaptation difficulties that sojourners face should be addressed adequately. This study explored the sociocultural adaptation of international students ($N = 267$, $M_{age} = 24.5$, $SD = 4.7$) in Hungary. The exploratory factor analysis of the Sociocultural Adaptation Scale yielded five factors: Affiliative Relations, Bureaucracy and Services, Power Relations, Cultural Understanding, and Academic Performance. The students' countries of origin (post-Soviet countries versus others) and locations of residence (the capital versus small cities) were determinants of sociocultural adaptation. Depressive symptoms, perceived stress, and lower life satisfaction were associated with greater sociocultural adaptation difficulties. Resilient coping was linked with a lower level of difficulties in academic performance ($r_s = -.20$) and cultural understanding ($r_s = -.15$). Our findings supported that the students' countries of origin, places of residence, and mental health should be considered in improving counseling and educational programs targeting international students.

Keywords: higher education, Hungary, international students, post-Soviet countries, psychological adaptation, sociocultural adaptation

The global international student population increased 165% from an estimated 2,000,000 in 2000 to 5,300,000 in 2017 (UNESCO, 2019). A vital question for international students studying abroad is how they manage everyday life in their host countries or, in other words, how successful their sociocultural adaptation is (Berry, 1997). Coming from different cultural backgrounds, they encounter great challenges, including difficulties with the language barrier, educational and practical stressors, and adaptation to the cultural norms in a new culture (Smith & Khawaja, 2011). A substantial amount of research exists regarding cross-cultural adaptation among various samples of sojourners, examining the effects of different factors on the adaptation process (e.g., Su et al., 2019; Wang & Hannes, 2014; Ward & Kennedy, 1993, 1999; Wilson, 2013; Wilson et al., 2017). These studies found significant differences in sociocultural adaptation across samples, suggesting sociocultural difficulties increase with a high cultural distance between the host and home cultures. This study extends the conceptualization and assessment of sociocultural adaptation of an underrepresented group within a new sociocultural environment while also focusing on international students' countries of origin.

In acculturative studies, acculturation refers to cultural and psychological changes that result from intercultural contact (Berry et al., 2006), while adaptation is commonly understood as an outcome of the acculturation process. There are different concepts addressing acculturation issues such as "culture shock" or "acculturative stress" (Berry, 1997) and cross-cultural adjustment stress (Cross, 1995); however, the recent trends focus on adaptation processes of sojourners. Adaptation pertains to the level of fit between the individual and the host cultural environment (Berry, 1997). Sociocultural adaptation is conceptually distinct from psychological adaptation (Searle & Ward, 1990; Ward & Kennedy, 1999). Psychological adaptation is grounded in stress and coping theory (Lazarus & Folkman, 1984). This approach considers coping resources as emotional and problem-focused efforts to manage stressful situations. Grounded in a culture-learning framework, sociocultural adaptation assumes that cross-cultural difficulties happen because sojourners struggle to learn social skills to fit in to a new cultural context (Argyle, 1969).

Sociocultural adaptation could be assessed by measuring social difficulties, whereas psychological adaptation could be measured by mood changes or the assessment of depressive symptoms (Ward & Kennedy, 1993). Previous studies have demonstrated that cultural distance, language fluency, length of residence, and acculturation strategies mostly affect sociocultural adaptation (Searle & Ward, 1990; Ward & Kennedy, 1999).

However, life changes, personality variables, and situational factors such as social support strongly influence psychological adaptation (Ward & Kennedy, 1993).

Both forms of adaptation have been studied in relation to several factors, for instance, life satisfaction (Sam et al., 2015), academic adaptation (Cemalcilar et al., 2005), cultural distance (Demes & Geeraert, 2014), and perceived discrimination (Berry et al., 2006). Psychological and sociocultural adaptations significantly predicted academic adaptation when measured with the academic performance (Cemalcilar et al., 2005). Perceived discrimination had negative association with psychological ($r = -.31$) and sociocultural ($r = -.30$) adaptations (Berry et al., 2006). Cultural distance had a relationship with a lower level of both types of adaptation (Demes & Geeraert, 2014).

Studies on Measurement of Sociocultural Adaptation

Within the framework of acculturation research, sociocultural adaptation is measured by assessing social skills and the ways individuals react in everyday social situations in a new culture. Several self-report measures, such as the Social Situations Questionnaire (Furnham & Bochner, 1986) and the modified version of it, the Sociocultural Adaptation Scale (SCAS; Ward & Kennedy, 1999), have been used to examine sociocultural adaptation levels.

The SCAS is believed to be a "flexible instrument that can be modified according to the characteristics of the sojourning sample" (Ward & Kennedy, 1999, p. 662). Grounded in a culture-learning framework, it consequently emphasizes both the behavioral and cognitive dimensions of adaptation. The SCAS has been used across various cross-sectional and longitudinal studies and has been found to be a reliable instrument in multiple cultural contexts (Ward & Kennedy, 1993, 1999). It measures the amount of perceived difficulty in many situations, such as "making friends" and "coping with academic work." Additional features of the instrument are its short length and being developed specifically for measuring sojourners' adaptation.

Psychosocial adaptation changes over time. According to previous studies, international students had greater amounts of difficulty with sociocultural adaptation during their first months of residence in a host country and it decreased significantly over time (Wilson, 2013; Wilson et al., 2017). In contrast, Berry et al. (2006) did not find any relationship between the length of residence and both sociocultural and psychological adaptation scores.

Regarding the impacts of age and gender on sociocultural adaptation, previous studies have had mixed results. Some studies found a significant difference between males' and females' sociocultural adaptation subtypes (Güzel & Glazer, 2019; Mahmood & Galloway Burke, 2018), whereas others indicated no gender differences (Su et al., 2019). Younger participants demonstrated a higher amount of sociocultural adaptation problems; however, the strength of this association was weak ($r = .12$; Wilson, 2013), and some researchers found no support for a link between age and sociocultural adaptation (Searle & Ward, 1990).

International students' countries of origin influence sociocultural adaptation difficulties encountered in new cultures (Güzel & Glazer, 2019; Simic-Yamashita & Tanaka, 2010). For instance, East Asians had fewer sociocultural difficulties on the academic level in Japan (Simic-Yamashita & Tanaka, 2010). For this group of students, cultural similarities might lead to successful adaptation outcomes.

Based on our literature review, no nonprobability sampling-based quantitative research has been conducted to explore different aspects of sociocultural adaptation for international students from post-Soviet countries. However, 8% of all international students around the world are from post-Soviet countries (Chankseliani, 2016). Furthermore, a previous study on Russian-speaking international students in Hungary emphasized an existing cultural distance between post-Soviet countries and Hungary (Samokhotova, 2018). Therefore, we aimed to assess the relationship between participants' countries of origin, especially post-Soviet countries, and the sociocultural adaptation difficulties they might encounter.

International students' English language proficiency was related to their having fewer sociocultural adaptation difficulties (Mahmood & Galloway Burke, 2018; Wilson, 2013) and better psychological well-being (Sam et al., 2015). A low level of English language competence is an important factor, affecting international student's academic achievement. However, few studies have linked a higher competence in a local language to better adaptation outcomes (e.g., Wang & Hannes, 2014). In this study, we assessed the impact of both English-language competence and proficiency in the Hungarian language on sociocultural adaptation difficulties.

A few studies have been conducted to examine the relationship between international students' places of residence in their host countries and their sociocultural adaptation. Students who settled in rural areas had more difficulties in interpersonal adaptation than those who lived in urban ones (Su et al., 2019). Urban regions are more developed and have more frequent population movements than rural ones. People living in rural areas might be less exposed to culturally diverse environments, which may influence their preservation of their own culture. Similarly, in this study, we measured how the participants' locations in Hungary linked to their sociocultural adaptation difficulties.

Financial satisfaction has a positive association with psychological adaptation across varied samples (e.g., Sam et al., 2015). International students worrying about their financial security may have less time to spend on their studies and fewer internal resources for adaptation. However, few studies have determined the relationship between sociocultural adaptation and financial satisfaction. In this study, we measured this association and predicted that financial dissatisfaction would be linked to sociocultural adaptation difficulties.

Many studies have measured psychological adaptation with various instruments and have found a moderate association with sociocultural adaptation (Searle & Ward, 1990; Wilson, 2013; Wilson et al., 2017); the effect size of the correlation in one such study was $r = .42$ (Wilson, 2013).

Psychological adaptation might be affected by coping resources (Lazarus & Folkman, 1984). Resilient coping is the ability to use cognitive appraisal skills effectively to cope with stressful circumstances and to adapt easily to consequences of culture change (Sinclair & Wallston, 2004), which is relevant in the case of international students. By immersion in a new culture, sojourners may experience psychological stress or "culture shock" (Cross, 1995). As for sociocultural adaptation, a few studies (e.g., Sumer, 2009) have measured its relationship with coping resources, finding a positive association between them. Hence, we wanted to examine the association between resilient coping, perceived stress, and adaptation outcomes.

Aims and Hypotheses of the Study

The aims of this study were to identify the underlying structure of the SCAS for international students studying in Hungary and to reveal how sociodemographic factors affect different types of sociocultural adaptation. We also attempted to gain a deeper understanding of both internal and external factors associated with sociocultural adaptation difficulties. Although many studies have revealed that international students have greater difficulties than domestic students in a host country, remarkably few studies have compared groups of international students based upon their countries of origin, especially those coming from post-Soviet countries. We formulated several hypotheses regarding the anticipated association between sociocultural adaptation and different variables.

1. Sociocultural adaptation difficulties are expected to correlate positively with more depressive symptoms and higher stress and to correlate negatively with lower life satisfaction and lower resilient coping.
2. Negative associations are expected between sociocultural adaptation difficulties and age, financial satisfaction, and language proficiencies in English and Hungarian.
3. A positive relationship is hypothesized between the length of residence and sociocultural adaptation concerns.
4. More sociocultural adaptation difficulties are expected for female students than male students.
5. Fewer sociocultural problems are hypothesized for international students from post-Soviet countries than international students from other countries of origin.
6. We anticipate more sociocultural difficulties for international students who live in Hungarian cities other than the capital than those who reside in the capital city.

METHOD

Participants and Procedure

We applied a convenience sampling method based on the following variables: country of origin and location of residence in Hungary. We recruited participants via advertising on social media and personal invitation. Ethical approval for this study was granted by the Research Ethics Committee at the authors' institution.

We collected data from undergraduate international students attending one of the Hungarian higher institutions. We informed subjects via a written form that participation in the study was anonymous and voluntary. Of the 474 international students who participated in the online survey, we dropped data for 207 participants because of the high number of missing values. An acceptable percentage of missing values in the data set was 10% because analysis may be biased with a higher amount (Bennett, 2001). The final sample comprised 267 participants (105 males and 162 females). The age range of participants was 18–41 years ($M =$ 24.5, $SD = 4.7$).

As for the participants' countries of origin, 48% of the international students were from post-Soviet countries. The rest (52%) were from other regions: East Asia, 13.7%; South and Southeast Asia, 21.6%; Middle East and Africa, 46%; Europe, 8.6%, Central and South America, 5%; and North America, 5%.

The length of residence in Hungary at the time of completing this survey was less than 6 months for 7.1%, between 6 months and 1 year for

31.8%, 1–2 years for 28.8%, 2–3 years for 16.5%, 3–4 years for 7.9%, and longer than 4 years for 7.9% of the sample.

Bachelor's degree students constituted 40.1% of the sample, master's degree students constituted 35.6%, doctoral degree students constituted 16.9%, and the rest were doing a foundation year or preparatory courses. The majority of the participants (76%) studied in the capital city of Hungary at the time of completing this survey, and the rest (24%) studied in other cities. Regarding financial satisfaction, 6.4% of the sample were very dissatisfied with their financial situations, 15.4% were somewhat dissatisfied, 26.2% were neither satisfied nor dissatisfied, 40.4% were somewhat satisfied, and 11.6% were very satisfied. As for the self-estimation of English language proficiency, 1.5% of the sample assessed themselves as poor, 4.5% as fair, 30% as good, and 55.1% as excellent; 9% were native speakers. Most of the participants participated in classes taught in the English language. Regarding Hungarian language competence, 48.3% of the sample scored as not speaking this language at all, 38.2% as a little, 9.4% as somewhat, 3.7% as slightly well, and 0.4% as very well.

Measures
Sociodemographic Information

We collected data regarding age, gender, country of origin, length of residence, degree, financial satisfaction, location of residence in Hungary, and language competence in English and Hungarian.

Sociocultural Adaptation

The SCAS (Ward & Kennedy, 1999) is a 28-item scale that assesses the amount of difficulty experienced in various sociocultural situations, with emphasis on the behavioral and cognitive domains. Participants rate the amount of difficulty they have experienced with the statements based on a 5-point Likert scale (1 = *no difficulty* to 5 = *extreme difficulty*). The alpha coefficient of internal consistency for the scale was .85 in the original publication (Ward & Kennedy, 1999). In this study, Cronbach's alpha for the overall SCAS was excellent ($\alpha = .91$).

Psychological Adaptation Measures

We assessed psychological adaptation using negative and positive indicators of adaptation, the Center for Epidemiologic Studies Depression Scale (Radloff, 1977), and the Satisfaction With Life Scale (Diener et al., 1985). The Center for Epidemiologic Studies Depression Scale is a 20-item self-report scale that measures depressive symptoms, emphasizing the affective components. We used an eight-item version of the original scale that was developed and used in previous studies (e.g., Hone et al., 2014). The participants indicated the frequency and severity of depressive symptoms on a scale ranging from 1 (*rarely or none of the time*) to 4 (*all or almost all of the time*). Six items measured various depressive affects and somatic and retarded activity. Two items were phrased in a positive direction ("I enjoyed life" and "I was happy") and were reverse scored. The internal consistency was found to be good in this research ($\alpha = .83$). The other indicator of psychological adaptation was the Satisfaction With Life Scale, which assesses subjective well-being and global life satisfaction. It consists of five items, inviting participants to indicate their level of agreement with each item based on a 7-point Likert scale (1 = *strongly disagree* to 7 = *strongly agree*). The alpha coefficient of internal consistency for the scale was .87 in the original paper (Diener et al., 1985). In this study, Cronbach's alpha was good ($\alpha = .89$).

Perceived Stress

We measured perceived stress using the Perceived Stress Scale (Cohen et al., 1983). The short version of the scale comprises four items (Numbers 2, 6, 7, and 14) assessing the subjective measure of the appraised event. It invites participants to indicate the frequency of feelings and thoughts during the last month based on a 5-point Likert scale ranging from 0 (*never*) to 4 (*very often*). Two positively worded items are scored in the reverse direction. The Cronbach's alpha of the four-item scale was .72 in the original publication (Cohen et al., 1983) and .57 in this study.

Resilient Coping

We assessed coping resources with the Brief Resilient Coping Scale (Sinclair & Wallston, 2004), a four-item scale designed to measure resilient coping resources, such as tenacity, optimism, creativity, and problem-solving. Each item is positively phrased, and the statements are measured using a Likert scale ranging from 1 (*does not describe me at all*) to 5 (*describes me very well*). The Brief Resilient Coping Scale demonstrated acceptable reliability for the four-item scale in the original paper ($\alpha = .70$; Sinclair & Wallston, 2004). The internal consistency was also acceptable in this research ($\alpha = .71$).

Data Analysis

We used exploratory factor analysis (EFA) with Mplus 8.0 (Muthén & Muthén, 1998–2017) to explore the underlying latent structure of the SCAS. We performed all analyses with maximum likelihood parameter estimates with standard errors and chi-square test statistics that were robust to the nonnormality of observations (Muthén & Muthén, 1998–2017, p. 484). The oblique rotation of geomin was used by the default. We determined the appropriate number of factors based on eigenvalues greater than 1, the goodness of model fit, and the interpretability of the factors. A reasonably good fit of the model requires the comparative fit index (CFI) and the Tucker–Lewis Index (TLI) values to be higher than .90 and the root-mean-square error of approximation (RMSEA) to be below .05 (Hu & Bentler, 1999). The standardized root-mean-square residual (SRMR) should be below .08 for a good model fit (Kline, 2011). In a relatively small sample, a lower value for the Akaike information criterion (AIC) indicates a better model fit in comparison to alternative models (Akaike, 1987).

We used IBM SPSS Statistics to further the data analyses. We compared the differences in the participants' sociocultural adaptation scores using a two-sample t test after conducting a descriptive analysis. For the effect size indices (Cohen's d), 0.20 was considered a small effect size, 0.50 a medium effect size, and 0.8 a large effect size (Cohen, 1988). In the final step, we used Spearman's correlation to examine formulated hypotheses and assess whether some of the factors affect selected factors of the SCAS.

RESULTS

Factor Analysis

We performed an EFA to explore the underlying factors of the SCAS. We ascertained one to seven factors could be extracted by EFA. Six factors had eigenvalues greater than 1 (9.00, 1.89, 1.39, 1.20, 1.16, and 1.08). Although the eigenvalues suggested that six factors should be retained, six-factor and seven-factor solutions were not identifiable in Mplus 8. The results of the analysis demonstrated that out of the given five models, the degree of fit for a five-factor model was best in comparison to alternative models: $\chi^2(248) = 407.1$, CFI = .925, TLI = .886, RMSEA = .049 with 90%CI [.040, 0.57], SRMR = .035, AIC = 20,157.

Factor determinacy values for each factor of the five-factor model were close to .90 or higher, indicating good determinacy. We used a loading of .40 as the cutoff criteria for item inclusion. We defined a factor structure by eliminating items that had small loadings or cross-loadings on more than one factor. Initial factor loadings for the five-factor model ranged from .40 to 1.00 (see Table 1). Item 1 (.54), Item 3 (.76), Item 4 (.54), and Item 5 (.51) had moderately positive loadings on Factor 1. Factor 2 consisted of three items (7, 8, and 12). Both Factors 3 and 4 consisted of five items each, and Factor 5 had three items, from moderately

Table 1. Initial Factor Loadings for the Five-Factor Model of the Sociocultural Adaptation Scale

Item No.	Item	F1	F2	F3	F4	F5
1	Making friends	**.54**	-.03	-.04	.03	.08
2	Using the transport system	.24	-.03	.00	.08	.17
3	Making yourself understood	**.76**	.10	.00	-.05	.01
4	Understanding jokes and humor	**.54**	.00	.09	.19	-.03
5	Dealing with someone who is unpleasant/cross/aggressive	**.51**	.12	.13	.07	-.07
6	Getting used to the local food/finding food you enjoy	.07	.22	.19	.16	-.02
7	Dealing with people in authority	.12	**.58**	.15	-.05	.08
8	Dealing with the bureaucracy	-.01	**.84**	-.02	.04	-.05
9	Adapting to local accommodation	.04	.26	.21	.31	.04
10	Communicating with people of a different ethnic group	-.01	.04	.28	.16	.23
11	Relating to members of the opposite gender	-.09	.09	**.41**	.09	.14
12	Dealing with unsatisfactory service	.08	**.46**	.03	.19	.02
13	Finding your way around	.11	.03	.06	.29	.29
14	Dealing with the climate	.05	-.05	**.50**	.00	.11
15	Dealing with people staring at you	.23	-.02	.18	.18	.09
16	Understanding the local accent/language	.28	.22	-.03	.03	.09
17	Living away from family members overseas/independently from your parents	.06	.02	.27	.14	.11
18	Adapting to local etiquette	-.03	.06	**.45**	.32	.05
19	Relating to older people	.04	.05	**.73**	-.12	.00
20	Dealing with people of higher status	.07	.01	**.72**	.00	-.01
21	Understanding what is required of you at university	-.14	.13	.15	.13	**.54**
22	Coping with academic work	.02	.00	-.05	-.10	**1.00**
23	Expressing your ideas in class	.02	-.21	.21	.19	**.48**
24	Living with your flatmate/roommate	.08	-.10	.14	**.40**	.01
25	Understanding the local value system	.12	.08	.01	**.58**	.05
26	Seeing things from the locals' point of view	.07	-.01	-.04	**.70**	.04
27	Understanding cultural differences	-.04	.12	-.02	**.76**	.02
28	Being able to see two sides of an intercultural issue	-.01	-.08	.35	**.49**	-.08
Correlations between factors						
F1 - Affiliative Relations			.39	.49	.44	.28
F2 - Bureaucracy and Services				.40	.32	.28
F3 - Power Relations					.60	.48
F4 - Academic Performance						.52
F5 - Cultural Understanding						
Eigenvalue		9.00	1.89	1.39	1.20	1.16
Factor Determinacy		0.89	0.89	0.91	0.92	0.95

Note. $N = 267$. Factor solution was estimated with MLR method in Mplus. Factor loadings higher than 0.40 are boldfaced.

Table 2. Final Factor Loadings for the Five-Factor Model of the Sociocultural Adaptation Scale

Item No.	Item	F1	F2	F3	F4	F5
1	Making friends	**.54**	-.01	-.05	.08	.02
3	Making yourself understood	**.76**	.09	-.01	.01	-.05
4	Understanding jokes and humor	**.59**	-.03	.06	.01	.17
5	Dealing with someone who is unpleasant/cross/aggressive	**.50**	.14	.12	-.09	.11
7	Dealing with people in authority	.12	**.60**	.14	.09	-.03
8	Dealing with the bureaucracy	.00	**.79**	.01	-.04	.05
11	Relating to members of the opposite gender	-.05	.08	.32	.18	.10
12	Dealing with unsatisfactory service	.09	**.47**	.00	.05	.20
14	Dealing with the climate	.09	-.05	.38	.19	.01
18	Adapting to local etiquette	-.01	.08	.38	.09	.34
19	Relating to older people	.02	.06	**.71**	.01	-.05
20	Dealing with people of higher status	.05	.01	**.74**	.01	.03
21	Understanding what is required of you at university	-.12	.14	.06	**.66**	.09
22	Coping with academic work	.02	.01	-.11	**.91**	-.06
23	Expressing your ideas in class	.05	-.20	.11	**.59**	.15
24	Living with your flatmate/roommate	.13	-.10	.07	.09	.36
25	Understanding the local value system	.14	.07	.01	.07	**.56**
26	Seeing things from the locals' point of view	.05	-.01	-.02	.04	**.71**
27	Understanding cultural differences	-.02	.12	-.02	.00	**.77**
28	Being able to see two sides of an intercultural issue	-.01	-.07	.34	-.06	.51
Correlations between factors						
F1 - Affiliative Relations			.38	.49	.32	.43
F2 - Bureaucracy and Services				.36	.28	.28
F3 - Power Relations					.51	.54
F4 - Academic Performance						.56
F5 - Cultural Understanding						
Eigenvalue		6.93	1.76	1.31	1.13	1.08
Factor Determinacy		0.89	0.88	0.90	0.92	0.92

Note. N = 267. Factor solution was estimated with MLR method in Mplus. Model fit: χ^2 (248) = 407.1, CFI = .925, TLI = .886, RMSEA = .049 with 90%CI [.040, 0.57], SRMR = .035, AIC = 20,157.

low to high positive loadings on the factor. Item 4 ("dealing with the climate"), which moderately loaded on Factor 3, did not have a substantive relevance and meaning compared to other items. Item 22 ("coping with academic work") had a loading of 1.00 on Factor 5, indicating that the variable strongly influenced the factor. Because several items (2, 6, 9, 10, 13, 15, 16, and 17) were dropped in the preceding step, we reran the EFA in the same sample (n = 267) for further analysis.

In the second EFA, the eigenvalues suggested that five factors should be retained, where Factor 1 demonstrated the most variance (see Table 2). Factor determinacy values indicated good determinacy.

Factor 1 consisted of the same four items (1, 3, 4, and 5) with slight changes in the loadings related to interpersonal contact. We named this factor "Affiliative Relations." Items clustered in Factor 2 were related to bureaucracy (Items 7 and 8) and the delivery of public services (Item 12); accordingly, we entitled this factor "Bureaucracy and Services." Factor 3 consisted of only two items (19 and 20) that had salient loadings. Other items were below the cutoff criteria for inclusion, and we decided to keep this factor because the items had large positive loadings on this factor. Both items represented power and status relations; therefore, we labeled the factor "Power Relations." Factor 4 consisted of three items related to academic life (Items 21, 22, and 23) and we defined this factor as "Academic Performance." The loading of Item 22 decreased slightly from the first EFA. The last factor consisted of three items (25, 26, and 27) associated with understanding cultural differences. All of the items had relatively high positive loadings on the factor. We did not include Items 18 and 24 because of low communalities, and Item 28 had a cross-loading on Factor 3. The fifth factor was named "Cultural Understanding."

Sociodemographic Determinants of Sociocultural Adaptations

We employed an independent samples t test to examine significant differences between the sociocultural adaptation subtypes of the participants and sociodemographic variables. Gender, country of origin, and location of residence in Hungary were chosen as sociodemographic data. We found no significant relation between the sociocultural adaptation subtypes and students' gender (see Table 3). We found significant differences in sociocultural adaptation difficulties regarding countries of origin. International students from other countries of origin ($M = 2.69$, $SD = 0.84$) had more difficulties with affiliative relations than students coming from post-Soviet countries ($M_{\text{post-Soviet}} = 2.23$, $SD_{\text{post-Soviet}} = 0.89$; $t = 4.41$, $p = <.001$). The effect size of the difference was medium ($d = 0.54$). Substantial differences were revealed in the power relations ($M = 2.05$, $SD = 1.04$; $M_{\text{post-Soviet}} = 1.63$, $SD_{\text{post-Soviet}} = 0.82$), academic performance ($M = 2.22$, $SD = 1.00$; $M_{\text{post-Soviet}} = 1.85$, $SD_{\text{post-Soviet}} = 0.75$), and cultural understanding subscales ($M = 2.20$, $SD = 0.85$; $M_{\text{post-Soviet}} = 1.84$, $SD_{\text{post-Soviet}} = 0.75$), indicating international students coming from other countries of origin encounter more difficulties than international students from post-Soviet countries. The effect sizes of those differences were medium ($d = 0.45$, 0.42, and 0.44, respectively).

As for location of residence in Hungary, those participants who lived in the capital city had fewer difficulties in affiliative relations ($M = 2.35$, $SD = 0.81$) and cultural understanding ($M = 1.95$, $SD = 0.79$) compared to those who lived in other cities ($M = 2.87$, $SD = 1.02$; $M = 2.34$, $SD = 0.94$, respectively). The differences between these groups were equivalent to medium effect sizes of 0.60 and 0.48, respectively.

Table 3. Independent Samples *t* Test for the Sociocultural Adaptation Subscales

Factors	M (SD)	M (SD)	t (p)	Cohen's d
	Gender differences			
	Males n = 105	Females n = 162		
Affiliative Relations	2.35 (0.81)	2.55 (0.93)	1.80 (.073)	0.23
Bureaucracy and Services	2.62 (0.93)	2.68 (1.03)	0.54 (.589)	0.07
Power Relations	1.94 (1.06)	1.79 (0.89)	1.20 (.230)	0.15
Academic Performance	2.00 (0.85)	2.09 (0.97)	0.79 (.430)	0.10
Cultural Understanding	2.05 (0.91)	2.03 (0.80)	0.16 (.875)	0.02
	Differences between countries of origin			
	Other countries of origin n = 139	Post-Soviet countries n = 127		
Affiliative Relations	2.69 (0.84)	2.23 (0.89)	**4.41 (<.001)**	0.54
Bureaucracy and Services	2.74 (1.01)	2.56 (0.97)	1.43 (.153)	0.18
Power Relations	2.05 (1.04)	1.63 (0.82)	**3.67 (<.001)**	0.45
Academic Performance	2.22 (1.00)	1.85 (0.75)	**3.39 (<.001)**	0.42
Cultural Understanding	2.20 (0.85)	1.84 (0.75)	**3.59 (<.001)**	0.44
	Locations of residence in Hungary			
	The capital city n = 203	Other Hungarian cities n = 62		
Affiliative Relations	2.35 (0.81)	2.87 (1.02)	**4.15 (<.001)**	0.60
Bureaucracy and Services	2.63 (1.00)	2.75 (0.96)	0.83 (.409)	0.12
Power Relations	1.79 (0.93)	2.06 (1.05)	1.95 (.052)	0.28
Academic Performance	2.00 (0.89)	2.25 (0.99)	1.83 (.068)	0.27
Cultural Understanding	1.95 (0.79)	2.34 (0.94)	**3.28 (.001)**	0.48

Note. Due to multiple testing Bonferroni correction was applied and *t* (*p*) values are bolded if they remained significant with the more restrictive p value ($p = .00333$)

Table 4. Correlation Analysis Results

	1	2	3	4	5	6	7	8	9	10	11	12	13	14	15
1. Age	-														
2. Gender	.10	-													
3. Length of residence	**.23**	-.06	-												
4. English language proficiency	.02	.03	.05	-											
5. Hungarian language proficiency	.00	*-.15*	**.28**	.04	-										
6. Financial satisfaction	-.11	-.05	-.01	.08	-.05	-									
7. Affiliative Relations	.03	.10	.05	.01	.02	**-.19**	-								
8. Bureaucracy and Services	.10	.03	**.16**	.07	.02	-.08	**.46**	-							
9. Power Relations	-.05	-.03	-.01	-.01	.08	**-.20**	**.45**	**.42**	-						
10. Cultural Understanding	-.01	.01	.00	*-.12*	-.01	*-.13*	**.50**	**.39**	**.50**	-					
11. Academic Performance	*-.16*	.02	-.06	*-.13*	-.01	*-.14*	**.33**	**.30**	**.41**	**.48**	-				
12. Depression (CES-D)	-.08	-.02	-.01	.08	.01	**-.27**	**.31**	.17	**.29**	**.31**	**.27**	-			
13. Perceived stress (PSS)	*-.14*	.12	.03	.03	-.02	**-.16**	**.26**	*.15*	*.15*	*.13*	**.26**	**.50**	-		
14. Life satisfaction (SWLS)	.02	.06	.02	-.02	.11	**.31**	-.23	*-.16*	**-.17**	**-.23**	**-.24**	**-.52**	**-.35**	-	
15. Resilient coping (BRCS)	.07	-.06	.07	.08	.04	.09	-.05	.03	-.08	*-.15*	**-.20**	**-.18**	**-.19**	**.26**	-

Note. $N = 267$. The bolded correlation coefficients are significant at the 0.01 level (2-tailed). Correlations with italic are significant at the 0.05 level (two-tailed). Gender: 1 = male; 2 = female; CES-D = Center for Epidemiologic Studies Depression Scale; PSS = Perceived Stress Scale; SWLS = Satisfaction With Life Scale; BRCS = Brief Resilient Coping Scale.

Mental Health Indices and Sociocultural Adaptations

We performed a Spearman's correlation to measure the association between the determined factors of the SCAS and other indicators of adaptation profiles of the participants (see Table 4). As we hypothesized, we found correlations between all determined factors of sociocultural adaptation and psychological adaptation. All factors of sociocultural adaptation difficulties correlated positively with depressive symptoms (measured with the Center for Epidemiologic Studies Depression Scale) and negatively with life satisfaction (measured with the Satisfaction With Life Scale). The perceived stress (measured with the Perceived Stress Scale) also correlated positively with all sociocultural adaptation difficulties; therefore, higher stress might be explained by the increasing number of difficulties the students experienced in various sociocultural situations. The Brief Resilient Coping Scale had a negative association with only two factors: difficulties in cultural understanding ($r_s = -.15$, $p < 0.05$) and in academic performance ($r_s = -.20$, $p < 0.01$). Additionally, the third hypothesis was partially supported—difficulties in academic performance were negatively correlated with age ($r_s = -.16$, $p < 0.05$), English language proficiency ($r_s = -.13$, $p < 0.05$), and financial satisfaction ($r_s = -.14$, $p < 0.05$). Hence, the smaller number of difficulties the students experienced in academic performance might be explained by higher ages, higher levels of English language competence, and greater financial satisfaction. No support was found for a relationship between the students' Hungarian language proficiency and sociocultural adaptation concerns. Difficulties in cultural understanding were associated negatively also with English language proficiency ($r_s = -.12$) and financial satisfaction ($r_s = -.13$). Difficulties in affiliative relations negatively associated with the students' financial satisfaction ($r_s = -.19$, $p < 0.01$). Length of residence correlated positively with difficulties in bureaucracy and services ($r_s = .16$, $p < 0.01$). No support was found for an association between gender and sociocultural adaptation difficulties, as we anticipated.

DISCUSSION

We examined the underlying structure of the SCAS and the factors influencing the sociocultural adaptation difficulties of international students studying in Hungary. We chose to investigate the association between sociodemographic variables—gender, location of residence in Hungary, and country of origin—of the participants and sociocultural adaptation subscales.

The results of previously conducted factor analyses explained multiple domains of the SCAS. Ward and Kennedy (1999) identified a two-factor solution related to the cognitive and behavioral domains. Further factor analyses of the SCAS demonstrated a three-factor solution (Simic-Yamashita & Tanaka, 2010), a four-factor solution (GulRaihan & Sandaran, 2018), and others identified six factors (Su et al., 2019).

In this study, a five-factor solution showed the best model fit and included Affiliative Relations, Bureaucracy and Services, Power Relations, Cultural Understanding, and Academic Performance. The first factor, Affiliative Relations—explaining the greatest amount of variance—was connected to difficulties in interpersonal relations, whereas the factor Cultural Understanding referred to understanding cultural differences. Both factors corresponded to results found in previous studies (Su et al., 2019; Ward & Kennedy, 1999). The factor Academic Performance was related to difficulties in university life and was similar to factors found in earlier studies (GulRaihan & Sandaran, 2018; Simic-Yamashita & Tanaka, 2010). Items related to the factors Bureaucracy and Services and Power Relations were clustered variously in previous findings (e.g., Ward & Kennedy, 1999).

We found significant differences in regard to countries of origin and location of residence in Hungary. International students from other countries of origin had more difficulties in affiliative relations, power relations, academic performance, and cultural understanding than those coming from post-Soviet countries (H5). Since many of post-Soviet countries are relatively collectivist cultures (Hofstede & Hofstede, 2005), social and relational ties may be stronger and students may value order and duties more than other international students. Furthermore, Russian-speaking students may have a larger in-group in Hungary, which provides them with a sense of community and social support. It might explain why international students from post-Soviet countries have fewer difficulties in affiliative and power relations. For difficulties in cultural understanding and academic achievement, due to their common political pasts, post-Soviet countries and Hungary might have a relatively smaller cultural distance. Our findings were supported with the results from previous studies that also found significant differences in participants' countries of origin (GulRaihan & Sandaran, 2018; Simic-Yamashita & Tanaka, 2010). These results might be contingent on a range of contextual factors, such as countries of origin and/or the country of destination, and such factors should be carefully considered for further interpretations of adaptation processes (Wilson, 2013).

In line with our sixth hypothesis, international students who lived in Hungarian cities other than the capital had more sociocultural adaptation difficulties in affiliative relations and cultural understanding than those who resided in the capital city. A capital city is usually more diverse and provides more opportunities to meet people with international experience and language skills. These results reflect the impact of cultural diversity on international students' concerns in interpersonal relations and their cultural understanding in Hungary.

Similar to prior studies (Güzel & Glazer, 2019; Su et al., 2019), we found no support for a relationship between gender and sociocultural adaptation difficulties (H4). However, one study found a small correlation between gender and sociocultural adaptation ($r = .12$), indicating lower sociocultural adaptation for females (Wilson, 2013).

Sociocultural adaptation difficulties were confirmed through small to moderate correlations with measures of psychological adaptation (depression and life satisfaction) (H1). These results were in accordance with earlier studies (Demes & Geeraert, 2014; Wilson et al., 2017). Individuals who reported having greater difficulties in affiliative relations also appeared to have greater depressive symptoms ($r_s = .31, p < 0.01$) and lower life satisfaction ($r_s = -.23, p < 0.01$). The same previous study mentioned above also identified that the interpersonal communication subscale of the SCAS-R was related to both depression ($r = -.39, p < 0.01$) and life satisfaction ($r = .43, p < 0.01$; Wilson, 2013). Another notable difference found in this study was between difficulties in academic performance and psychological adaptation, corresponding to a larger correlation with depression ($r = .27$, $p < 0.01$) than life satisfaction ($r = -.24$, $p < 0.01$). Depression is importunate in the academic and social lives of international students, because it can make acquiring new knowledge and performing at universities more difficult.

Perceived stress also strongly associated with sociocultural adaptation concerns because it correlated positively with all sociocultural adaptation subscales, as we anticipated (H1). Studying abroad can be seen as producing chronic stress, which makes the adaptation process more difficult for sojourners. However, only a few studies have measured perceived stress and its relation with sociocultural adaptation difficulties. Some found a negative association between psychological distress and sociocultural adaptation (b $= -.31$, $p < .001$; Brisset et al., 2010). Furthermore, resilient coping correlated negatively with only two subscales of sociocultural adaptation: difficulties in cultural understanding and in academic performance.

Student sojourners have a large number of sociocultural adaptation difficulties at the beginning of their residence in a host country (Ward & Kennedy, 1999; Wilson et al., 2017). In this study, we tested the relationship between the length of residence in Hungary and sociocultural adaptation problems (H3). However, we confirmed only difficulties related to bureaucracy and services, despite the anticipation of a positive relationship with all sociocultural adaptation subscales. Other studies also did not find any link between the length of residence and sociocultural adaptation (Berry et al., 2006; Simic-Yamashita & Tanaka, 2010).

We anticipated negative associations between sociocultural adaptation difficulties and age, financial satisfaction, and English and Hungarian language proficiency (H2). However, English language proficiency correlated negatively only with difficulties in academic performance and in cultural understanding. Other studies also found a relationship between English language proficiency and difficulties in academic performance and other subtypes of the SCAS (see Mahmood & Galloway Burke, 2018; Wilson et al., 2017). Some previous studies found a relationship between a local language and sociocultural adaptation difficulties (e.g., Simic-Yamashita & Tanaka, 2010). However, this study did not confirm a negative relationship between sociocultural adaptation concerns and Hungarian language proficiency.

In line with some previous studies (e.g., Wilson 2013), we found that younger participants demonstrated a higher number of difficulties in academic performance ($r_s = -.16$). We found no support for the relationship between other subtypes of sociocultural adaptation and age.

The results of previous studies were mixed: Some found an association between age and sociocultural adaptation (e.g., Mahmood & Galloway Burke, 2018), whereas others did not indicate such a relationship (e.g., Su et al., 2019).

The current study confirmed a relationship between financial satisfaction and difficulties in affiliative relations, cultural understanding, and academic performance. To the best of our knowledge, no studies have been conducted to test this relationship. Additionally, some linked financial satisfaction to worse psychological adaptation outcomes (e.g., Sam et al., 2015).

Limitations and Future Implications

The findings in the study should be regarded with caution due to the cross-sectional design and its uncertainty in the causal relationship. This study cannot explain whether depressive symptoms, perceived stress, and life satisfaction were antecedents or consequences of sociocultural adaptation difficulties. We cannot exclude the possibility that international students already had more depressive symptoms, higher perceived stress, and lower life satisfaction before coming to Hungary. This study also cannot address the certainty in the relationship between resilient coping and sociocultural adaptation difficulties.

The participants might have been influenced by social desirability bias, answering questions inaccurately to be viewed favorably by others. We cannot exclude the possibility of a sample selection bias that does not accurately reflect the targeted population. The analysis should be tested on another independent sample to verify the structure obtained by the exploratory factor analysis in this study.

Despite several limitations, this study explored the underlying structure of the SCAS and attempted to get a deeper understanding of the internal and external factors associated with sociocultural adaptation difficulties. The results offer new insights by comparing two groups of international students—based on their countries of origin—in a new sociocultural context. Only a small number of studies have been conducted to examine the sociocultural adaptation difficulties of international students from post-Soviet countries. We suggest conducting cross-national comparisons to explore sociocultural adaptation of those group of students and to investigate cultural differences. Understanding the adaptation difficulties international students face in their host countries could help universities organize programs and activities that provide these students more opportunities for better socialization. Teaching and administrative staff are encouraged to focus on cultural awareness.

Acknowledgments

The third author was supported by the National Research, Development and Innovation Office of Hungary (K-120 433, and ELTE Thematic Excellence Programme 2020 – TKP2020-IKA-05).

REFERENCES

Akaike, H. (1987). Factor analysis and AIC. *Psychometrika, 52*, 317–332.

Argyle, M. (1969). *Social interaction.* Methuen.

Bennett, D. A. (2001). How can I deal with missing data in my study? *Australian and New Zealand Journal of Public Health, 25*(5), 464–469.

Berry, J. W. (1997). Immigration, acculturation, and adaptation. *Applied Psychology: An International Review, 46*(1), 5–34. https://doi.org/10.1080/026999497378467

Berry, J. W., Phinney, J. S., Sam, D. L., & Vedder, P. (2006). Immigrant youth: Acculturation, identity, and adaptation. *Applied Psychology, 55*(3), 303–332. https://doi.org/10.1111/j.1464-0597.2006.00256.x

Brisset, C., Safdar, S., Lewis, J. R., & Sabatier, C. (2010). Psychological and sociocultural adaptation of university students in France: The case of Vietnamese international students. *International Journal of Intercultural Relations, 34*(4), 413–426. https://doi.org/10.1016/j.ijintrel.2010.02.009

Cemalcilar, Z., Falbo, T., & Stapleton, L. M. (2005). Cyber communication: A new opportunity for international students' adaptation? *International Journal of Intercultural Relations, 29*(1), 91–110. https://doi.org/10.1016/j.ijintrel.2005.04.002

Chankseliani, M. (2016). Escaping homelands with limited employment and tertiary education opportunities: Outbound student mobility from post-Soviet countries. *Population, Space and Place, 22*(3), 301–316. https://doi.org/10.1002/psp.1932

Cohen, J. (1988). *Statistical power analysis for the behavioral sciences* (2nd ed.). Lawrence Erlbaum.

Cohen, S., Kamarck, T., & Mermelstein, R. (1983). A global measure of perceived stress. *Journal of Health and Social Behavior, 24*(4), 385–396. https://doi.org/10.2307/2136404

Cross, S. E. (1995). Self-construals, coping, and stress in cross-cultural adaptation. *Journal of Cross-Cultural Psychology, 26*(6), 673–697. https://doi.org/10.1177/002202219502600610

Demes, K. A., & Geeraert, N. (2014). Measures matter: Scales for adaptation, cultural distance, and acculturation orientation revisited. *Journal of Cross-Cultural Psychology, 45*(1), 91–109. https://doi.org/10.1177/0022022113487590

Diener, E., Emmons, R. A., Larsen, R. J., & Griffin, S. (1985). The Satisfaction With Life Scale. *Journal of Personality Assessment, 49*(1), 71–75. https://doi.org/10.1207/s15327752jpa4901_13

Furnham, A., & Bochner, S. (1986). *Culture shock: Psychological reactions to unfamiliar environments.* Methuen.

GulRaihan, M., & Sandaran, S.C. (2018). Sociocultural adaptation challenges of international students at a higher learning institution in Malaysia. *LSP International Journal, 4*(2), 85–101.

Güzel, H., & Glazer, S. (2019). Demographic correlates of acculturation and sociocultural adaptation: Comparing international and domestic students. *Journal of International Students, 9*(4), 1074–1094. https://doi.org/10.32674/jis.v10i1.614

Hofstede, G., & Hofstede, G. J. (2005). *Cultures and organizations: Software of the mind.* McGraw-Hill USA.

Hone, L., Jarden, A., & Schofield, G. (2014). Psychometric properties of the Flourishing Scale in a New Zealand sample. *Social Indicators Research, 119*(2), 1031–1045. https://doi.org/10.1007/s11205-013-0501-x

Hu, L., & Bentler, P. M. (1999). Cutoff criteria for fit indexes in covariance structure analysis: Conventional criteria versus new alternatives. *Structural Equation Modeling, 6*, 1–55. https://doi.org/10.1080/10705519909540118

Kline, R. B. (2011). *Principles and practice of structural equation modeling* (3rd ed.). Guilford Press.

Lazarus, R., & Folkman, S. (1984). *Stress, appraisal, and coping.* Springer.

Mahmood, H., & Galloway Burke, M. (2018). Analysis of acculturative stress and sociocultural adaptation among international students at a non-metropolitan university. *Journal of International Students, 8*(1), 284–307. https://doi.org/10.32674/jis.v8i1.166

Muthén, L. K., & Muthén, B. O. (1998–2017). *Mplus user's guide* (8th ed.). Muthén & Muthén.

Radloff, L. S. (1977). The CES-D Scale: A self-report depression scale for research in the general population. *Applied Psychological Measurement, 1*(3), 385–401. https://doi.org/10.1177/014662167700100306

Sam, D. L., Tetteh, D. K., & Amponsah, B. (2015). Satisfaction with life and psychological symptoms among international students in Ghana and their correlates. *International Journal of Intercultural Relations, 49*, 156–167. https://doi.org/10.1016/j.ijintrel.2015.09.001

Samokhotova, N. (2018). *Intercultural competence and sociocultural adaptation of Russian-speaking students in Hungary* [Unpublished master's thesis]. Eötvös Loránd University.

Searle, W., & Ward, C. (1990). The prediction of psychological and sociocultural adjustment during cross-cultural transitions. *International Journal of Intercultural Relations, 14*(4), 449–464. https://doi.org/10.1016/0147-1767(90)90030-Z

Simic-Yamashita, M., & Tanaka, T. (2010). Exploratory factor analysis of the Sociocultural Adaptation Scale (SCAS) among international students in Japan. *Journal of Humanities and Social Sciences, 29*, 27–38.

Sinclair, V. G., & Wallston, K. A. (2004). The development and psychometric evaluation of the Brief Resilient Coping Scale. *Assessment, 11*(1), 94–101. https://doi.org/10.1177/1073191103258144

Smith, R. A., & Khawaja, N. G. (2011). A review of the acculturation experiences of international students. *International Journal of Intercultural Relations, 35*(6), 699–713. https://doi.org/10.1016/j.ijintrel.2011.08.004

Su, A., He, W., & Huang, T. (2019). Sociocultural adaptation profiles of ethnic minority senior high school students in mainland China: A latent class analysis. *Sustainability, 11*(24), 1–16. https://doi.org/10.3390/su11246942

Sumer, S. (2009). *International students' psychological and sociocultural adaptation in the United States* [Doctoral dissertation]. Georgia State University. https://scholarworks.gsu.edu/cgi/viewcontent.cgi?article=1033&context=cps_diss

UNESCO. (2019). Institute for Statistics (UIS) database. http://data.uis.unesco.org

Wang, Q., & Hannes, K. (2014). Academic and socio-cultural adjustment among Asian international students in the Flemish community of Belgium: A photovoice project. *International Journal of Intercultural Relations, 39*, 66–81. http://dx.doi.org/10.1016/j.ijintrel.2013.09.013

Ward, C., & Kennedy, A. (1993). Where's the "culture" in cross-cultural transition?: Comparative studies of sojourner adjustment. *Journal of Cross-Cultural Psychology, 24*(2), 221–249. https://doi.org/10.1177/0022022193242006

Ward, C., & Kennedy, A. (1999). The measurement of sociocultural adaptation. *International Journal of Intercultural Relations, 23*(4), 659–677. https://doi.org/10.1016/S0147-1767(99)00014-0

Wilson, J. (2013). *Exploring the past, present, and future of cultural competency research: The revision and expansion of the sociocultural adaptation construct.* [Doctoral dissertation]. Victoria University of Wellington.

Wilson, J., Ward, C., Fetvadjiev, V. H., & Bethel, A. (2017). Measuring cultural competencies: The development and validation of a revised measure of sociocultural adaptation. *Journal of Cross-Cultural Psychology, 48*(10), 1475–1506. https://doi.org/10.1177/0022022117732721

Authors Bios

AIGERIM YERKEN is currently a PhD candidate in the Doctoral School of Psychology, Faculty of Education and Psychology, Eötvös Loránd University (ELTE) in Budapest, Hungary. She also works as a senior lecturer at M. Narikbayev KAZGUU University in Nur-Sultan, Kazakhstan. Her primary research interests lie in the area of cross-cultural and social psychology, with a focus on the adaptation and acculturation processes of newcomers, ethnic identity, and gender beliefs. Email: yerkenaigerim@gmail.com https://orcid.org/0000-0003-0753-1958

RÓBERT URBÁN works as a professor of psychology at Eötvös Loránd University (ELTE), Faculty of Education and Psychology. His research focuses on health-related behaviors (smoking, e-cigarette, eating behaviors, unhealthy use of alcohol, technology-related problem behaviors), psychosocial determinants of health and diseases (psychosocial epidemiology), measurement models, and psychometrics. Email: urban.robert@ppk.elte.hu   https://orcid.org/0000-0002-2058-5937

LAN ANH NGUYEN LUU is a professor of psychology and director of the Institute of Intercultural Psychology and Education at the Faculty of Education and Psychology, Eötvös Loránd University (ELTE) in Budapest, Hungary. Her main research interests are acculturation, ethnic identity, gender beliefs, and teachers' attitudes toward diversity. Email: lananh@ppk.elte.hu   https://orcid.org/0000-0003-2045-3763

Article

© *Journal of International Students*
Volume 12, Issue 2 (2022), pp. 889-908
ISSN: 2162-3104 (Print), 2166-3750 (Online)
https://doi.org/10.32674/jis.v12i4.3662
ojed.org/jis

Destination, Experience, Social Network, and Institution: Exploring Four Academic Exchange Pull Factor Dimensions at a University in the Republic of Korea

Kyungsuk Lee
Boise State University, USA

William H. Stewart
Hankuk University of Foreign Studies, Republic of Korea

ABSTRACT

Korean universities have shown a dramatic change in international student enrolment over the last 20 years. While a notable increase in enrolment is undeniable, factors related to international students at Korean universities are not well known or are poorly understood. In this exploratory correlational study, we investigated the relationship between gender and study level using the push–pull model among four pull factor dimensions: (a) Appeal of Korea, (b) Experiential Motivations, (c) Social Network Influences, and (d) Institutional Appeal. Short-term exchange students (N = 601) showed that Experiential Motivations was the most salient pull factor dimension in general. A 2x3 analysis of variance indicated statistically significant differences by gender and study level among the four pull factor dimensions. We conclude by discussing mobility programs and the need to account for the different motivations of potential students typologically in order to design policies and programs more effectively.

Keywords: exchange students, Korean learning, pull factors, student mobility

Student mobility paradigms have largely been characterized by movement from East to West and/or South to North (Habib et al., 2014; D. Kim et al., 2018; S. W. Lee, 2017; Park, 2019). However, the 21st century has seen changes to these directional trends, particularly in Asia (Chan, 2012). The Republic of Korea (hereafter Korea) is unique in this sense as international student enrollment has changed dramatically over the previous two decades (Jon, 2009; T. Kim, 2011; S. W. Lee, 2017). In 2000, only 3,963 international students were enrolled at Korean institutions nationwide (S. W. Lee, 2017). Yet by December 2019, Fall semester enrollment alone had grown to 111,858 (Higher Education in Korea, n.d.). As of late 2019, annual international student enrollment numbers started reaching over 140,000 (National Institute for International Education, n.d.). Reasons for this growth, unsurprisingly, are multifaceted.

At the governmental level, initiatives such as Brain Korea 21, Study Korea, and the World Class University project have been implemented to recruit and attract foreign students (Byun et al., 2013; Green, 2015; T. Kim, 2017). These programs often coincide with governmental financial assistance through the Global Korea Scholarship (GKS) and the Korean Government Scholarship Program (KGSP) (Krechetnikov & Pestereva, 2017). Other initiatives include the development of regional student multilateral mobility consortiums such as the Collective Action for Mobility Program of University Students in Asia (CAMPUS Asia) or University Mobility in Asia and the Pacific (UMAP) to increase interinstitutional study pathways (Hou et al., 2017; S. J. Kim, 2017). Moreover, it is not just international students who have been targeted; transnational branch campuses of foreign universities have been established at an education hub in Songdo, Incheon, which is currently home to one Belgian and four American universities (Jon et al., 2014). Although these branch campuses typically attract local Korean students at present, part of the educational hub's larger mission is to attract students from the Asian region (Jon et al., 2014). At the university level, recruiting targets have been increased in response to local enrollment shortfalls as a result of Korea's declining birth rate (Alemu & Cordier, 2017). The number of classes offered in English has similarly been expanded to attract and be more accessible to a more diverse student body (Byun & Kim, 2011; Chun et al., 2017). Nevertheless, while the increase in enrollment is undeniable, factors in general related to international students enrolled at Korean universities are not well known or are poorly understood (Alemu & Cordier, 2017).

While differences in motivation have been attributed to differing countries of origin in prior research (see S. W. Lee, 2017), complicating our understanding of international student enrollment in general is that international students are a heterogeneous group beyond just national origins. Further, different levels of study (noncredit, undergraduate, graduate) and mobility type (short- or long-term) have different motivating factors. Moreover, student decisions to study abroad result from a complex web of interactions between multiple sociocultural and socioeconomic dimensions in both the home (e.g., study abroad desire) and host country such as destination appeal (Altbach, 2015). As a result, the subsequent decisions leading to enrollment can be markedly different across numerous typological dimensions. In prior research, examples of conflated or overlooked student types are relatively easy to find (see Madge et al., 2015; Rensimer, 2016; Stewart, 2019). These complications are similarly present in international student research in the Korean context. While push and pull factors associated with degree-seeking students are better investigated (e.g., Alemu & Cordier, 2017), push factors are not necessarily applicable to exchange students given their relatively quick and intended return to their home countries. At the same time, it is not known what attracts short-term exchange students to study abroad specifically in Korea in the first place.

LITERATURE REVIEW

Although international students as a student category are heterogeneous, distinctions in the literature have been lacking (Madge et al., 2015; Rensimer, 2016), obfuscating research findings. Other student types are simply overlooked due to similar yet subtly different situational characteristics such as classifying expatriates (i.e., long-term labor/marriage migrants [and potentially their dependents]) as international students (Rensimer, 2016). Further, there are numerous ways to achieve international education through conventional movement where students physically move to the location of the university (Beech, 2015), as well as when the university moves to the location of the students (transnational education; Francois, 2016). While transnational education has often been viewed as an enterprise for local students, this is not always the case due to immigration (Dobos, 2011); the lines between international and transnational education can blur (Rensimer, 2016). The lines can become even more ambiguous when distance education can eliminate physical movement and borders altogether (Stewart, 2019). In this regard, virtual academic exchanges have long been possible yet the practice is relatively uncommon (Jager et al., 2019). While cross-border distance education in terms of short-term study abroad may seem paradoxical, COVID-19 has prompted new discussions (e.g., Altbach & de Witt, 2020) as mobility programs adapt and/or reinvent themselves, at least in the short term. In any case, one-way student mobility that can be investigated more clearly is by sampling short- or long-term international students separately, or by clearly identifying this difference as a demographic variable. Short-term mobility is characterized by temporary sojourns enabled by interuniversity or multilateral consortium agreements and subsequent credit transfer (DeLoach et al., 2019; Perez-Encinas & Ammigan, 2016). Long-term mobility, by contrast, typically involves directly enrolling at an institution in degree programs. Nevertheless, characterizing mobility by sojourn length is only one piece of the mobility puzzle; there are also different motivations related to student type (Rensimer, 2016; Wilkins et al., 2012). The theoretical lens of push–pull theory is one way of conceptualizing these influences (Altbach, 2015).

Push–Pull Model

The push–pull model of international student mobility describes external forces that act on students. Push factors are often an environmental pressure causing students to seek education abroad (Li & Bray, 2007). Typical push factors can often be an adverse condition in one's home country such as the lack of certain classes or programs. By contrast, pull factors are ones that attract students such as financial incentives (e.g., full or partial scholarships) or benefits (perceived or real)—for example, degree prestige in one's home country (Altbach & Knight, 2007; Mazzarol & Soutar, 2002; Nghia, 2019). While this conceptualization is useful, push–pull theory is not without its own limitations. For example, the push–pull model typically only considers external forces and does not explicitly take students' personal attributes or individual socioeconomic contexts into account (Li & Bray, 2007). In other words, internal attributes can also influence students' decisions to study abroad, or some students may have easier access to another country via heritage visas (Greenholtz & Kim, 2009) that facilitate the study, which is not accounted for in an external-only point of view. Moreover, the model is youth-centric and/or traditional-student oriented (Iloh, 2018); the simple dichotomy of push and pull likely does not adequately capture nontraditional student motivations or more subtle scenarios that surface through globalization, global nomadism, cultural hybridity, and immigration/expatriation (Greenholtz & Kim, 2009; Rensimer, 2016).

Current research (e.g., Altbach & Knight, 2007; Enright & Newton, 2005; Li & Bray, 2007; Mazzarol & Soutar, 2002; Nghia, 2019) has often explored push–pull factors from the perspective of degree-seeking (or long-term) international students, which also limits the applicability of findings to a certain degree when considering different typological student populations. For example, in the case of short-term mobility, different internal dynamics can be seen more clearly through the tourist/entertainment-like nature of academic exchanges (see Lam et al., 2011; Llewellyn-Smith & McCabe, 2008) and individual goals such as personal growth (Nilsson, 2015) compared to traditional international degree-seeking student counterparts who are pulled by the prestige of a degree or the name of a particular institution (Nghia, 2019). Further, pull factors, arguably, have much more relevance than push factors do in the context of short-term study abroad.

Pull Factors

The combinations of external determinants (push and/or pull), sojourn types (short or long), mobility methods (international or transnational), and motivations (intrinsic and/or extrinsic) produce complex and distinct educational scenarios that are not only bound to both a place and time, but relatively between home and destination countries (Enright & Newton, 2005). In Australia, for example, Mazzarol and Soutar (2002) investigated the push and pull factors of predominantly long-term international undergraduate degree students, finding that pull factors included positive perception of the degree, as well as the university and its faculty. Lam et al. (2011) produced similar results among graduate students in Malaysia who viewed the academic reputation of the university, along with its research reputation, to be the most salient pull factors. Nghia (2019) also noted that degree-seeking students often factor in the possibility of staying in the host country after graduation for work or residence, which is another potential pull factor that does not apply to short-term students. Weirs-Jennsen (2020) highlighted the absence of tuition fees in Norway as a strong pull factor for degree-seeking students, which similarly would not apply to exchange students whose tuition is already waived. In the case of Korea, long-term Chinese international students have been attracted by lower entrance standards (Park, 2019) as well as geographical proximity to home (Alemu & Cordier, 2017).

Such pull factors, arguably, are not relevant for short-term exchange students given their lack of official admission status (i.e., they are not degree students at the host university) and relatively quick returns to their home countries. For example, short-term exchange students in Australia were attracted by desirable tourist destinations and considered the characteristics of the destination country to be more relevant than the appeal of the institution (Llewellyn-Smith & McCabe, 2008). Lesjak et al. (2015) found differences by gender among exchange students in the European Union with respect to their motivations for conducting an exchange, as well as reasons for selecting a particular exchange destination. Recent research also suggests that K-pop and Hallyu (the Korean Wave) are also pull factors to some degree for international students, though popular media is more likely the avenue through which students have become aware of Korea rather than it being a determinant for studying abroad in the nation itself (S. W. Lee, 2017). Given the rather recent increase in international student enrollment in Korea (see S. W. Lee, 2017), related research is very much still developing.

International Education Research in Korea

When it comes to prior international education research in Korea, much has focused on students engaged in long-term mobility (i.e., degree-seeking international students), the majority of whom come from China or East Asia (e.g., Bae & Song, 2017; Jon et al., 2014; S. W. Lee, 2017; J. Lee et al., 2017; Park, 2019). In this sense, international student research in Korea is perhaps more accurately characterized as regional. When sampling has been diverse by nationality or region of origin, it has still predominantly sampled long-term degree students. For example, Alemu and Cordier's (2017) multi-institutional survey investigating international student satisfaction in Korea only received 20% of responses from exchange students. In other words, there is a gap in extant literature regarding other types of international students, and with international students originating from other regions in the world. Further, there are growing calls for research with foreign residents in Korea (Shin & Moon, 2019) and exchange students are a part of this broader population, even if only residing short-term. As Korea's presence on the global mobility landscape is comparatively new, prior studies are not only timely and valuable, but ongoing empirical research is needed.

Since differences in pull factors have been documented in prior literature by student type (i.e., Llewellyn-Smith & McCabe, 2008; Mazzarol & Soutar, 2002), and other exchange student research in Korea has been situated in different mobility program contexts (i.e., short 4–5 week summer programs) investigating local students' perspectives of interacting with exchange students (e.g., Jon, 2009) or primarily with long-term degree students (e.g., Alemu & Cordier, 2017), there is a gap to fill regarding short-term students.

METHOD

Since there is little known about the phenomenon of short-term exchange students in Korea, we used an exploratory correlational approach to investigate the factors related to exchange students in Korea. Further, since exchange students are engaged in temporary and comparatively short educational sojourns, we focused on identifying the specific pull factors and their larger pull dimensions that were influential in their decisions to participate in an exchange. To determine appropriate pull factors, we consulted relevant literature on international student destination choice (e.g., Ahmad & Buchanan, 2016; Ahmad et al., 2016; S. W. Lee, 2017; Li & Bray, 2007; Llewellyn-Smith & McCabe, 2008; Mazzarol & Soutar, 2002; Park, 2019; Wilkins et al., 2012). Then, we aggregated pull items and refined them based on the Korean context. This process occurred in conjunction professionals working in the Office of International Affairs, and the Office of International Admissions and Management, leading to eight demographic questions and 30 pull factor statements to measure the following four pull dimensions: (a) Appeal of Korea (AK; 10 items), (b) Experiential Motivations (EM; five items), (c) Social Network Influences (SNI; five items), and (d) Institutional Appeal (IA; 10 items). The questionnaire (see Appendix A) was written in both English/Korean and piloted in a private social media group (which is managed by the Office of International Affairs) for formative evaluation and content validity prior to implementation (Archer, 2008; Bennett & Nair, 2010; Burford et al., 2009; Edwards et al., 2009). Based on the resulting four pull dimensions and exploratory nature of the study, we sought to answer the following research questions:

- RQ1: Are there gender differences in short-term mobility pull factor dimensions?
- RQ2: Are there study level differences in short-term mobility pull factor dimensions?
- RQ3: Are there any interaction effects between gender and study level short-term mobility pull factor dimensions?

Participants

We conducted the study at a large private research university in northern Seoul, which has enrollment of around 20,000 students, and 3,300 of which are international. To capture a current snapshot of exchange student perceptions, we recruited five semesters worth of students from 2018 to 2020, resulting in a survey population of $N = 1{,}423$. The reason for the specific timeframe was due the overlapping of exchange periods with various students from 2018 completing their exchanges in 2019, while others were ending soon/had recently begun in 2019, or who were about to start in Spring 2020 when the study was conducted. The Office of International Affairs granted permission and assistance to create a mailing list from their internal database. Total enrollment of both new and continuing exchange students ranged from 300–500 each semester, often representing 50–100 nationalities. Moreover, exchange students are able to enroll across almost all colleges (with three exceptions), in addition to the university's language institute, meaning they have diverse academic backgrounds, language abilities, and thus possibly diverse motivations.

Data Collection

We collected data from late Fall 2019 through early Spring 2020 for 2 months. We emailed notice of the questionnaire to students 2 weeks in advance of data collection. The email included information about the study, the principal investigator, and the approximate length of time needed (5 minutes) to complete it. Respondents were asked to rate pull factor statements on a five-point scale (i.e., 1 = *strongly disagree*, 2 = *disagree*, 3 = *neutral*, 4 = *agree*, 5 = *strongly agree*). Reminder emails to nonrespondents were automated in Survey Monkey at various intervals to promote participation (Waclawski, 2012). Students reviewed an informed consent page and submitted an "I agree" response to participate. They did not receive any compensation for participation.

Descriptive Statistics

The survey population yielded 1,406 valid email addresses because 17 were either invalid or had bounced. We received 611 complete responses for a 43.4% complete response rate. Out of 55, 24 nations represented roughly 88% of all respondents, and students' home university regions typically varied between 3%–4% with the population total. Response percentages by region were proportional to the student body demographics with Europe at 46.7%, Asia at 33.3%, and the Americas at 20%. Thus, around 67% of respondents originated from outside of Asia (this percentage increases to about 85% if only compared to East Asia only). Such diversity is a stark contrast to international degree-seeking students in Korea (see Bae & Song, 2017; Jon et al., 2014; J. Lee et al., 2017; S. W. Lee, 2017; Park, 2019). Respondent characteristics (female [83%], aged 18–34 [$M = 22.2$], taking undergraduate [66.1%] courses for 4–6 months [76%] at the university's main campus [95.3%]) were confirmed to be consistent with the program as a whole by the university's Office of International Affairs.

For the four dimensions on the questionnaire, Cronbach's Alpha (a scale reliability test) was calculated for each dimension with the AK at .731, EM at .784, SNI at .751, and IA at .712. The internal consistency of the questionnaire's four pull factor dimensions can be considered reliable since they are $\geq .7$.

The distribution of students by gender and level of study is presented in Table 1.

Table 1: CrossTab for Gender ´ Level of Study

Gender	Language	Undergraduate	Graduate	Total
Male	16	71	14	101
Female	145	326	29	500
Total	161	397	43	601

RESULTS

In order to answer the study's three research questions, a 2´3 ANOVA procedure was applied with two levels of gender (male and female) and the three levels of study (language institute, undergraduate, and graduate). Where significant differences in study levels appeared, Sheffe's post hoc test was conducted to determine the differences between groups.

General Analysis

A comparison of pull factor dimension scores is illustrated in Figure 1. Notable is that EM (4.55) was the most salient pull dimension among students, particularly when compared with IA (3.67) and SNI (3.0). Pearson's correlation analysis resulted in significantly positive correlations among pull factor dimensions. Specifically, AK was positively correlated with EM, SNI, and IA. These dimensions' Pearson's correlation coefficients were .423, .260, and .426, respectively. The EM dimension also had positive correlations (.136) with SNI and with IA, which was .309. Lastly, SNI had a positive correlation with IA, with a correlation coefficient of .358.

Figure 1. Comparison of Pull Factor Dimension Scores

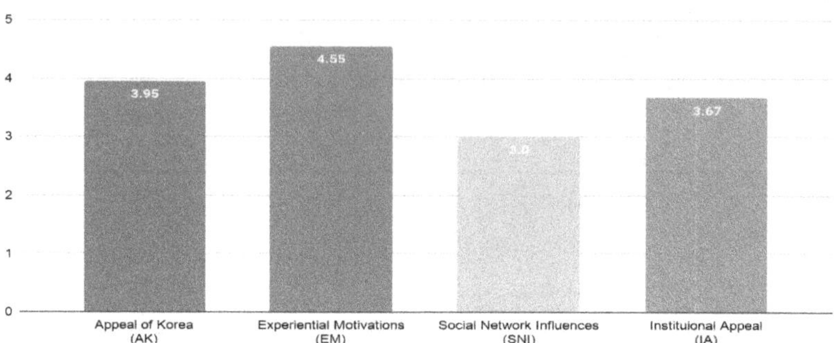

Analyses for Research Questions

A 2x3 ANOVA was conducted to see if there were differences by gender and study level across the four pull factor dimensions, but no statistically significant differences were found. However, there were differences found by gender and study level across individual pull factor dimensions. An analysis of each of the four dimensions is presented below within the context of the study's three research questions.

AK Factor

To see if there were any gender and study level differences, as well as an interaction effect for the factor AK, we applied a 2x3 ANOVA. The statistical analysis produced significant differences in terms of participants' gender (Type III Sum of Squares = 96.667, df = 1, MS = 96.667, F = 5.337, p = .021) and study level (Type III Sum of Squares = 147.894, df = 2, MS = 73.947, F = 4.083, p = .017); however, no significant interaction effect between gender and study level was found.

Female participants' mean scored 39.57 on the AK dimension, whereas their male counterparts scored 37.91. In terms of study level, graduate students had a score of 37.07, which was lower than regular undergraduate students or those attending the university's language center. Sheffe's post hoc analysis revealed the nature of the significant differences where graduate students showed lower scores than participants in the language and undergraduate study by 2.91 (p = .000) and 2.18 (p = .006), respectively.

EM Factor

To see if there were gender and study level differences and an interaction effect for the EM pull factor dimension, a 2x3 ANOVA procedure was applied. The statistical analysis showed significant differences in terms of participants' study levels (Type III Sum of Squares

= 155.093, *df* = 2, MS = 77.546, *F* = 14.797, *p* = .000), though no significant differences were found by gender. Further, no significant interaction effect between gender and study level was found.

Participants attending the language school EM had a mean score of 23.83, which is higher than participants in undergraduate and graduate levels by 1.31 (*p* = .000) and 2.53 (*p* = .000), respectively, which turned out to have significant differences by Sheffe's post hoc analysis. In addition, undergraduate students scored higher than graduate students by 1.22 (*p* = .004). In simpler terms, the higher level of study, the less pull there was by EM.

SNI Factor

To see if there were gender and study level differences and an interaction effect for the SNI pull dimension, a 2x3 ANOVA procedure was applied. The results showed significant differences among participants' gender (Type III Sum of Squares = 122.405, *df* = 1, MS = 122.405, *F* = 16.869, *p* = .009), but there were no significant differences in study level. Further, no significant interaction effect between gender and study level was found. The mean score for male participants on the SNI pull factor dimension was 16.05, higher than female participants by 1.23. The Sheffe's post hoc analysis indicated a significant difference between participants in the language school with a score of 1.13 (*p* = .017).

IA Factor

A 2x3 ANOVA procedure was applied to check differences in the IA dimension by participants' gender and study level. The result showed no significant differences.

Research Question 1 asked if there were differences by gender among the four pull factor dimensions, and differences were found in two dimensions: AK and SNI. Female participants' score on the AK dimension was 39.57 (male participants' score was 37.91). On the SNI dimension, male participants' score was 16.05 (higher than female participants by 1.23). Research Question 2 asked if the participants' levels of study were related to differences in pull factor dimensions, and results were positive for AK and EM. In the AK dimension, graduate students had lower scores than undergraduate or language institute students. In the EM dimension, participants in the language institute showed higher scores than both undergraduate and graduate students, while graduate students had a higher score than undergraduate students. Lastly, to answer Research Question 3, there were no significant interaction effects between gender and study level in any of the four pull factor dimensions.

DISCUSSION AND CONCLUSION

In this study, language students were pulled more by EM, and female students were more likely to be studying at the university's language institute. Thus given that EM was the greatest pull dimension, it would seem a relatively easy return on investment to develop or increase cultural activities, programs, or experiences for both male and female students. Further, given that the vast majority of exchange students in this study were female (and often disproportionately are in exchange programs, see Lesjak et al., 2015; Li & Bray, 2007; Llewellyn-Smith & McCabe, 2008; Mazzarol & Soutar, 2002; Nghia, 2019), it would also be beneficial to develop and/or integrate experiential programming into language programs since female students were more likely to be enrolled in them. Nevertheless, this need not be limited to language programs or female students; experiential programming can be integrated into undergraduate and graduate programs through extracurricular clubs and activities that center on intercultural and international experiences for students of both genders at different levels of study since their pull factors were correlated differently. This type of strategic programming might manifest through student-driven organizations such as an International Student Organization, or in conjunction with government-supported community programs, in addition to university International Affairs offices. We recognize, however, that this requires staffing, funding, and expertise that may not be readily available, or easily acquired for all universities.

At present in Korea, most universities likely need to invest resources to develop such programming, especially outside of the capital metropolitan area. In simpler terms, one size does not fit all, but with limited resources, budgets, and staffing, strategic implementation of experiential programming may be very effective for any university and lead to increased interest and subsequent enrollment, fostering a positive feedback loop. In this study, exchange students were attracted to destination characteristics more than institutional ones, which confirms previous research findings (e.g., Llewellyn-Smith & McCabe, 2008). Ultimately, rather than homogenize international students as a singular entity, mobility programs should take the different motivations of potential students by type into account, in addition to other characteristics such as national/regional origins in order to design policies and programs more effectively. Thus, institutions or departments may want to focus efforts first and foremost on experiences for short-term exchange students as a practical starting point; this would be particularly pragmatic if only limited financial or human resources are available. Related research findings regarding positive perceptions of personal development by means of short-term academic exchanges have also been found in prior research (see

Nilsson, 2015). One the one hand, other study abroad research has shown that gender influences the decision to study abroad as well as the study destination, with a stronger relationship among female students (see Lesjak et al., 2015; Nghia, 2019), and the results from this study support this finding from the perspective of pull factors and pull factor dimensions. However, the same study did not find differences by study level and exchange motivations, suggesting that students found exposure to other countries and cultures to be more valuable and important. While this is both plausible and likely accurate for many students (see Llewellyn-Smith & McCabe, 2008; Nilsson, 2015), the findings from our study are semi contradictory. While we also found EM to be the most salient pull-dimension overall, the results regarding level of study were negatively correlated to the AK as well as EM for graduate students. We posit that this may be related to age (or at least a proxy for age) as graduate students are typically older than their undergraduate counterparts. Such students may have more established academic or career goals in mind when compared with undergraduate or language school students. Nevertheless, no significant differences were found in regard to study level and IA, which is paradoxical since we might expect older students, or students studying at the graduate level, to be more attracted by the institutional qualities (see Lam et al., 2011). However, in the case of older (or even nontraditional) short-term exchange students in Korea, the reasons for this remain unclear and is an open area of research.

We recognize that findings from this study have limitations. First, respondents were not only pulled from a single institution, but one that is only similar to a handful of large metropolitan universities in Korea at present. Moreover, pull factors or pull factor dimensions are a moving target to some degree; their applicability should also be considered in the context of both the time and place they originate. Increasing the sample size to include multiple institutions would also strengthen inferences from pull dimensions among exchange students. Moreover, as a correlational study, it is possible that gender may be a proxy for another variable that is directly related to our results. Given these limitations, future research should be conducted in mixed method designs, with more rigorous quantitative approaches, as well as with qualitative approaches such as case studies, to provide reference points for the underlying perspectives that such students have, and which influence their decisions to come to Korea temporarily for study. For example, graduate students could share their insights about the appeal of Korea as a study destination, as well as the specific appeal of their chosen host university given the paradoxical results we found with this subcategory of exchange student.

We conclude by reiterating that not all international students are the same typologically, and consequently the factors that attract them to study abroad are different. While this is no different in the context of Korea, this study contributes to the literature in several ways. First, it provides a conceptual contribution by specifically examining not only a clearly delineated subtype (i.e., exchange) of international student and their specific pull factors, but granularly so by level of study and gender. Prior research, by contrast, has focused largely on degree-seeking international students. Second, it provides an empirical contribution with a data point for the Korean context where ongoing research is needed to better understand the growing inflow of international students. In turn, this can assist Korean universities (and other universities in similar positions elsewhere in the world) to not only expand their programs or partnerships by developing programs and policies to attract students in strategic ways, but to further refine them based on the most salient pull factor dimensions that students have.

REFERENCES

Ahmad, S. Z., & Buchanan, F. R. (2016). Choices of destination for transnational higher education: "Pull" factors in an Asia Pacific market. *Educational Studies, 42,* 163–180 https://doi.org/10.1080/03055698.2016.1152171.

Ahmad, S. Z., Buchanan, F. R., & Ahmad, N. (2016). Examination of students' selection criteria for international education. *International Journal of Educational Management, 30,* 1088–1103. https://doi.org/10.1108/IJEM-11-2014-0145

Alemu, A. M., & Cordier, J. (2017). Factors influencing international student satisfaction in Korean universities. *International Journal of Educational Development, 57,* 54–64. https://doi.org/10.1016/j.ijedudev.2017.08.006

Altbach, P. G. (2015). Knowledge and education as international commodities. *International Higher Education, 28,* 2–5. https://ejournals.bc.edu/index.php/ihe/article/download/6657/5878

Altbach, P. G., & de Wit, H. (2020, March). COVID-19: The internationalisation revolution that isn't. *University World News.* https://www.universityworldnews.com/post.php?story=20200312143728370

Altbach, P. G., & Knight, J. (2007). The internationalization of higher education: Motivations and realities. *Journal of Studies in International Education, 11,* 290–305. http://doi.org/10.1177/1028315307303542

Archer, T. M. (2008). Response rates to expect from web-based surveys and what to do about it. *Journal of Extension, 46.* https://archives.joe.org/joe/2008june/rb3.php

Bae, S. Y., & Song, H. (2017). Intercultural sensitivity and tourism patterns among international students in Korea: Using a latent profile analysis. *Asia Pacific Journal of Tourism Research, 22*, 436–448. https://doi.org/10.1080/10941665.2016.1276087

Beech, S. E. (2015). International student mobility: The role of social networks. *Social & Cultural Geography, 16*, 332–350. http://doi.org/10.1080/14649365.2014.983961

Bennett, L., & Nair, C. S. (2010). A recipe for effective participation rates for web-based surveys. *Assessment & Evaluation in Higher Education, 35*, 357–365. http://doi.org/10.1080/02602930802687752

Burford, B., Hesketh, A., Wakeling, J., Bagnall, G., Colthart, I., Illing, J., Kergon, J., Morrow, G., Spencer, J., & van Zwanenberg, T. (2009). Asking the right questions and getting meaningful responses: 12 tips on developing and administering a questionnaire survey for healthcare professionals. *Medical Teacher, 31*, 207–211. http://doi.org/10.1080/01421590802225762

Byun, K., Jon, J. E., & Kim, D. (2013). Quest for building world-class universities in South Korea: Outcomes and consequences. *Higher Education, 65*, 645–659. http://doi.org/10.1007/s10734-012-9568-6

Byun, K., & Kim, M. (2011). Shifting patterns of the government's policies for the internationalization of Korean higher education. *Journal of Studies in International Education, 15*, 467–486. http://doi.org/10.1177/1028315310375307

Chan, S. (2012). Shifting patterns of student mobility in Asia. *Higher Education Policy, 25*, 207–224. https://dx.doi.org/10.1057/hep.2012.3

Chun, S., Kim, H., Park, C. K., McDonald, K., Sun Ha, O., Kim, D. L., & Lee, S. M. (2017). South Korean students' responses to English-medium instruction courses. *Social Behavior and Personality, 45*, 951–965. https://doi.org/10.2224/sbp.6049

DeLoach, S. B., Kurt, M. R., & Olitsky, N. H. (2019). Duration matters: Separating the impact of depth and duration in study abroad programs. *Journal of Studies in International Education, 25*, 100–118. https://doi.org/10.1177/1028315319887389

Dobos, K. (2011). "Serving two masters"—Academics' perspectives on working at an offshore campus in Malaysia. *Educational Review, 63*, 19–35. https://doi.org/10.1080/00131911003748035

Edwards, P. J., Roberts, I., Clarke, M. J., DiGuiseppi, C., Wentz, R., Kwan, I., Cooper, R., Felix, L. M., & Pratap, S. (2009). Methods to increase response to postal and electronic questionnaires. *Cochrane Database of Systematic Reviews, 3*, Article MR000008. https://doi.org/10.1002/14651858.MR000008.pub4

Enright, M. J., & Newton, J. (2005). Determinants of tourism destination competitiveness in Asia Pacific: Comprehensiveness and universality. *Journal of Travel Research, 43*, 339–350. http://doi.org/10.1177/0047287505274647

Francois, E. J. (2016). What is transnational education? In E. J. Francois, M. B. M. Avoseh, & W. Griswold (Eds.), *Perspectives in transnational higher education* (pp. 639–653). Sense Publishers.

Green, C. (2015). Internationalization, deregulation and the expansion of higher education in Korea: An historical overview. *International Journal of Higher Education, 4*, 1–13. http://dx.doi.org/10.5430/ijhe.v4n3p1

Greenholtz, J., & Kim, J. (2009). The cultural hybridity of Lena: A multi-method case study of a third culture kid. *International Journal of Intercultural Relations, 33*, 391–398. https://doi.org/10.1016/j.ijintrel.2009.05.004

Habib, L., Johannesen, M., & Øgrim, L. (2014). Experiences and challenges of international students in technology-rich learning environments. *Journal of Educational Technology & Society, 17*, 196–206. https://www.jstor.org/stable/pdf/jeductechsoci.17.2.196.pdf

Higher Education in Korea. (n.d.). Status of foreign students (university). Retrieved December 01, 2019, from https://www.academyinfo.go.kr/uipnh/unt/unmcom/RdViewer.do

Hou, A. Y. C., Hill, C., Chen, K. H. J., Tsai, S., & Chen, V. (2017). A comparative study of student mobility programs in SEAMEO-RIHED, UMAP, and Campus Asia: Regulation, challenges, and impacts on higher education regionalization. *Higher Education Evaluation and Development, 11*, 12–24. http://doi.org/10.1108/HEED-08-2017-003

Iloh, C. (2018). Toward a new model of college "choice" for a twenty-first-century context. *Harvard Educational Review, 88*, 227–244. https://doi.org/10.17763/1943-5045-88.2.227

Jager, S., Nissen, E., Helm, F., Baroni, A., & Rousset, I. (2019). *Virtual exchange as innovative practice across Europe. Awareness and use in higher education. EVOLVE Project Baseline Study.* University of Groningen. https://www.rug.nl/research/portal/files/128139457/Baseline_study_rep ort_Final_Published_Incl_Survey.pdf

Jon, J. E. (2009). 'Interculturality' in higher education as student intercultural learning and development: A case study in South Korea. *Intercultural Education, 20*, 439–449. https://dx.doi.org/10.1080/14675980903371308

Jon, J. E., Lee, J. J., & Byun, K. (2014). The emergence of a regional hub: Comparing international student choices and experiences in South Korea. *Higher Education, 67*, 691–710. http://doi.org/ 10.1007/s10734-013-9674-0

Kim, D., Bankart, C. A., Jiang, X., & Brazil, A. M. (2018). Understanding the college choice process of Asian international students. In Y. Ma & M. A. Garcilla-Murillo (Eds.), *Understanding international students from Asia in American universities* (pp. 15–41). Springer.

Kim, S. J. (2017). Leveraging process evaluation for project development and sustainability: The case of the CAMPUS Asia program in Korea. *Journal of Studies in International Education, 21,* 315–332. http://doi.org/10.1177/1028315317696961

Kim, T. (2011). Globalization and higher education in South Korea—Towards ethnocentric internationalization or global commercialization of higher education? In R. King, S. Marginson, & R. Naidoo (Eds.), *Handbook of globalization and higher education* (pp. 286–305). Edward Elgar Publishing.

Kim, T. (2017). Academic mobility, transnational identity capital, and stratification under conditions of academic capitalism. *Higher Education, 73,* 981–997. http://doi.org/10.1007/s10734- 017-0118-0

Krechetnikov, K. G., & Pestereva, N. M. (2017). A comparative analysis of the education systems in Korea and Japan from the perspective of internationalization. *European Journal of Contemporary Education, 6,* 77–88. http://doi.org/ 10.13187/ejced.2017.1.77

Lam, J., Ariffin, A., & Ahmad, A. (2011). Edutourism: Exploring the push-pull factors in selecting a university. *International Journal of Business and Society, 12,* 63–78. http://shdl.mmu.edu.my/3792/

Lee, J., Jon, J. E., & Byun, K. (2017). Neo-racism and neo-nationalism within East Asia: The experiences of international students in South Korea. *Journal of Studies in International Education, 21,* 136–155. http://doi.org/10.1177/1028315316669903

Lee, S. W. (2017). Circulating East to East: Understanding the push–pull factors of Chinese studying in Korea. *Journal of Studies in International Education, 21,* 170–190. http://doi.org/10/1177/10283153176797540

Lesjak, M., Juvan, E., Ineson, E. M., Yap, M. H., & Axelsson, E. P. (2015). Erasmus student motivation: Why and where to go? *Higher Education, 70,* 845–865. http://doi.org/10.1007/s10734-015-9871-0

Li, M., & Bray, M. (2007). Cross-border flows of students for higher education: Push–pull factors and motivations of mainland Chinese students in Hong Kong and Macau. *Higher Education, 53,* 791–818. http://doi.org/10.1007/s10734-005-5423-3

Llewellyn-Smith, C., & McCabe, V. S. (2008). What is the attraction for exchange students: The host destination or host university? Empirical evidence from a study of an Australian university. *International Journal of Tourism Research, 10,* 593–607. https://doi.org/10.1002/jtr.692

Madge, C., Raghuram, P., & Noxolo, P. (2015). Conceptualizing international education: From international student to international study. *Progress in Human Geography, 39,* 681–701. http://doi.org/10.1177/0309132514526442

Mazzarol, T., & Soutar, G. N. (2002). "Push-pull" factors influencing international student destination choice. *International Journal of Educational Management, 16,* 82–90. https://doi.org/10.1108/09513540210418403

National Institute for International Education. (n.d.). *For the development of human resources in the age of globalization.* Retrieved December 01, 2019, from http://www.niied.go.kr/eng/index.do

Nghia, T. L. H. (2019). Motivations for studying abroad and immigration intentions: The case of Vietnamese students. *Journal of International Students, 9,* 758–776. https://doi.org/10.32674/jis.v0i0.731

Nilsson, P. A. (2015). Expectations and experiences of inbound students: Perspectives from Sweden. *Journal of International Students, 5,* 161–174. https://www.ojed.org/index.php/jis/article/view/432

Park, S. (2019). The globalization of Korean universities and Chinese students: A comparative analysis between universities in Seoul and a provincial city. *Korean Anthropology Review, 3,* 253–291. http://s-space.snu.ac.kr/handle/10371/146918

Perez-Encinas, A., & Ammigan, R. (2016). Support services at Spanish and U.S. institutions: A driver for international student satisfaction. *Journal of International Students, 6,* 984–998. https://www.ojed.org/index.php/jis/article/view/330

Rensimer, L. (2016). International higher education for whom? Expatriate students, choice-making and international (im)mobility in the Northern United Arab Emirates. *FIRE, 3,* 79–96. http://dx.doi.org/10.18275/fire201603021092

Shin, G. W., & Moon, R. J. (2019). Korea's migrants: From homogeneity to diversity: An Asian survey special section. *Asian Survey, 59,* 595–606. https://doi.org/10.1525/as.2019.59.4.595

Stewart, W. H. (2019). The complexity of transnational distance students: A review of the literature. *Open Praxis, 11,* 23–39. http://dx.doi.org/10.5944/openpraxis.11.1.923

Waclawski, E. (2012). How I use it: Survey Monkey. *Occupational Medicine, 62,* 477–477. http://doi.org/10.1093/occmed/kqs075

Wiers-Jenssen, J. (2020). What brings international students to Norway? *Journal of International Students, 10,* ix–xii. https://doi.org/10.32674/jis.v10i1.1888

Wilkins, S., Balakrishnan, M. S., & Huisman, J. (2012). Student choice in higher education: Motivations for choosing to study at an international branch campus. *Journal of Studies in International Education, 16,* 413–433. http://doi.org/10.1177/1028315311429002

Appendix

Table A: Exchange Student Pull Factor Items

Dimensions/pull factors

Appeal of Korea (AK)

I am interested in Korean culture and lifestyle.

There are many interesting attractions to see in my free time.

Korea is a safe and convenient country to live in.

I want to learn Korean/improve Korean language skills.

Korea has a good reputation.

Korea is well situated for international/domestic travel.

It is easy to get a student visa.

Korea has strong ties to my home country.

I am interested in K-pop/Hallyu.

Korea is an affordable place to live.

Experiential Motivations (EM)

I want to see new places and have new cultural experiences.

I want to experience a new/different culture.

I want to experience a new/different lifestyle.

I want to meet new people from different countries.

I want to have new educational experiences.

Social Network Influences (SNI)

My professor(s) recommended studying in Korea.

My school advisor/counselor(s) recommended studying in Korea.

My friend(s) recommended studying in Korea.

My friend(s) also planned to study in Korea.

My family member(s) recommended studying in Korea

Institutional Appeal (IA)

There are many student support services (ISO, Buddy Program, etc.).

The university has a good reputation for its educational programs.

The university has a prestigious reputation.

The university has high quality professors/faculty.

The university offers classes that are not available in my home university.

It is easy to get admitted as an exchange student.

There are many different types of classes/programs that I can take.

The classes I want/need to take available in English.

The university's ranking is important to me.

There are many scholarships/financial supports available to me.

Authors Bios

KYUNGSUK LEE, PhD, is an Adjunct Professor of Korean language at Boise State University where she teaches beginner's and intermediate Korean. She has been teaching Korean in distance and in-person as well. She specializes in Korean language learning in informal settings where language intersects with culture. Email: kyungsuklee@boisestate.edu

WILLIAM H. STEWART, EdD, is the Inbound Exchange Student Program Manager at Hankuk University of Foreign Studies, where he coordinates all aspects of inbound exchanges. He specializes in transnational and international education, particularly where these fields intersect with distance education. His research focuses on student motivations for, and experiences with distance education in cross-border settings with a focus on the Korean context. He earned a doctorate in Educational Technology from Boise State University. Email: wstewart@hufs.ac.kr ORCid: https://orcid.org/0000-0002-8227-849X

Article
___

© *Journal of International Students*
Volume 12, Issue 4 (2022), pp. 909-932
ISSN: 2162-3104 (Print), 2166-3750 (Online)
https://doi.org/10.32674/jis.v12i4.2905
ojed.org/jis

International Students by Treaty: Common Space, Different Vulnerabilities

Cherry-Ann Smart
Information Smart Consulting, Jamaica

ABSTRACT

Nonnational students in the Anglophone Caribbean are often affected by natural or man-made disasters that affect their experiences in the host country. However, the region had never experienced pandemic disasters such as COVID-19. Its occurrence highlighted latent concerns such as prejudices, border issues, and weak institutional support despite the existence of geopolitical treaties. Using the concept of the looming vulnerability framework, and incorporating a transformative lens, the research examined factors that contributed to these students' vulnerabilities at institutions of higher education in the Caribbean during the pandemic. A qualitative research design using regional newspapers accounted for students' collective voices. The results showed that nonnational students' mental well-being was affected by factors including institutional role, management of communication, access to resources, their governments' expression of financial support, and perceived discrimination from the host community. The article highlights the potential for students' further marginalization in the absence of pragmatic disaster preparedness plans.

Keywords: Caribbean, COVID-19, developing nations, higher education, international students, looming vulnerability

During the COVID-19 pandemic, international students the world over were caught in a maelstrom of uncertainties that disrupted their studies and financial investments, which added stress to their already vulnerable status in a foreign country. In the Anglophone Caribbean, nonnational students faced similar challenges. Despite a semblance of protection under geopolitical treaties unlike their counterparts in the United States (Castiello-Gutiérrez & Li, 2020), similar uncertainties and diverse levels of institutional support added to existing challenges of their mobile study experience during the pandemic.

In the Caribbean, students attend tertiary level institutions within the region that range from 770 to 4,288 km from their home territories. Interisland air travel is facilitated by three carriers, with other alternatives being commercial transit through the United States. This alternate transit is expensive and requires travelers to possess a U.S. visa. Apart from the limited availability of flights, nonnational students were faced with border closures and strict lockdown measures in host and home territories. The nature of this pandemic meant resolutions undertaken during past natural disasters, such as home governments' swift repatriation of students by special flights (e.g., post passage of a Category 5 hurricane in Jamaica; "UWI Students Return," 2004) could not be implemented. To prevent contagion, governments instituted special security procedures at borders for citizens' readmission. Meanwhile, in host territories, island-wide curfews and stay-at-home orders restricted access to food, medicine, and other services. Correspondingly, at host institutions, housing accommodation, program continuity, financial worries, and uncertainties about the virus added to students' concerns.

Specific knowledge of international and nonnational students' vulnerabilities and capacities in the face of disasters in the Anglophone Caribbean is unknown. Although the region experiences annual disruptions of natural disasters such as hurricanes, earthquakes, volcanic eruptions, and pockets of civil disruptions such as states of emergencies because of crime and coups, their experience of biological hazards such as Severe Acute Respiratory Syndrome (SARS) and Middle East Respiratory Syndrome (MERS) is nonexistent. The purpose of this research, therefore, was to identify factors that contributed to the vulnerabilities of nonnational tertiary level students at host institutions in the Caribbean during the pandemic. Data culled from newspapers provided theoretical and methodological opportunities to examine social movement events (Earl et al., 2004) and were useful to examine information behavior (Tanacković et al., 2014). Themes were derived using content analysis. The article demonstrates the need for transformative strategies to understand and address the vulnerable status of nonnational students within tertiary institutions in the Caribbean in the event of disasters.

LITERATURE REVIEW

Reasons for Studying Abroad

Prospective students of international higher education consider different aspects in their decisions to study in a host country. Cubillo et al. (2006) identified some of these factors as safety, security, quality of life, and visa and entry requirements. Other authors pinpoint factors such as quality of education, proximity to home, and amicable political arrangements with the host country (Forbes-Mewett, 2020; Lam et al., 2017; Marginson, 2012). Studying abroad increases opportunities for research and to learn about different groups and ways of life, thus increasing intercultural sensitivity (Chien, 2015).

International Students' Wellbeing

Recent occurrences in international politics and violence against students on U.S. campuses emphasize the importance for universities to implement policies and programs to reduce risks and maintain safety and security for migrant students (Kapucu & Khosa, 2013). *Migrants in Countries in Crisis Initiative* suggested short-term migrants, including international students, face disproportionate struggles that affect their lives and security during a disaster (Perchinig, 2016). Their vulnerability is often intensified because of their marginalized status, and further emphasized through limited social networks, restrictions on mobility, discrimination, hostility, and xenophobia, to name a few (Guadagno et al., 2017; Rahming, 2019; Sherry et al., 2009). Guadagno et al. (2017) maintained the extent of migrants' vulnerability, during and after disasters, was often determined by the host university. This is possibly because the academy represents the first official port of information (Lam et al., 2017). Thorup-Binger and Charania (2019) affirmed this behavior in their qualitative study of international students after the 2010 Darfield earthquake in New Zealand. International students' belief that their institution would provide adequate support following the disaster emphasizes the importance of host institutions to honor this responsibility. It was only in the absence of a dedicated emergency hub (Izumi et al., 2020), or noncommunication, that students resorted to their respective embassies or consulates (Lam et al., 2017; Walters, 2018).

Higher Education amid COVID-19

Tran (2020) highlighted the fragility of current transactional higher education models amid COVID-19. Common topics in the literature have been the transition to online teaching modules and high levels of apprehension by tutors and students. In developing nations, the digital divide posed a unique barrier (Partridge, 2007), which further heightened skepticism among tutors about their ability to effectively teach online (Izumi et al., 2020). This focus on pedagogy was rivaled only by institutions' panic about pecuniary upsets (Dunkley-Willis, 2020), with the "personal realities" of postsecondary students a seemingly uncontested third, after crisis management (Castiello-Gutiérrez & Li, 2020). In the Caribbean, some institutions assumed an almost amorphous role, deferring responsibility for "their" nonnational students to home governments. This inherently "neutral approach" seems antithetical to international higher education within treaty arrangements, suggesting perhaps the injection of neoliberalist tendencies. However, authors such as Walters (2018) contended institutions need to come to terms with the politics of international education by assuming responsibility for international students. Castiello-Gutiérrez and Li (2020) concurred with this position, as they argued that international students were more than a business transaction. Despite the internationalization of higher education, this ethical and moral aspect, and its alignment with corporate social responsibility, remains largely unmediated and seldom addressed in the literature on international students. During unexpected hazards, such as disasters and civil disruption, failure by institutions to grok situates these students in precarious positions where their mental well-being may be adversely affected.

Student Vulnerability amid COVID-19

An individual's initial response to a disaster is perhaps panic, followed by an innate urge to escape, fight, freeze, or submit (Gilbert, 2016). Invariably, the barrage of media reporting that follows disasters sometimes serves to instill greater anxieties than provide comfort. During Hurricane Katrina, research showed the influence of the media and their tendency to overstep boundaries (Littlefield & Quenette, 2007). Inflammatory language exaggerated claims, which fueled the ongoing panic (Tierney et al., 2006). For international students, management of communication can reduce stress and build resilience (Forbes-Mewett, 2020; Thorup-Binger & Charania, 2019). Kapucu and Khosa (2013) stressed the need for tailored communication since insufficient, disjointed, or limited communication added to the panic and increased feelings of vulnerabilities. To this end, Izumi et al. (2020) advised that higher education institutions should conduct regular awareness programs on risks, preparedness, and responses for campus stakeholders. Ideally, this should include a comprehensive risk communication strategy, encompassing all disasters—natural, biological, and man-made. These are just a few of the measures to protect students' well-being as sojourners of international higher education.

Vulnerability as a Conceptual Framework

Human beings are vulnerable to specific hazards but credit their resilience as symptomatic of the generative capacity to survive. Diverse conceptual frameworks of vulnerability span multiple sectors from medicine to disaster management (Wisner, 2016), and are riddled with ambiguity (Peroni & Timmer, 2013). Wisner (2016) suggested this was because these models were definitions expanded to highlight how diverse sectoral processes negotiated their "loss and harm and obstacles to recovery" (p. 9). In their looming vulnerability model (LVM), the framework used in this study, Riskind and Rector (2018) suggested that an *individual's perception* of a threat, *if it occurs,* was as important as the imminent threat as it hindered the mind's response mechanism and contributed to the etiology of stress and anxiety. The "looming cognitive style" (LCS) is an evolutionary construct that refers to an individual's perceived bias toward prospection and perception of future threats. It is based on a mental image of the threat's rapid progression as it draws nearer and intensifies as it becomes more urgent (Yeo et al., 2020).

Although the concept falls under the suite of cognitive behavioral theories, it does not presuppose that students' exposure to these stresses is a corollary for psychological disorders such as depression. Rather, early detection of a hazard allows an individual to prepare for harmful stimuli and to engage in self-protective behaviors. However, Riskind and Rector (2018) maintained some individuals may be at greater risk of anxiety than others. So although the risk of direct infection with COVID-19 might be negligible, the imminent uncertainty could adversely affect international students' psychological state (Serafini et al., 2020).

The LCS joins other cognitive behavior models in psychology, which conceptualizes, identifies and assesses, and generates appropriate interventions for anxiety and other disorders. This construct differs from conditions such as embodied predictive coding where both sensory and interoceptive states modulate inferences (Pezzulo, 2004).

Cognitive behavioral theorists such as Aaron T. Beck (1976) highlighted anxiety as a response to an impending negative event. Anxiety is linked to stress and other psychological disorders and explored using lines of inquiry such as worry (Capobianco et al., 2018), uncertainty (Zlomke & Jeter, 2014), and depression (Weger & Sandi, 2018). Early detection of hazards allows individuals to prepare for harmful stimuli and engage in self-protective behaviors.

Cognitive theories augment and expand the understanding of human behavior and its environment. Piaget's model of cognitive development posited that knowledge gained from dynamic or operative knowledge was of greater importance to cognitive development than information derived from static properties (Riskind & Rector, 2018). Accordingly, Strenger (2012), in situating the LVM between the philosophical thoughts of Hume and the existentialism of Heidegger and Merleau Ponty, advocated for more integrative use of concepts and categories in psychotherapy. Human survival depends on actual bodily experiences where skepticism and doubts are cured or overridden by praxis and not by vicarious or utopian existences.

METHOD

A qualitative research design (Creswell, 2014) addressed the research question: What are the factors that influenced nonnational tertiary level Caribbean students' vulnerability during the COVID-19 pandemic at host institutions in the Caribbean? Newspapers were the data source because they were important to frame an understanding of collective actions and social issues exhibited within the public discourse. They function as an outlet for society in their dealings with quisquous institutions, shadow protests, and collective actions (Earl et al., 2004). Newspapers also acted as a recorder of the social construction of students' protests during the pandemic and are appropriate given their historically proven benefits in research traditions (Earl et al., 2004). Voices of the vulnerable population and affected stakeholders were heard through the reported narrative. In this way, they "collaborated" to suggest ways to transform the institutional culture (Farias et al., 2017).

Author Positionality

This inductive research assumes it can be viewed through the lens of the transformative framework to "interrogate patterns within personal or social meaning" (Clarke & Braun, 2017, p. 297). Thus, these findings are one possible interpretation based on my position as an Afro-Caribbean citizen and nonnational alumna of a regional university. I have observed, researched, and advocated for more equitable relational issues of foreign and international students. This experience contributed to meaning in the newspaper accounts.

Study Area and Population

The Anglophone Caribbean are islands whose coastlines border the Caribbean Sea. The area encompasses some 2.754 million km^2 with a population of approximately 44.42 million (as of 2019). The islands are popular tourism sites and relatively peaceful despite their disruptive origins as receptacles of trafficked African slaves from the 16th to the 19th century. Islands are sovereign states and require the presentation of a passport to gain entry. Some islands host several tertiary-level institutions.

The terms "international" and "foreign" are often used interchangeably in the literature. The International Organization for Migration considers international students as persons "living, working or staying in a country other than her or his country of citizenship, regardless of her or his legal status, the reason for entry in the country and length of stay" (Guadagno et al., 2017, p. 9). In this research, the terms are inclusive and describe nonnationals who are in the country specifically for education. In the Caribbean, the demarcation has implications for institutional treatment. For example, The University of the West Indies, which is featured in this study, categorizes students based on country status because of the treaty that established the institution (Caribbean Community, 2002). Students who originate from islands that are signatories are considered "foreign students"; students outside that arrangement are considered "international." This status has implications for tuition fees. Medical schools are located in Grenada, St. Kitts & Nevis, and Cuba that fall outside of this treaty arrangement, but fall within favorable geopolitical arrangements; their students may be regarded as regional transients.

Data Collection

Primary data were retrieved from daily newspapers (Downs, 1972). Nineteen articles dated from March to August 2020 were extracted from eight newspapers (see Table 1). The data was publicly available, without human engagement and did not require Institutional Review Board permission. Featured student subjects originated from or studied in Trinidad and Tobago, Jamaica, Cuba, Barbados, Grenada, Guyana, St. Kitts & Nevis, Anguilla, Antigua, Montserrat, St. Lucia, St. Vincent and the Grenadines, and The Bahamas. Specific search terms used to retrieve articles from the newspapers' websites were: "international students," "foreign students," "university," "COVID-19," "Caribbean," "Jamaica," "Trinidad and Tobago," "Guyana," "Grenada," and "pandemic."

The use of multiple newspaper publishers addressed validity and concerns of reporting standards and sensational and unbalanced accounts of events (Barranco & Wisler, 1999). Although validity problems can also occur with the news-value paradigm, the nascent origins and proximity among the Caribbean public posits cross-border transactions of students, and the activities of higher learning institutions are of regional concern. All newspapers had high degrees of reliability and credibility as premier national publications. One publication, *The Gleaner*, has been Jamaica's newspaper of record for more than a century (Bowen, 2009). Newsworthiness as evidenced by significant occurrences in these major newspapers were reported as continuing events and not unexpected, novel, or unique (Barranco & Wisler, 1999). Downs (1972) referred to this practice as the "issues-attention cycle" or "media attentional cycle" (pp. 38-39).

Table 1: Caribbean Newspaper Coverage March to August 2020

Name	Countries of collective narrative
Barbados Today	Trinidad and Tobago, Jamaica, Cuba,
Grenada	Barbados, Grenada, Guyana, St. Kitts
Jamaica Observer	& Nevis, Anguilla, Antigua,
Newsday [Trinidad & Tobago]	Montserrat, St. Lucia, St. Vincent and
Stabroek News [Guyana]	the Grenadines, The Bahamas.
The Gleaner [Jamaica]	
The Tribune [The Bahamas]	
Trinidad Express	

Table 2: Generated Themes and Subthemes

Major themes	Subthemes
Symptoms of mental stress	Feelings of isolation
	Anxiety
	Uncertainty
	Fear of the unknown
	Stress
	Depression
	Panic
Institutional positioning	Anxiety, uncertainty, stress
Management of communication	Anxiety, panic, stress
Expressions of positive experiences	Gratefulness, happiness, spirituality, patience
Access to resources	Food security, food shortage
Expressions of financial assistance	Gratefulness, anxiety, patience
Discrimination, stigma, and xenophobia	Perceived discrimination
	Stigma
	Xenophobia

Data Analysis

An analysis of themes involved "identifying, analyzing, and interpreting patterns of meaning" (Clarke & Braun, 2017, p. 297). It seemed an appropriate technique given its flexibility with "sample size and constitution, data collection method, and approaches to generating meaning" (p. 297). In this instance, recurrence and importance of themes (Buetow, 2010) were centered on the LVM.

Data analysis occurred in three phases after I uploaded the articles into the NVivo 12 Plus software. At Phase 1, I read each news article repeatedly and coded for patterns (Saldaña, 2015) from extracts of quotations from students and stakeholders. Coded items related to expressions of social life (i.e., perceptions, beliefs, and opinions); institutional responses (i.e., schools and governments); and environmental hazards related to COVID-19. In Phase 2, I refined codes and grouped for emergent themes related to behaviors or experiences expressed as a result of the pandemic. In Phase 3, I explored supporting and contrasting quotations to gain a richer understanding of the scene. A colleague voluntarily reviewed the codes. There was a minor disagreement about whether the term "racism" could be used with this population. Eventually, we agreed that "xenophobia" might be more appropriate. The analysis yielded seven major themes and 16 subthemes (see Table 2).

RESULTS

Symptoms of Mental Stress

Students expressed varying levels of stress brought about by the uncertainty of disruptions surrounding the pandemic. These were manifested through feelings of anxiety, depression, panic, confusion, and fear. Some situational factors were room confinement that forced self-isolation. Border closures limited freedom of movement, and the nature of the virus required persons to maintain physical distancing, which limited social contact.

Psychological Impact of Quarantine

Being locked in now because you have to, has produced the psychological feeling that you are trapped. (Salmon, 2020)

COVID-19 has created a spirit of anxiety in me. (Salmon, 2020)

Financial Support

Students' transient status was exacerbated by thoughts of imminent disruption to finances. Concerns extended beyond their circumstances to worries about family members being affected by actual or potential job loss. Results showed governments and institutional support were uneven thus contributing to levels of anxiety.

> If I get kicked out, she said, I have no money and I'm in a foreign place. (Gioannetti, 2020)

> As a student, I have been dependent on my relatives in TT [Trinidad and Tobago], and like most citizens who are not essential workers, the lockdown has affected their ability to work. (Fraser, 2020)

> I can only speak on behalf of myself, I am eternally grateful for the aid which we received and I do not stand by the statements that were recently made in the news report regarding feeling neglected by our Government. In my opinion, we were seen and treated as a top priority and I wish to say again, thank you very much. (Webb, 2020)

Institutional Positioning

Each institution's position as it related to outward engagement with its nonnational student population varied and contributed in part to ease or aggravate students' vulnerabilities. Institutional positioning was posited to be a result of their resources, student focus, risk aversion, nationalism, and global outlook. Reports varied among institutions.

> The situation is stressful on many levels but SGU [St. George's University] has done all it can to accommodate and help those stranded. The university is paying for the flight, so they just awaiting government approval. (Gioannetti, 2020)

> Surely the university [UWI] would have let the students know what the closures—at the campus, country, and border levels—would mean for them?

> And why did the students feel they had to directly contact the Ministries of Foreign Affairs and National Security? One would imagine that the university [UWI] takes responsibility for the welfare of its registered students and that it would have

been directly engaging them to ascertain their needs. Shouldn't the university have been communicating both with its students and the governments involved?" [Stakeholder comment] (Hunte, 2020)

Management of Communication

Nonnational students were affected by the quantity, mode, and handling of the communication during the pandemic. The lag in institutional communication laid the groundwork for the dissemination of exaggerated and contradictory, not necessarily fake news, which fueled students' anxiety.

> Rumors of an infected patient at the campus hospital circulated in mid-February,…"mass hysteria" among students has not subsided. (Smith, 2020)

> I think it's because there's so much information out there on the virus that people don't always know what to believe. (Smith, 2020)

> We thank you, our students, for your patience and resilience as you adapted to the significant changes over the last couple of months. We are aware that we should have communicated with you sooner. We apologize for this. [Principal's response to criticism from the Student Guild] (Randall, 2020)

While government information from the host and home countries was channeled through official channels such as government websites or newspapers, social media posts were unmanageable. The lack of a dedicated communication channel from institutions meant an inability to check dubious information (Pennycook et al., 2020). In addition to concerns about personal safety, students worried about limited official news about the status of their academic program.

> Negligible communication from the institution to its primary charges: its students. [Stakeholder comment]. (Hunte, 2020)

> Whereas I welcomed the move to reintroduce face-to-face learning via the blended approach, it is disappointing that the first place our students get confirmation is via a newspaper. Just

> last week I wrote to senior administration about the importance of communication. (Randall, 2020)

> It's really about tightening up the communication between students and the university. [Comment by a High Commissioner] (Fraser, 2020)

Expressions of Positive Experiences

Some students thought it was important to maintain focus on their original goal and channel pent up uncertainties on their studies. Spirituality and faith were important to maintain a calm attitude.

> There's really nothing we can do besides pray and try to stay in our rooms. (Smith, 2020)

> …writing journal entries, listening to music, exercising and watching plays have helped him through the often-lonely experience. On the other hand, wisdom has found that being involved in her studies takes her mind off the pandemic. (Salmon, 2020)

The announcement of the pandemic in March occurred soon after the resumption of classes in the New Year. Students circumvented their limited mobility, social isolation, and loss of peer network by using social media to create new networks.

> The situation in Grenada has been scary. (Gioannetti, 2020)

> We can't do much about it besides trying to stay clean and not letting people cough on you. (Smith, 2020)

> We have tried to band together during this time by engaging in different activities such as exercising, cooking and studying together. I also keep frequent contact with my family and friends who are back home …. Their support definitely keeps me going. (Salmon, 2020)

Access to Resources

Nonnational students' inability to access resources such as food, cleaning products, and medication contributed to feelings of powerlessness and anxiety from this looming threat. Individual countries implemented disparate methods for persons to access supplies by limiting shopping days or instituting shop-by-surname days. Some students complained of depleted supplies while waiting in line. Since maintenance of hygiene was a prime precaution against spread of the virus, inaccessibility and inflated costs for these items were of concern.

> The supermarkets on campus are empty. We can't get wipes, sanitisers, [rubbing] alcohol or medication. (Smith, 2020)

> New measures include that certain basic food and items will be rerouted to the bodega; it is common knowledge that these items in the bodega can only be sought with the use of a booklet. Foreign national students do not have access nor can they utilize the same. ("Covid-19: Guyanese doctors," 2020)

> I was out of food during April when Grenada only allowed you to go to the grocery two days for the week (and) it was by last-name basis. (Gioannetti, 2020)

International trade and supply chains were disrupted due to border closures and embargoes. In times of crisis and scarcity, as often happens, locals have a home-court advantage. No special provisions were made for foreign students who had to compete with natives' local knowledge.

> Cuba has recently been plunged into even more difficulties following the exacerbation and intensification of the embargo placed by the USA. This has caused a lack of and/or shortage of basic food, goods, personal care products, necessities and services. These elements have all been compounded by the recent introduction of the COVID-19 epidemic locally. ("Covid-19: Guyanese doctors," 2020)

> We are living off the food that we brought up here from Jamaica before the pandemic, and we have very limited amounts now. (Bailey, 2020)

> So we cannot get access to things like rice, sugar, soap or toothpaste now because they are not available in the other markets. (Hunte, 2020)

Expressions of Financial Assistance

Expressions of financial assistance were either a source of comfort or distress. Governments' decision to repatriate their students, or wire funds for their upkeep, was an acknowledgment of students' vulnerable status in the foreign country. These expressions were, however, individual decisions, and inconsistently applied across board.

> I was extremely grateful when I heard that the government was sending money to students trapped in other countries during this pandemic. (Fraser, 2020)

> The government chartered a plane to Jamaica on Saturday for Bahamian students studying in the region….The only reason we did this is because the largest cluster of Bahamian students outside of this country is in those three countries. We're going to have to review this policy about going for Bahamian students wherever they happen to be. Parents and students must realise once you leave this country, getting back here is your responsibility. (Rolle, 2020)

Some institutions expressed their univocal relationship with students through reminders of financial obligations.

> Students who are away from the halls have been given various options to store their belongings for a fee while they are away. Some students have chosen the option of their belongings remaining in their room undisturbed, for which the applicable storage fee will apply. (Wilson-Harris, 2020)

However, external stakeholders appeared reluctant to accept the aleatory interest institutions demonstrated toward nonnational students. There was an inference that institutions held some responsibility for their safeguard.

> There are students locked down at the various halls of residence; students who are struggling to pay rent because they could not get back to their homelands, whose families are hard-pressed now to fund them; what arrangements have been made to help them get by? [Stakeholder comment] (Baksh, 2020)

Discrimination, Stigma, and Xenophobia

In the early stages of the pandemic, there was some level of stigma and discrimination brought about by ignorance and trending information. Nonnationals perceived their status attracted discrimination. Treatment from locals heightened or lessened feelings of vulnerability. The silence of authorities in the light of claims of stigma and xenophobia affected students' feelings of vulnerability.

> They just have a little soap and we were hearing that the taxi operators aren't accepting work from UWI students because they don't want to get infected. (Smith, 2020)

> "The Cubans are of the opinion that these items are for the locals and have openly objected to our presence in their lines," the letter said. ("Covid-19: Guyanese doctors," 2020)

> The student said that some Jamaicans have experienced high levels of discrimination from residents and grocery store clerks who prevent them from buying supplies. (("Covid-19: Guyanese doctors," 2020)

DISCUSSION

This research explored factors that influenced the vulnerabilities of nonnational tertiary level students at host institutions in the Caribbean at the start of the pandemic using the LV framework. Descriptions of students' vulnerability in the findings were unique to nonnational students in the respective territories and comparable to the literature on mobile students (Lam et al., 2017; Thorup-Binger & Charania, 2019). Although the number of students who remain and receive higher education in the Caribbean is larger than the numbers that study overseas, they receive incomparable levels of scholarly interest. Therefore, they represent a largely unexplored demographic in the landscape of international higher education. Often the literature demonstrates a common error of conflating Caribbean students with the African American or African demographic, treating their issues or expectations as homogeneous. The lessons to learn and unlearn the distinctions are treated with less avidity by those for whom this singularity is beneficial and fuels the paucity of research that suppresses the voices of transient Caribbean students. For example, through issues on identity as "foreign-born Caribbean Blacks" (Mouzon & McLean, 2017) with unfeasible categories of "foreign-born European

Whites." Additionally, the representativeness of Caribbean students is sometimes narrated from the "soft power" perspective of the educational institutions. These discrepancies lack percipience as they suggest mobile students' experiences within the Caribbean are perhaps phlegmatic, given the region's marketing as a tourist destination. However, these perceptions avoid critical questions about this market such as students' reception in territories with geopolitical accommodation, their vulnerabilities within neoliberal (Anglo-Caribbean) or socialist (Cuba) higher education sectors, or the condition of universities within the Caribbean. Regional universities were established on a claim of postcolonial social justice and democracy. Their establishment was important to regional economic development although Echols (1996) argued the inability to create borderless higher education institutions was short-sighted.

The literature illustrated international students sought host countries that were secure, nearby, had favorable geopolitical arrangements, and were low risk (Cubillo et al., 2006; Lam et al., 2017; Marginson, 2012). Findings from this study support the notion given the genesis of tertiary arrangements. However, while the Caribbean is perceived as highly homogeneous based on its history and geography, each island is heterogeneous in its outlook and culture. Over the years, there has been a greater focus on nationalism instead of regionalism, which is attributed to the polarizing nature of Caribbean politics and neoliberalism (Hinds, 2006). Disputes between island states have resulted in a boycott of goods, services, and rising xenophobia, which have weakened assurances in geopolitics. This knowledge, coupled with the unpredictability of the pandemic, is proposed to contribute to students' decision to flee or engage in self-protective behaviors (Gilbert, 2016; Riskind & Rector, 2018).

These disruptions to the region's cultural homogeneity have affected locals' reactions to intraregional visitors. In some ways, the pandemic served as a spark to this tinder, as the findings highlighted overt hostility and discriminatory tendencies among some locals. Locals' interpretation of the imminent threat was to resort to a protective "fight" mode (Gilbert, 2016), as looming threats can trigger anger reactions (Risking & Rector, 2018). Unfortunately, migrant students are often exposed to microaggression and territorialism by locals during and after disasters (Guadagno et al., 2017). Home-court disadvantage was compounded by the lack of social networks and communities and the closure of escape routes that triggered anxiety of this never-experienced SARS. More research is required to ascertain if micro aggressive tendencies are habitual behaviors during normal times. Nevertheless, COVID-19 was unique as there were no minimal cues. Perceptions were derived from a combination of diverse visual and auditory inputs from the media and fueled by imagination. These effects on mental well-being support the LVM that some individuals, more than others, are at greater risks for anxiety (Riskind & Rector, 2018; Yeo et al., 2020). Here, the individual's cognitive style was important as a negative cognitive style was more susceptible to anxiety disorders versus a highly resilient individual.

Resilience was pegged to trust, and trust in institutions was significant to ensure migrants' safety during a crisis (Sullivan & Kashubeck-West, 2015. Migrant students' ability to trust their tertiary institution to provide adequate support in the event of a disaster (Thorup-Binger & Charania, 2019) was not fully supported in the findings. Across the region, institutional responses were uneven. Some universities were prepared to sponsor students' desire to escape while others adopted a position of neutrality. Neutrality inferred a withdrawal of support, which is posited to be a response to the disruption of students' fiduciary obligations (Castiello-Gutiérrez & Li, 2020). It was only when students' public protest via the newspapers posed a public relations risk that they mobilized with efforts at mitigation. Sunstein (2003) coined the phrase "probability neglect" to describe a pattern where the amount of concern may be inadequately sensitive to the probability of harm. The more universities align their products with international counterparts, the greater students' perception and expectation of synchronized services. Accordingly, the availability of newsfeeds (Littlefield & Quenette, 2007) exposes and allows for comparisons about students' treatment in other territories. There is also the matter of failed expectations, which can result in disappointment, frustration, resentment, and increased anxiety levels. Stakeholders' anticipation that the university would safeguard migrant students was largely unmet but introduced other concerns that can add to the stress, such as faith-based questions (Edwards-Joseph & Baker, 2014) and a plethora of crises—such as identity, legitimacy, and self-worth.

This study is limited by its research design. However, it contributes to the body of knowledge of nonnational students in the Anglophone Caribbean and the larger arena of student mobility. It is also limited in its intentional "silencing" of the voice of institutions and governments to justify their decisions. Overall, this work is not generalizable as qualitative studies are designed to increase understanding of a phenomenon.

Implications for Practice, Policy, and Research

In the quest to protect and ensure the safety of migrant students who study within the Caribbean, higher education institutions need to create disaster plans that encompass physical, economic, environmental, and social factors (Füssel, 2006). Social factors especially will address students' well-being, security, and resemble good governance. Too often disaster plans focus on crisis management, with strategies designed to protect the institution rather than their main stakeholders—students. In preparation for disasters, institutions need to create a stakeholder map, devise risk reduction strategies, create an emergency communication plan, and leverage technology in their implementation.

Stakeholder Map

Higher education institutions need to ascertain the stakeholders to whom they must pay attention. Since the establishment of the Treaty in the Caribbean, institutional cultures and associated sociocultural imperatives have transformed with globalization. This brought fundamental shifts in the way migrant students are treated, and implications for the way students experience stressors that contribute to vulnerabilities.

Risk Reduction Strategies

There is a need to develop or revisit mechanisms to identify, evaluate, monitor, and, importantly, action plans to reduce risks and manage the consequences of imminent disasters. The Caribbean is at risk annually for natural disasters. However, weak institutional responses suggest that existing plans are one-dimensional and unable to handle looming threats such as this biological hazard. Plans should also be culturally inclusive and not inosculate the needs of nonnational students with those of domestic students.

Emergency Communication Management Plan

An institutional emergency risk disaster plan needs to contain specifically tailored instructions, be written in language to mitigate fear, empower its audience, and be accessible to all students. This plan should contain avenues to initiate unique two-way communication channels that should be functional and fully operational during an emergency. This is especially when strategic communication lines are established between governments and the institution to ensure their citizens' safety. Institutions should be cognizant that while Consuls and High Commissions are the government representatives on islands, educational contracts are inter- and intranegotiated. Additionally, the government communicating with itself in a foreign country may be an ineffective approach.

Leverage Technology

As much as possible, universities need to leverage technology to keep track of their nonnational population. This is particularly important when communicating with governments or family stakeholders and to ensure students' safety. It is also important for accurate reporting in the event of death, or as in this research, the dispensation of much-needed funds to ensure survival. As mentioned earlier, values of compassion should be endogenous to universities in their treatment of nonnational students.

CONCLUSION

The experiences of nonnational students in the Anglophone Caribbean are an underresearched area in the literature on student mobility. The etiology of COVID-19 was an anomaly for a region more inured to natural disasters such as hurricanes and earthquakes and man-made crises such as coups, curfews, and even crime. Despite the ability of these events to create vulnerable situations, they are predictive inferences with definitive responses. However, the amorphous structure of COVID-19 made it difficult to appraise this impending threat. The lack of a specific disaster readiness plan to ensure nonnational students' security and safety, protection from hardships, and mitigation of risks was evident.

The conceptual framework of LV presented is intended to alert researchers of mobile students' vulnerability when faced with imminent threats. Its application requires those concerned with international higher education to understand that heightened vulnerability occurs regardless of location and geopolitical arrangements. Further, the findings underscore how minority student groups are always at risk for microaggression. Moving forward, this study demonstrates the need for organizational stakeholder mapping. Ideally, this map should be an authentic analysis of the environment to distinguish salient groups. An examination of changing relationships of educational institutions within expanding neoliberalism is also required.

REFERENCES

Bailey, T. (2020, April 27). Slamming shortages, med students in Cuba plead to come home. *The Gleaner.* http://jamaica-gleaner.com/article/news/20200427/slamming-shortages-med-students-cuba-plead-come-home

Baksh, V. (2020, May 1). Caring for students. *Trinidad Express.* https://trinidadexpress.com/opinion/columnists/caring-for-students/article_d3a8872e-8c05-11ea-84df-534bb77b3b56.html

Barranco, J., & Wisler, D. (1999). Validity and systematicity of newspaper data in event analysis. *European Sociological Review, 15*(3), 301–322.

Beck, A.T. (1976). *Cognitive therapy and the emotional disorders.* Penguin.

Bowen, G. A. (2009). Document analysis as a qualitative research method. *Qualitative Research Journal, 9*(2), 27–40.

Buetow, S. (2010). Thematic analysis and its reconceptualization as 'saliency analysis.' *Journal of Health Services Research & Policy, 15*(2), 123–125.

Capobianco, L., Morris, J. A., & Wells, A. (2018). Worry and rumination: Do they prolong physiological and affective recovery from stress? *Anxiety, Stress, & Coping, 31*(3), 291–303.https://doi.org/10.1080/10615806.2018.1438723

Caribbean Community. (2002). *Revised Treaty of Chaguaramas establishing the Caribbean community including the CARICOM single market & economy*. CARICOM Secretariat.

Castiello-Gutiérrez, S., & Li, X. (2020). We are more than your paycheck. *Journal of International Students, 10*(3), i–iv. https://doi.org/10.32674/jis.v10i3.2676

Chien, Y. Y. G. (2015). International postgraduate students in Britain: Reasons for studying abroad and issues related to adjustment. *International Journal of Technology and Inclusive Education, 2*(1), 737–748.

Clarke, V., & Braun, V. (2017). Thematic analysis. *The Journal of Positive Psychology, 12*(3), 297–298. http://dx.doi.org/10.1080/17439760.2016.1262613

Covid-19: Guyanese doctors, students seeking evacuation from Cuba, say conditions deteriorating. (2020, April 20). *Stabroek News.* https://www.stabroeknews.com/2020/04/20/news/guyana/covid-19-guyanese-doctors-students-seeking-evacuation-from-cuba-say-conditions-deteriorating/

Creswell, J.W. (2014). *Research design: Qualitative, quantitative, and mixed methods approaches* (4th ed.). SAGE.

Cubillo, J. M., Sanchez, J., & Cervino, J. (2006). International students decision-making process. *International Journal of Educational Management, 20*(2), 101–115.

Downs, A. (1972). Up and down with ecology-the "issue-attention cycle". *Public Interest, 28*(Summer), 38–50.

Dunkley-Willis, A. (2020, April 9). UWI seeks help. *Jamaica Observer.* http://www.jamaicaobserver.com/news/uwi-seeks-principal-outlines-measures-being-taken-amid-covid-19_191571?profile=1470

Earl, J., Martin, A., McCarthy, J. D., & Soule, S. A. (2004). The use of newspaper data in the study of collective action. *Annual Review of Sociology, 30*, 65–80. https://doi.org/10.1146/annurev.soc.30.012703.110603

Echols, M. A. (1996). Regional economic integration and higher education: An idea for a university. *Law & Policy in International Business, 27*(4), 903–926.

Edwards-Joseph, A., & Baker, S. (2014). Factors Caribbean overseas students perceive influence their academic self-efficacy. *Journal of International Students, 4(*1), 48–59.

Farias, L., Rudman, D. L., Magalhães, L., & Gastaldo, D. (2017). Reclaiming the potential of transformative scholarship to enable social justice. *International Journal of Qualitative Methods, 16*(1). https://doi.org/10.1177/1609406917714161

Forbes-Mewett, H. (2020). Vulnerability and resilience in a mobile world. *Journal of International Students, 10*(3), ix–xi. https://doi.org/10.32674/jis.v10i3.2002

Fraser, N. (2020, May 24). TT students at UWI Mona 'stressed and confused' as they cannot access grants. *Newsday.* https://newsday.co.tt/2020/05/24/tt-students-at-uwi-mona-stressed-and-confused-as-they-cannot-access-grants/

Füssel, H. (2006). Vulnerability: A generally applicable conceptual framework for climate change research. *Global Environmental Change, 17*(2007), 155–167.

Gilbert, P. (2016). *Human nature and suffering.* Routledge.

Gioannetti, A. (2020, July 3). TT students in Grenada: We need to come home too. *Newsday.* https://newsday.co.tt/2020/07/03/tt-students-in-grenada-we-need-to-come-home-too/

Guadagno, L., Fuhrer, M., & Twigg, J. (2017). Introduction: A case for migrant-inclusive disaster risk reduction. In L. Guadagno, M. Fuhrer, & J. Twigg (Eds.), *Migrants in disaster risk reduction: Practices for inclusion* (pp. 9–12). IOM and France, Council of Europe.

Hinds, D. (January 01, 2006). Domestic non-cooperation and regional integration: Problems of Caribbean regionalism. *Social and Economic Studies, 3*, 32–48.

Hunte, C. (2020, June 27). T&T students beg to come home. *Trinidad Express.* https://trinidadexpress.com/news/local/t-t-students-beg-to-come-home/article_37214b3e-b815-11ea-88cd-7fc838767649.html

Izumi, T., Sukhwani, V., Surjan, A., & Shaw, R. (2020). Managing and responding to pandemics in higher educational institutions: Initial learning from COVID-19. *International Journal of Disaster Resilience in the Built Environment, 12*(1). https://doi.org/10.1108/IJDRBE-06-2020-0054

Kapucu, N., & Khosa, S. (2013). Disaster resiliency and culture of preparedness for university and college campuses. *Administration & Society, 45*(1), 3–37. https://doi.org/10.1177/0095399712471626

Lam, J. M., Tong, D. Y. K., & Ariffin, A. A. M. (2017). Exploring perceived risk and risk reduction strategies in the pursuit of higher education abroad: A case of international students in Malaysia. *Journal of Studies in International Education, 21*(2), 83–104.

Littlefield, R. S., & Quenette, A. M. (2007). Crisis leadership and Hurricane Katrina: The portrayal of authority by the media in natural disasters.

Journal of Applied Communication Research, 35(1), 26–47. https://doi.org/10.1080/00909880601065664

Marginson, S. (2012). Including the other: Regulation of the human rights of mobile students in a nation-bound world. *Higher Education, 63*, 497–512. https://doi.org/10.1007/s10734-011-9454-7

Mouzon, D. M., & McLean, J. S. (2017). Internalized racism and mental health among African-Americans, US-born Caribbean Blacks, and foreign-born Caribbean Blacks. *Ethnicity & Health, 22*(1), 36–48. http://dx.doi.org/10.1080/13447858.2016.1196652

Partridge, H. (2007). *Establishing the human perspective of the information society* [Doctoral dissertation]. Queensland University of Technology.

Pennycook, G., McPhetres, J., Zhang, Y., Lu, J. G., & Rand, D. G. (2020). Fighting COVID-19 misinformation on social media: Experimental evidence for a scalable accuracy-nudge intervention. *Psychological Science, 31*(7), 770–780. https://doi.org/10.1177/0956797620939054

Perchinig, B. (2016). *Migrants in countries in crisis initiative: Supporting an evidence-based approach for effective and cooperative state action* (Research Brief). International Centre for Migration Policy Development.

Peroni, L., & Timmer, A. (2013). Vulnerable groups: The promise of an emerging concept in European human rights convention law. *International Journal of Constitutional Law, 11*(4), 1056–1085.

Pezzulo, G. (2014). Why do you fear the bogeyman? An embodied predictive coding model of perceptual inference. *Cognitive, Affective, & Behavioral Neuroscience, 14*(3), 902–911.

Rahming, S. (2019). Social support and stress-related acculturative experiences of an English-speaking Afro-Caribbean female student in U.S. higher education. *Journal of International Students, 9*(4), 1055–1073.

Randall, F. (2020, July 17). COVID-19 leads to freeze of tuition and some hall fees at UWI Mona. *Jamaica Observer.* http://www.jamaicaobserver.com/

Riskind, J. H., & Rector, N. A. (2018). *Looming vulnerability: Theory, research and practice in anxiety.* Springer.

Rolle, R. (2020, March 23). Plane sent to Jamaica to bring back 61 students. *The Tribune.* http://www.tribune242.com/news/2020/mar/23/plane-sent-jamaica-bring-back-61-students/

Saldaña, J. (2015). *The coding manual for qualitative researchers.* SAGE.

Salmon, D. (2020, May 17). UWI Caribbean students feel trapped, abandoned in Ja. *The Sunday Gleaner.* http://jamaica-gleaner.com/article/news/20200517/uwi-caribbean-students-feel-trapped-abandoned-ja

Serafini, G., Parmigiani, B., Amerio, A., Aguglia, A., Sher, L., & Amore, M. (2020). The psychological impact of COVID-19 on the mental health in the general population. *Qjm: An International Journal of Medicine, 11*(8), 531–537.

Sherry, M., Thomas, P., & Chui, W. (2009). International students: A vulnerable student population. *High Education, 60,* 33–46. https://doi.org/10.1007/s10734-009-9284-z

Smith, K. (2020, March 13). Bajan students in Jamaica short on supplies as country records first COVID-19 cases. *Barbados Today.* https://barbadostoday.bb/2020/03/13/bajan-students-in-jamaica-short-on-supplies-as-country-records-first-covid-19-cases/

Strenger, C. (2012). Existential foundations of looming vulnerability: Thoughts about John Riskind's work with anxiety. *Journal of Psychotherapy Integration, 22*(2), 163–165.

Sullivan, C., & Kashubeck-West, S. (2015). The interplay of international students' acculturative stress, social support, and acculturation modes. *Journal of International Students, 5*(1), 1–11.

Sunstein, C. R. (2003). Terrorism and probability neglect. *Journal of Risk and Uncertainty, 26*(2–3), 121–136.

Tanacković, S. F., Krtalić, M., & Lacović, D. (2014). *Newspapers as a research source: Information needs and information seeking of humanities scholars.* IFLA Lyons.

Thorup-Binger, C., & Charania, N. A. (2019). Vulnerability and capacities of international students in the face of disasters in Auckland, New Zealand: A qualitative descriptive study. *International Journal of Disaster Risk Reduction, 39,* Article 101136. https://doi.org/10.1016/j.ijdrr.2019.101136

Tierney, K., Bevc, C., & Kuligowski, E. (2006). Metaphors matter: Disaster myths, media frames, and their consequences in Hurricane Katrina. *The ANNALS of the American Academy of Political and Social Science, 604*(1). https://doi.org/10.1177/0002716205285589

Tran, L. T. (2020). Teaching and engaging international students. *Journal of International Students, 10*(3), xii–xvii. https://doi.org/10.32674/jis.v10i3.2005

UWI students return after Ivan passes Jamaica. (2004, September 17). *Searchlight.* http://testwp09.newsmemory.com/searchlight/news/news/2004/09/17/uwi-students-return-after-ivan-passes-jamaica/

Walters, J. L. (2018). International education is political! Exploring the politics of international student mobilities. *Journal of International Students, 3*(3), 1459–1478. http://jistudents.org/doi:10.5281/zenodo.1254611

Webb, Y. (2020, May 13). Grateful Cave Hill students: 'We're being treated as top priority.' *Newsday.* https://newsday.co.tt/2020/05/13/grateful-cave-hill-students-were-being-treated-as-top-priority/

Weger, M., & Sandi, C. (2018). High anxiety trait: A vulnerable phenotype for stress-induced depression. *Neuroscience & Biobehavioral Reviews, 87,* 27–37.

Wilson-Harris, N. (2020, May 28). Boycott threat on 138 Student living over storage fees. *The Gleaner.* http://jamaica-gleaner.com/article/lead-stories/20200528/boycott-threat-138-student-living-over-storage-fees

Wisner, B. (2016). Vulnerability as concept, model, metric, and tool. *Oxford Research Encyclopedia of Natural Hazard Science.* https://doi.org/10.1093/acrefore/9780199389407.013.25

Yeo, G. C., Hong, R. Y., & Riskind, J. H. (2020). Looming cognitive style and its associations with anxiety and depression: A meta-analysis. *Cognitive Therapy and Research, 44*(3), 445–467.

Zlomke, K. R., & Jeter, K. M. (2014). Stress and worry: Examining intolerance of uncertainty's moderating effect. *Anxiety, Stress & Coping, 27*(2), 202–215. https://doi.org/10.1080/10615806.2013.835400

Author Bio

CHERRY-ANN SMART, PhD, is an independent researcher resident in Jamaica, West Indies. Her research interests focus on the international experience of Caribbean students, border issues as they affect human migration, social identity, inclusivity, and diversity in the field of information and the wider society. Email: cherian_29@yahoo.com https://orcid.org/0000-0002-1322-8835

© *Journal of International Students*
Volume 12, Issue 4 (2022), pp. 933-954
ISSN: 2162-3104 (Print), 2166-3750 (Online)
https://doi.org/10.32674/jis.v12i4.3877
ojed.org/jis

OJED
OPEN JOURNALS IN EDUCATION

International Students' Suggestions for What Universities Can Do to Better Support Their Mental Wellbeing

Samantha Marangell
Chi Baik
The University of Melbourne, Australia

ABSTRACT

This article aims to expand understanding of how to support international students' mental wellbeing in Australian higher education. It presents findings from a study that explored international students' own suggestions for how universities could improve their wellbeing. Qualitative responses were analyzed from 601 international students at one large, metropolitan university in Australia. Findings emphasize the relationship between course experience and student wellbeing and suggest that universities could improve international students' wellbeing by focusing on improving their learning experiences and fostering a sense of belonging.

Keywords: Australia, higher education, international students, mental health, support, wellbeing

The COVID-19 pandemic and subsequent shift to remote teaching and learning practices across higher education sectors globally has highlighted the importance of supporting international students' mental wellbeing. In Australia, for example, there has been heightened attention on challenges of isolation, separation from support networks, and ineligibility for federal aid during the height of the crisis. Although these circumstances may seem to increase the risk of psychological distress among international students, the importance of understanding and addressing their mental health has been a concern in Australia for over a decade, with several prepandemic studies indicating that international students are at high risk of experiencing mental health difficulties (Orygen, 2017; Shadowen et al., 2019; Veness, 2016).

Despite recognition of international students as a high-risk group (Russell et al., 2010; Skromanis et al., 2018), only a few of the growing number of empirical studies on university students' mental wellbeing have focused on international students specifically (e.g., Shadowen et al., 2019). Of those, the tendency has been to explore the efficacy of international students' actions and behaviors, such as their attitudes toward and inclinations to seek mental health support (e.g., Clough et al., 2019; Ling & Tran, 2015). Alternatively, literature has focused on the problems associated with international students' mental health and only tangentially acknowledged suggestions for improvement.

This article presents an alternative perspective and reports the findings from a prepandemic study that identified factors in the university environment that, from the students' perspective, could better support their wellbeing. The study was part of a larger research project that aimed to address the question, "What can universities do to better support international students' mental health and wellbeing?"

This question is critical for universities given the increasing proportion of students reporting extremely high levels of psychological distress (e.g., Larcombe et al., 2016; Stallman 2010). It is important not just because of universities' obligations to ensure the safety and wellbeing of all students, but also from an educational perspective. It is well established in published research that mental health can have a powerful impact on every aspect of a student's physical, cognitive, emotional, and interpersonal functioning (Kitzrow, 2003). When psychological distress is prolonged, it can severely impact a student's ability to learn and can lead to disengagement with studies, lower self-efficacy, decreased motivation, and withdrawing from studies (Lipson & Eisenberg, 2018; Thorley, 2017). In a recent study of the first-year experience, wellbeing was the most common reason that both international and domestic students gave for seriously considering deferring or withdrawing (Baik et al., 2015).

In this article, we used a socioecological perspective to explore ways that international students can be better supported in the higher education environment rather than focusing on international students' help-seeking or self-management. We believe it elevates the voices of international students by focusing on their suggestions for what universities can do to better support student wellbeing.

LITERATURE REVIEW

International students comprised almost one third of the higher education student population in Australia in 2020, representing an increase from around 108,000 students in 2000 to over half a million in 2020 (Department of Education, Skills and Employment, 2020). There has likewise been an expansion in literature that explores the unique challenges experienced by international students. Notable among these is Marginson et al.'s seminal 2010 study of international students' lived experiences in Australian universities, which identified challenges related to cultural adjustment, English language skills, housing, loneliness, and racism, among other issues. Subsequent studies have similarly identified distinct difficulties that can put international students' safety and wellbeing at risk, such as their financial circumstances (Arkoudis et al., 2018), employment (Blackmore et al., 2014), and lack of secure accommodation (Ryan et al., 2016).

Challenges Influencing International Students' Wellbeing

Among the challenges that international students face, their difficulties with English language skills have received particular attention in the literature, as these skills have been shown to influence both international students' academic performance and their social experiences (Arkoudis & Baik, 2014; Mori, 2000). Even highly proficient speakers may be unfamiliar with local idioms, slang, or nuance (Akanwa, 2015). This can both inhibit smooth academic adjustment and contribute to a lack of deep interaction with local students (Arkoudis & Baik, 2014), which can lead to feeling as if one does not belong at the university. This is an important issue as establishing positive relationships with peers and having a strong sense of belonging can help to promote positive mental wellbeing, and, conversely, social isolation can undermine wellbeing and exacerbate mental health difficulties (Baik et al., 2017). The institutional context can often heighten this feeling of loneliness, as well (Sawir et al., 2008).

Sümer et al.'s (2008) study on the predictors of depression and anxiety elaborates on the possible influence of poor English language proficiency on students' mental wellbeing. Their study involving 440 international students in the United States found that lower levels of self-assessed English proficiency are associated with higher levels of reported depression and anxiety. This finding has important implications for countries like Australia where the largest percentage of international students come from East and Central Asian regions where English is an additional language.

In addition to identifying the influence that language proficiency has on international students' wellbeing, international students' displacement and isolation from support networks can put their mental health at risk (Orygen, 2017; Veness, 2016). For example, Cemalcilar and Falbo's (2008) longitudinal study of 90 international students in the United States demonstrated that relocating to another country negatively affected the mental health of even those students who had come from relatively similar cultures to the United States.

On top of this, international students are also vulnerable to a range of stressors in the community, including racism, prejudice, and workplace exploitation (Brown & Jones, 2013). Brown and Jones (2013) found that one third of the international postgraduate students in their study in the United Kingdom had experienced some form of racism, often in the form of verbal abuse. These experiences of racism, the researchers found, had a "strong and lasting impact on well-being" (p. 1013) and frequently led to participants' reluctance to return later to the United Kingdom as tourists. In the United States, Lee and Rice (2007) found that international students encountered incidents of verbal abuse and racist remarks both on campus and in the surrounding community. International students of color in Australia were also found to be more vulnerable to exclusion and attack than their white counterparts (Marginson et al., 2010).

More recently, Shadowen et al. (2019) explored a range of academic and social factors associated with international students' mental health. They found that perceived discrimination, poor English-language skills, and increased acculturative stress were each significantly correlated with international students' levels of depressive symptoms. Studies that have compared international and domestic students' experiences have seemed to indicate that these correlates are particularly notable for international students. For example, the international students ($n = 383$) in Skromanis et al.'s (2018) study in Australia reported lower global life satisfaction and poorer perceived social support than the domestic students ($n = 1,013$).

Help-Seeking Behavior

One common issue that has drawn some attention in the literature on students' mental health is the help-seeking behavior of international students. Research, such as that by McLachlan and Justice (2009) in the United States, has suggested that international students are particularly unlikely to seek assistance for their mental health and that they often "suffer quietly" instead (p. 30). The researchers investigated the processes that international students used to "survive and thrive" (p. 28) during their time in the United States and found that the tendency to not seek assistance was prevalent among international students from many backgrounds. There are numerous potential reasons for this, including lack of awareness of services, difficulty in accessing services, language or cultural barriers, or embarrassment. For example, in Russell et al.'s (2010) study, 38% of students reported feeling a need to seek help but had decided not to do so mainly because they believed their problem was not important enough or because they did not know about available services. Similarly, Skromanis et al. (2018) reported that international students in their Australian study were less likely than domestic students to seek help for mental health and related problems. Compared with more than half of domestic students who had sought help, less than one in five international students reported that they had sought help. These findings pose the question of how international students might be better supported if many are averse to seeking help from existing services.

The Role of Universities in Supporting International Students' Mental Wellbeing

Several recent studies (e.g., Bore et al., 2016; Larcombe et al., 2016) have supported the idea that the university, and educators specifically, can play a valuable role in reducing students' levels of psychological distress. For example, Bore and colleagues (2016) recommended introducing a full university subject on resilience into the curriculum. Larcombe et al. (2016) suggested that helping students develop effective study skills would also be warranted. At the classroom level, academic teachers' approachability, communication skills, and quality of individual feedback were aspects that university students in Baik et al.'s (2019) recent study indicated would improve their psychological wellbeing. However, these studies tend to focus on students generally, rather than on the specific needs of international students.

With the exception of a few studies (e.g., Rosenthal et al., 2006; Skromanis et al., 2018), there is very little research in the Australian context that investigates international students' psychological distress and wellbeing, and fewer still that have considered students' perspectives on what universities could do to better support their mental wellbeing. This is critical as students hold understanding of their learning experiences and insights that researchers do not have (Flynn 2015). Without knowing what international students' themselves believe about how their wellbeing could be improved, it is difficult to fully understand the realities of their experiences. Students' perspectives can offer a valuable complement to the ideas and perspectives of teachers and staff (Keddie, 2015), offer warnings on what needs to be improved (Busher, 2012), or provide a new way of approaching education policy development (Cook-Sather, 2002).

Consciously encouraging students' voices can itself help improve the student experience. For example, by encouraging student feedback on their learning environment, students gain more ownership over their learning and will therefore be more engaged with it (Riley & Rustique-Forrester, 2002). The encouragement of students' voices is thus believed to reduce dropout rates (Levin, 2000, as cited in Bland & Atweh, 2007). The validation of students' voices also offers benefits to the educational environment, including by establishing an "open" school culture (Quinn et al., 2009), a more inclusive school environment (Demetriou & Wilson, 2010, as cited in Busher, 2012), and environments that foster respect, empowerment, and citizenship (Busher, 2012), which can have a positive effect on students' mental health and wellbeing. In addition, as Quinn et al. (2009) acknowledged, student narratives can reduce stigma around mental health issues. This article aims to actively incorporate students' voices and it expands existing understanding of international student wellbeing by presenting international students' own suggestions for how their wellbeing could be improved.

METHOD

This study was conducted in a large metropolitan Australian university where international students account for 38% of total enrolments. It was part of a Student Wellbeing and Course Experience Survey that was conducted at the university in late 2017 and reported by Larcombe et al. (2021). The project received approval from the university's Human Research Ethics Committee and each participant self-identified as either an international or domestic student.

Research Approach

This exploration of students' suggestions was informed by a socioecological approach utilizing a version of Bronfenbrenner's (1979, 2005) ecological model, which describes the human development process in terms of systematic interactions between people and their environment. In particular, we drew on two levels of systems: the microsystem and macrosystem. In the higher education context, the microsystem can be associated with the course activities, social roles, and interpersonal relationships students have with staff and peers in their courses. In the most recent understanding of Bronfenbrenner's ecological systems theory, the microsystem is the most influential to development (Rosa & Tudge, 2013). The macrosystem level in the higher education context can be considered the broader structural and cultural environments in which the microsystem operates. This might include institutional policies or communications and services.

Our study considered the various ecological systems of the learning environment that influence students' mental wellbeing. This approach recognizes the importance of social environments and systems on students' mental health and wellbeing. It also emphasizes the importance of students' subjective experiences, an emphasis that Wosnitza and Beltman (2012) said may be overemphasized in such approaches but that aligns with the need, identified above, to incorporate students' voices into the conversation about their wellbeing.

In addition, this study utilized a qualitative research approach that aligned with the socioecological perspective. Although the larger study incorporated a mixed methods approach, a qualitative approach was best suited to exploring students' subjective experience in the substudy (Cohen et al., 2011). It also allowed for students' own voices to be recognized (Cohen et al., 2011).

Data Collection

As part of the larger study, an electronic survey was designed to explore students' levels of psychological distress and positive wellbeing and to identify course-related factors that were associated with students' mental wellbeing. None of the questions were compulsory and participants could cease participation at any time. While the questions themselves were not expected to cause distress for students, the survey included clearly visible contact details to the university's psychological and counseling service, as well as links to websites that offer support and assistance for psychological wellbeing, such as those of Beyond Blue, Lifeline, and Orygen.

The survey was predominantly quantitative; however, it also included an open-ended question that collected qualitative data on students' own ideas about what the university could do to improve their wellbeing. This article derives from our analysis of the responses to this open-ended question.

Participants

The research team contacted the course coordinators of all schools and faculties at the university who then decided whether their students would participate in the study. Coordinators from 10 programs assented and shared the electronic survey with the students in their respective programs. A total of 1,233 international students responded to the survey, which represents a 27% response rate. Of these, 601 international students responded to the open-ended question about how their wellbeing could be improved (see Table 1). The largest number of students were enrolled in undergraduate programs in science (25.8%) and commerce (23.5%), each comprising approximately one quarter of the sample. Postgraduates in engineering (18.5%) comprised the next most frequent cohort.

Table 1. Disciplinary Cohorts as Proportion of Sample ($n = 601$)

Course	n	%
Undergraduate	384	63.9&
Science	155	25.8%
Commerce	144	23.5%
Arts	55	9.2%
Biomedicine	27	4.5%
Fine arts	3	0.5%
Music	3	0.5%
Postgraduate	200	33.3%
Engineering	111	18.5%
Veterinary medicine	70	11.6%
Teaching	12	2.0%
Education	7	1.2%
Other course	17	2.8%

Data Analysis

Students' qualitative responses were coded, analyzed, and classified into seven categories pertaining to the student experience. Given the exploratory nature of this study and the aim to incorporate diverse student voices, all responses to this question were included in the study and analyzed.

In alignment with a socioecological framework (Bronfenbrenner, 1979, 2005), students' responses were coded based on the domains of students' experiences where each suggestion was based (e.g., teaching and learning, student services, etc.). The guiding question in the coding process was the area of the university where a suggestion would be enacted. In addition, inductive coding was used for the specific suggestions in order to let students' responses drive the analysis (Cohen et al., 2011).

To ensure consistency in the coding, responses were independently recoded by a second researcher. Results between coders were compared and revised until there was 90% agreement in coding classifications between the coders. Agreement considered both the specific nature of the suggestion and the environmental dimension under which it was categorized. Through an iterative process of comparison and classification (Cohen et al., 2011), the codes were finalized. Frequencies were calculated both for codes and categories.

The identified categories are represented in Table 2. The frequencies presented in the table represent the percentage of the 601 respondents who mentioned a suggestion relating to that category. It was possible that an individual respondent made multiple suggestions that each related to a different category, and so the percentages given for the categories are not cumulative. Furthermore, if a participant made multiple suggestions related to the same category, they were only counted once under the frequency for that category. A total of 750 discrete recommendations were identified. Categories under which at least 15% of respondents made comments are each discussed in the Results section next, followed by the implications of these findings as analyzed through a socioecological lens.

RESULTS

This section presents findings from the analyses of international students' suggestions for improving their wellbeing. For context, over one quarter of participants (29.8%) recorded a "severe" or "extremely severe" score on one or more of the subscales on the Depression, Anxiety and Stress Scale (DASS-21; Lovibond & Lovibond, 1995). Although the percentage of international students reporting severe or extremely severe symptoms of psychological distress was similar to the percentage reported by the domestic students in the same study and to those found in other studies of university student populations (e.g., Larcombe et al., 2021; Naylor, 2020), it is significantly higher than the percentage of those reporting a severe or extremely severe score (5%–7%) in normative community samples (see Lovibond & Lovibond, 1995). With so many international students reporting high levels of psychological distress, it is especially important to study their suggestions for how their wellbeing could be improved.

Teaching and Learning

The largest proportion of students (34.3%) mentioned that changes relating to teaching and learning would improve their wellbeing. They did not include comments related to learning spaces or general references to staff. Students' recommendations about aspects relating to teaching practice tended to focus on the quality of feedback, clarity of explanations, and perceived quality of lecture delivery. For example,

Table 2. Coding Categories for Student Recommendations

Category	Description	Frequency ($n = 601$)
Teaching & learning	Recommendations related to teachers and teaching practice; teacher attributes and characteristics; course design and curriculum; assessment; workload; student advice; and the academic calendar.	34.3%
Academic services	Recommendations related to developing stronger academic or language skills; improving or increasing existing student services; and awareness of existing services.	16.6%
Mental health support & skills	Recommendations related to supporting mental health; reduction of stigma associated with mental health; improving existing mental health services; and increasing students' skills in dealing with mental health issues.	16.0%
University community & relationships	Recommendations related to feeling part of the university community; making friends; building closer relationships with teachers, students, or staff; and bonding or fitting in.	15.6%
Finances	Recommendations related to students' financial circumstances; reducing the costs associated with university study; and requests for financial support.	6.3%
Orientation & organized activities	Recommendations related to helping new students transition to the university; increasing or improving planned campus activities; helping new students transition to the new culture; and increasing opportunities for students to socialize and relax.	6.2%
Employability & careers	Recommendations related to future career prospects; career services; development of practical skills; and existing employment opportunities.	5.3%

> Explain the knowledge during the lectures and not provide just one or two formulas without saying what we need to know in advance for that (like in math). (arts student)

> Tutors should engage more with the students instead of just blindly teaching or reading of the slides or notes that they have. (commerce student)

In addition to comments about teaching practice, there were also comments related to teachers' attitudes toward and approach to the students. For example, one participant wrote that it would be helpful if "teachers tried to form more personal relationships with students, even those who are shy/reserved" (science student). There were similar comments about the need for teachers to "genuinely care for students" (commerce student), and, specifically, to know their students' names. The following quote demonstrates the comments made about this sentiment:

> I feel my general sense of wellbeing would be improved if lecturers made more of an effort to get to know and engage with students. It's hard to feel valued and motivated when there is no interaction. (science student)

The last type of teacher-related recommendations focused on the role that teachers could play in facilitating interaction in the classroom. Such recommendations emphasized the importance of fostering interaction and connection among students in the learning environment, such as in the following quote:

> As there are only 20 students in class, I feel that there could be more group work and arrange us in different groups where we can have a chance to work with every classmate. This could help to improve our relationship with each classmate as we do not have much time to get to know each other during lectures. (fine arts student)

Under this category, many participants mentioned that there were not many opportunities for building connection through their learning experiences. Specifically, participants suggested "more class bonding in tutorials" (arts student) and more opportunities to establish deeper relationships with peers.

Students' comments about ways that teachers could improve students' wellbeing point to the strong role that the teacher has in students' learning experience, highlighting that the individual teacher "can make or break a subject" (science student). These responses support the suggestion by Baik et al. (2019) that implementation of well-established best practices in teaching may help support student wellbeing within the learning environment.

Other suggestions about improvements related to teaching and learning referred to aspects of the curriculum and degree structure that were often outside individual teachers' control. They pertained primarily to matters of workload and elements of the course structure that students found stressful or unfair. For example, students commented on a lack of flexibility in attendance requirements, overlapping assessment schedules between subjects, and frustration with the academic calendar. A comment that was echoed by multiple respondents was that the workload was concentrated within too short and intense a period. Participants felt that it would be helpful if the workload were more balanced, both during the semester and across the length of the program; for example,

> I feel that students' general sense of wellbeing would be improved if assignments' deadlines across different subjects are not so close together, so as to allow us enough time to finish them properly. (commerce student)

It is notable that one third of participants felt that some change to the teaching and learning dimension would improve their wellbeing, and this prevalence further supports the role that the learning experience plays in international students' mental health and wellbeing.

Academic Services

The next most frequent category dealt with recommendations about academic services and skills-based support. Just over 16% of participants made comments that were included in this category, which pertained primarily to recommendations to improve such services and requests for improving specific skills such as time management and language skills. Some of the comments were requests for greater access to existing academic services. Other comments pertained specifically to the unique needs of international students, including services to help develop English-language skills or assistance with understanding visa requirements and implications; for example,

> Provide more activities to help students develop English language skills for international students is a good way. (commerce student)

> More guidance specific to this course in the process of repeating a year, especially for international students. Dealing with many steps in that process such as visas, re-enrolling, etc. (veterinary medicine student)

Although it is not surprising that students mentioned academic support services when answering a question about how the university could better support their wellbeing, it is significant that these students mentioned that support with their academic skills would improve their wellbeing. These responses therefore reinforce the importance of students' academic skills, preparedness, and success in supporting their wellbeing. They also emphasize the importance of the microsystem of the learning environment. Along with the comments about learning and teaching, described above, these comments further indicate the considerable role that students believe their learning experiences play in shaping their mental wellbeing.

Mental Health Support and Skills

A similar proportion of participants (16%) made recommendations that pertained specifically to mental health services and support. Students' comments addressed both microlevel and macrolevel systems. For example, students focused on the need for improvements in immediate services, for better awareness of existing resources, and on the role of stigma and university culture in mental health support.

A notable set of comments mentioned the need for better access to the existing counseling services, that there were not enough appointment slots available, and that the number of offered counseling sessions was too small to be helpful. Other students felt that the services sufficed but that awareness could be improved or that there was a need for more understanding of how to respond or manage mental health matters, such as in the following comment:

> Outreach to students with mental health issues can be improved...Students going through depression often cannot identify what they are experiencing let alone seek the help they require...It is important not only to make these resources (counseling services, workshops) more readily available, but to make their presence known to students through more campus-wide awareness program. (science student)

Some students pointed out the need for services to address the specific needs of international students; for example:

> I think my general sense of wellbeing would be improved if there are more workshops/consultations/psychology services that focus on international students' wellbeing, provide us with more knowledge/skills/information about how to integrate into the local society and how to confront the dilemmas that international students commonly have. (biomedicine student)

Despite the recent campaigns across universities to raise awareness of mental health difficulties, it seems that stigma remains a concern. Numerous students made suggestion about the importance of reducing the stigma around mental health challenges:

> Reducing stigma about not coping/mental illness. This is obviously hard to do since it seems to be ingrained in our society that being mentally ill equals failure. (commerce student)

> Internal pressures were talked about, things like anxiety and fear of failure and a constant second guessing of the self be discussed openly and in a helpful manner. Not like there's something wrong with you just that it's something some people struggle with and that there are ways to stop it from taking over you. (commerce student)

While the comments above were about societal stigma, others mentioned ways the university specifically could help reduce stigma, for example by offering "more events or activities catered to student wellbeing" (arts student) and "public lectures about stress and anxiety" (commerce student). In general, students requested more information, through explicit communication or the addition of specific lectures, both on aspects of mental wellbeing and on availability of existing resources.

University Community and Relationships

Another commonly mentioned issue (16% of respondents) pertained to students' sense of university community and their connection to it, further highlighting the importance of strong microsystem to support students' wellbeing. Students highlighted the importance of making friends, particularly local Australian friends, and of feeling understood and valued by teachers, classmates, and the university, such as in the following comment:

> International students who come to [X] University face a lot of loneliness. It is a time of great change and many students struggle to find emotional support they need to excel in school. It

> would be great if the university held more bonding camps or activities among students so that they have an opportunity to meet each other outside of class. (commerce student)

This supports research that "establishing friendships with local students is critical for reducing feelings of loneliness and homesickness" (Arthur, 2017, p. 891). Importantly, there was notable overlap between commentary on lack of belonging and experiences in the learning environment:

> I feel sense of belonging if all my classes are made up of people doing the same course with me, whom I will see every semester and get to know them better instead of just seeing them for one semester and the next semester I have to start over again and make new friends. (science student)

Among similar comments were recommendations for how changes to the learning environment could improve students' sense of connection to the university community and, in turn, their wellbeing, a link which the following science student describes poignantly:

> A simple fix? Tutorials that aren't 300 student lectures guided by quick poll questions. Giving students an opportunity to connect in the context of their academic studies aids learning and engenders a greater sense of community and belonging. It's not difficult to see how a stronger sense of community may contribute to better student wellbeing. (science student)

The responses under this category provide important insight into the ways that students believe their sense of connection to the university and relationships with peers is related to their wellbeing. Importantly, they also support the significant role that the learning environment plays in developing that sense of connection and, ultimately, influencing their wellbeing.

Other Suggestions

Other comments, made by a smaller proportion of students, included recommendations related to students' finances, orientation and organized activities, and employability and career matters. Of note, only a small proportion of students made suggestions pertaining to finances and employment prospects (6% and 5%, respectively). This challenges previous research in Australia that found that half of international university students feel distressed over their financial circumstances (Arkoudis et al., 2018) and that financial pressures were associated with students' increased risk of mental health difficulties (Orygen, 2017). It was possible that students did not view these aspects as being within the role of universities to manage and, therefore, offered suggestions instead for the areas where they felt change was possible. The predominance of recommendations related specifically to learning and course experience support previous findings that students' experiences in the teaching and learning environment can influence their wellbeing. Additionally, they emphasize the importance of the microlevel systems within the university context.

DISCUSSION

Our study confirms that the main area where universities could enhance the wellbeing of international students is through improving their course experiences. This aligns with Bronfenbrenner's socioecological theory and the fundamental role that the environment plays, not only in terms of the context itself but a person's interaction with the environment, in this case the learning and teaching environments in students' courses. Like other studies (e.g., Larcombe et al., 2021; Naylor, 2020) that have shown a strong connection between course experience and wellbeing, our study shows that a significant portion of international students believe that aspects of their immediate environment could be improved to better support their wellbeing. Our study further supports and expands that idea by emphasizing the role of social relationships within that microsystem, including relationships with teaching staff.

From the student perspective, university teachers have the potential to enhance and support student mental wellbeing, and, conversely, to have a negative effect on wellbeing. In our study, the most frequently mentioned suggestions for improving their wellbeing were related to academic teachers and the kinds of teaching and learning environments they created. Their approachability and demonstrated interest in students are perceived to be important in improving student wellbeing. Prior research has also identified approaches to enhancing student wellbeing through intentional curriculum design and wellbeing-supportive teaching practices (e.g., Baik et al., 2017). Our study supported these findings and further demonstrated that "good" teaching practices can reduce students' stress and support their overall sense of wellbeing, as also suggested by Baik et al. (2019).

In addition, findings from this study reinforce the relationship between students' sense of belonging and their wellbeing. International students' sense of belonging has been raised as a critical issue by several researchers (e.g., Arkoudis et al., 2019; Gomes & Tran, 2017), and, as discussed above, international students' vulnerability during the recent pandemic has highlighted the importance of investigating their senses of belonging, isolation, and wellbeing. Specifically, findings from the study presented in this article further emphasize the benefit of fostering a sense of belonging within the learning environment. Academic educators have a key role to play in fostering students' sense of belonging to their class and learning community. Research suggests that students' sense of belonging is strengthened when teachers show interest in students and create welcoming and empathic learning environments (Wilson et al., 2018).

Implications for Universities

The findings from our study offer important insight for university educators and administrators into how international students' mental wellbeing can be better supported. In particular, understanding the perspectives of international students can have important implications for design and provision of university programs (Shadowden et al., 2019). This study highlights the significance of the teaching and learning contexts and students' interactions with teachers and peers within the learning environment. In the mid- and postpandemic context where much teaching and learning continues to take place remotely, it will be even more challenging for universities to foster a sense of community and to help international students feel a sense of belonging to the university. To support and enhance students' subjective wellbeing, ongoing purposeful attention to students' own perspectives and bolstering of students' voices will be particularly important.

Our study also highlights the importance of universities finding ways to enhance and stabilize the microsystems of the learning environment during times of considerable change. Findings from this study suggest that the microlevel systems are important for students' metal wellbeing; however, they are also elements that might be most directly affected by change, such as the opportunities for interaction with teachers and classmates.

Another well-known challenge for institutions is ensuring that those in need of support seek help and access the services. However, contrary to other studies (e.g., Shadowen et al., 2019; Skromanis et al., 2018) that suggest international students are less likely than domestic students to seek assistance for mental-health related issues, the larger study from which this article derived (Larcombe et al., 2021) found that a higher proportion of international students utilized the university's services for mental wellbeing than domestic students. Such findings make exploring students' perspectives, as presented in this article, especially important because they offer insight into how to support student wellbeing beyond providing access to wellbeing services.

CONCLUSION

By seeking international students' own suggestions, this exploratory study elevates students' voices and illuminates elements of the social and institutional dimensions of the university context that could better support their mental wellbeing.

Although these findings contribute to improving our understanding of international student wellbeing, our study was limited primarily by its single-institution design and by the single-question source of data. These two aspects meant that it was not possible to ask students for elaboration or clarification of their suggestions. In addition, this study was conducted in a prepandemic context, and, although there are valuable insights for institutions to consider, it is possible that some of the students' ideas, needs, and suggestions might have changed.

Future research would be needed to add more nuance to these findings. For example, our understanding of international students' mental health and wellbeing would benefit additionally from future research that explored the perspectives of international student subgroups and those in remote or regional universities. Considering differences across disciplines may provide additional insights. It would also be useful to explore students' perspectives and suggestions post the COVID-19 pandemic.

In the context of the large body of research on the unique issues and challenges experienced by international students, the findings in this study suggest that a greater focus on improving learning and course experiences is key to better supporting international student mental wellbeing. Incorporating the international student voice more strongly into the conversation around student wellbeing is an important step in meeting this aim.

Acknowledgments
We would like to thank all the students who participated in the study. We also thank Dr. Wendy Larcombe for her leadership in designing the survey study of which the analysis in this article is a part. The research was funded by a grant from The University of Melbourne.

REFERENCES

Akanwa, E. E. (2015). International students in western developed countries: History, challenges, and prospects. *Journal of International Students, 5*(3), 271–284. https://doi.org/10.32674/jis.v5i3.421

Arkoudis, S., & Baik, C. (2014). Crossing the interaction divide between international and domestic students in higher education. *HERDSA Review of Higher Education, 1*, 47–62.

Arkoudis, S., Dollinger, M., Baik, C., & Patience, A. (2019). International students' experience in Australian higher education: Can we do better? *Higher Education, 77*, 799–813. https://doi.org/10.1007/s10734-018-0302-x

Arkoudis, S., Marangell, S., Baik, C., Patrick, C., Bexley, E., & James, R. (2018). *University student finances 2017*. Universities Australia.

Arthur, N. (2017). Supporting international students through strengthening their social resources. *Studies in Higher Education, 42*(5), 887–894. https://doi.org/10.1080/03075079.2017.1293876

Baik, C., Larcombe, W., & Brooker, A. (2019). How universities can enhance student mental wellbeing: The student perspective. *Higher Education Research & Development, 38*(4), 1–14. https://doi.org/10.1080/07294360.2019.1576596

Baik, C., Larcombe, W., Brooker, A., Wyn, J., Allen, L., Field, R. & James, R. (2017). *Enhancing student mental wellbeing*. Melbourne Centre for the Study of Higher Education. http://melbourne-cshe.unimelb.edu.au/__data/assets/pdf_file/0006/2408604/MCSHE-Student-Wellbeing-Handbook-FINAL.pdf

Baik, C., Naylor, R., & Arkoudis, S. (2015). *The first year experience in Australian universities: Findings from two decades, 1994-2014*. Melbourne Centre for the Study of Higher Education, The University of Melbourne.

Blackmore, J., Gribble, C., Farrell, L., Rahimi, M., Arber, R., & Devlin, M. (2014). *Australian international graduates and the transition to employment*. Deakin University. https://www.voced.edu.au/content/ngv:72900

Bland, D., & Atweh, B. (2007). Students as researchers: Engaging students' voices in PAR. *Educational Action Research, 15*(3), 337–349. https://doi.org/10.1080/09650790701514259

Bore, M., Pittolo, C., Kirby, D., Dluzewska, T., & Marlin, S. (2016). Predictors of psychological distress and well-being in a sample of Australian undergraduate students. *Higher Education Research & Development, 35*(5), 869–880. https://doi.org/10.1080/07294360.2016.1138452

Bronfenbrenner, U. (1979). *The ecology of human development: Experiments by nature and design*. Harvard University Press.

Bronfenbrenner, U. (2005). *Making human beings human: Bioecological perspectives on human development*. SAGE.

Brown, L., & Jones, I. (2013). Encounters with racism and the international student experience. *Studies in Higher Education, 38*(7), 1004–1019. https://doi.org/10.1080/03075079.2011.614940

Busher, H. (2012). Students as expert witnesses of teaching and learning. *Management in Education, 26*(3), 113–119. https://doi.org/10.1177/0892020612445679

Cemalcilar, Z., & Falbo, T. (2008). A longitudinal study of the adaptation of international students in the United States. *Journal of Cross-Cultural Psychology, 39*(6), 799–804. https://doi.org/10.1177%2F0022022108323787

Clough, B. A., Nazareth, S. M., Day, J. J., & Casey, L. M. (2019). A comparison of mental health literacy, attitudes, and help-seeking intentions among domestic and international tertiary students. *British Journal of Guidance & Counselling*, *47*(1), 123–135. https://doi.org/10.1080/03069885.2018.1459473

Cohen, L., Manion, L., & Morrison, K. (2011). *Research methods in education* (7th ed.). Routledge.

Cook-Sather, A. (2002). Authorizing students' perspectives: Toward trust, dialogue, and change in education. *Educational Researcher*, *31*(4), 3–14. https://doi.org/10.3102%2F0013189X031004003

Department of Education, Skills and Employment (2020). *International student data summary: End of year summary of international student data 2019.* https://bit.ly/3PbdSVo

Flynn, P. (2015). Whose voice, who's listening? Student voices in research and practice; embedding a culture of listening in education discourse. In B. Mooney (Ed.) *Education matters yearbook 2015-2016.* Education Matters.

Gomes, C., & Tran, L. T. (2017). International student (dis)connectedness and identities: Why these matter and the way forward. In L. T. Tran & C. Gomes (Eds.), *International student connectedness and identity* (pp. 283–290). Dordrecht: Springer.

Keddie, A. (2015). Student voice and teacher accountability: Possibilities and problematics. *Pedagogy, Culture & Society*, *23*(2), 225–244. https://doi.org/10.1080/14681366.2014.977806

Kitzrow, M. A. (2003). The mental health needs of today's college students: Challenges and recommendations. *NASPA Journal*, *41*(1), 167–181. https://doi.org/10.2202/1949-6605.1310

Larcombe, W., Baik, C., & Finch, S. (2021). Exploring course experiences that predict psychological distress and mental wellbeing in Australian undergraduate and graduate coursework students, *Higher Education Research & Development.* Advance online publication. https://doi.org/10.1080/07294360.2020.1865284

Larcombe, W., Finch, S., Sore, R., Murray, C. M., Kentish, S., Mulder, R. A., Lee-Stecum, P., Baik, C., Tokatlidis, O., & Williams, D. A. (2016). Prevalence and socio-demographic correlates of psychological distress among students at an Australian university. *Studies in Higher Education, 41*(6), 1074–1091. https://doi.org/10.1080/03075079.2014.966072

Lee, J. J., & Rice, C. (2007). Welcome to America? International student perceptions of discrimination. *Higher education*, *53*(3), 381–409. https://doi.org/10.1007/s10734-005-4508-3

Ling, C., & Tran, L. T. (2015). Chinese international students in Australia: An insight into their help and information seeking manners. *International Education Journal: Comparative Perspectives, 14*(1), 42–56.

Lipson, S. K., & Eisenberg, D. (2018). Mental health and academic attitudes and expectations in university populations: Results from the healthy minds study. *Journal of Mental Health, 27*(3), 205–213. https://doi.org/10.1080/09638237.2017.1417567

Lovibond, S. H., & Lovibond, P. F. (1995). *Manual for the Depression Anxiety Stress Scales*. (2nd ed.). Psychology Foundation.

Marginson, S. Nylan, C., Sawir, E. & Forbes-Hewett, H. (2010). *International student security*. Cambridge University Press.

McLachlan, D. A., & Justice, J. (2009). A grounded theory of international student well-being. *Journal of Theory Construction & Testing, 13*(1), 27–32.

Mori, S. C. (2000). Addressing the mental health concerns of international students. *Journal of Counseling & Development, 78*(2), 137–144. https://doi.org/10.1002/j.1556-6676.2000.tb02571.x

Naylor, R. (2020). Key factors influencing psychological distress in university students: the effects of tertiary entrance scores. *Studies in Higher Education*. Advanced online publication. https://doi.org/10.1080/03075079.2020.1776245

Orygen. (2017). *Under the radar. The mental health of Australian university students*. https://www.orygen.org.au/Policy/Policy-Reports/Under-the-radar/Orygen-Under_the_radar_report?ext=.

Quinn, N., Wilson, A., MacIntyre, G., & Tinklin, T. (2009). 'People look at you differently': Students' experience of mental health support within higher education. *British Journal of Guidance & Counselling, 37*(4), 405–418. https://doi.org/10.1080/03069880903161385

Riley, K. A., & Rustique-Forrester, E. (2002). *Working with disaffected students: Why students lose interest in school and what we can do about it*. SAGE.

Rosa, E. M., & Tudge, J. (2013). Urie Bronfenbrenner's theory of human development: Its evolution from ecology to bioecology. *Journal of Family Theory & Review, 5*(4), 243–258. https://doi.org/10.1111/jftr.12022

Rosenthal, D. A., Russell, J., & Thomson, G. (2006). The health and wellbeing of international students at an Australian university. *Higher Education, 55*(1), 51–67. https://doi.org/10.1007/s10734-006-9037-1

Russell, J., Rosenthal, D., & Thomson, G. (2010). The international student experience: Three styles of adaptation. *Higher Education, 60*(2), 235–249. https://doi.org/10.1007/s10734-009-9297-7

Ryan, R., Dowler, B., Bruce, S., Gamage, S., & Morris, A. (2016). *The wellbeing of international students in the city of Sydney*. University of Technology Sydney, Institute for Public Policy and Governance.

Sawir, E., Marginson, S., Deumert, A., Nyland, C., & Ramia, G. (2008). Loneliness and international students: An Australian study. *Journal of Studies in International Education, 12*(2), 148–180. https://doi.org/10.1177%2F1028315307299699

Shadowen, N. L., Williamson, A. A., Guerra, N. G., Ammigan, R., & Drexler, M. L. (2019). Prevalence and correlates of depressive symptoms among international students: Implications for university support offices. *Journal of International Students, 9*(1), 129–148. https://doi.org/10.32674/jis.v9i1.277

Skromanis, S., Cooling, N., Rodgers, B., Purton, T., Fan, F., Bridgman, H., Harris, K., Presser, J., & Mond, J. (2018). Health and well-being of international university students, and comparison with domestic students, in Tasmania,

Australia. *International Journal of Environmental Research and Public Health, 15*(6), 1147–1160. https://doi.org/10.3390/ijerph15061147

Stallman, H. M. (2010). Psychological distress in university students: A comparison with general population data. *Australian Psychologist, 45*(4), 249–257. https://doi.org/10.1080/00050067.2010.482109

Sümer, S., Poyrazli, S., & Grahame, K. (2008). Predictors of depression and anxiety among international students. *Journal of Counseling & Development, 86*(4), 429–437. https://doi.org/10.1002/j.1556-6678.2008.tb00531.x

Thorley, C. (2017). *Not by degrees: Improving student mental health in the UK's universities.* IPPR. www.ippr.org/publications/not-by-degrees

Veness, B. (2016). *The wicked problem of university student mental health.* Monash University Winston Churchill Trust.

Wilson, R., Murray, G. & Clarke, B. (2018). The RMIT belonging strategy: Fostering student engagement in higher education. In D. Wache & D. Houston (Eds.), *Research and development in higher education: (Re)valuing higher education, 41* (pp. 257–266), HERDSA.

Wosnitza, M., & Beltman, S. (2012). Learning and motivation in multiple contexts: The development of a heuristic framework. *European Journal of Psychology of Education, 27*(2), 177–193. https://doi.org/10.1007/s10212-011-0081-6

Author Bios

SAMANTHA MARANGELL, PhD, is a lecturer at the Melbourne Centre for the Study of Higher Education at The University of Melbourne in Australia. Her major research interests comprise the student experience, university internationalization, and wellbeing.
Email: samantha.marangell@unimelb.edu.au

CHI BAIK, DEd, is a professor in higher education at the Melbourne Centre for the Study of Higher Education at The University of Melbourne in Australia. Her broad research interests center on the quality of the student experience and factors affecting the educational experiences and outcomes of students from diverse backgrounds. Email: cbaik@unimelb.edu.au

Article

© *Journal of International Students*
Volume 12, Issue 4 (2022), pp. 955-972
ISSN: 2162-3104 (Print), 2166-3750 (Online)
https://doi.org/10.32674/jis.v12i4.3829
ojed.org/jis

Understanding Post-Graduation Decision of Caribbean International Students to Remain in the United States

Trevis Belle
Susan Barclay
Thomas Bruick
Phillip Bailey
University of Central Arkansas, USA

ABSTRACT

We utilized Schlossberg's transition theory (1984) as the framework for understanding how international students from the Caribbean arrive at the decision to remain within the United States after completing their highest earned degree and joining the diaspora. Using a phenomenological research design with a sample of six international students who remained within the United States after completing their highest earned degree, we examined the underlying considerations participants made during their decision-making process. Results revealed that all six participants relied on economic, political, and social considerations, which contributed to their decision to remain in the United States.

Keywords: brain drain, Caribbean, international students, transition

Brain drain relates mainly to the migration of high professionals, such as engineers, physicians, scientists, IT personnel, and others who tend to have gained a university education. Javed et al. (2019) defined *brain drain* as the global migration of human capital assets from one area of the world to another, specifically the migration of educated individuals from developing countries to developed ones. Johnson (2009) discussed the consequences of brain drain as the unequal distribution of advantages and disadvantages of global migration, where the source country bears most of the losses (e.g., skilled labor, intellect) and, in Johnson's estimation, has yet to be compensated adequately for the net contributions their natives have made to the hosting countries. For the purpose of this article, skilled labor and intellect refers to individuals who are native to the Caribbean regions, moved to the United States to pursue higher education, and remained after completing their highest earned degree.

According to the Migration Policy Institute (2020), in the school year 2017–2018, 11,300 Caribbean students were enrolled in U.S. higher educational institutions, representing 1% of the total 1.1 million international students. Once international students complete their studies within the United States, they are faced with the decision of either staying or returning to their home country. The brain drain phenomenon intensifies once the international student chooses the former, which increases the negative impact on the source country.

In this study, the source country or region refers to the Caribbean and the host country refers to the United States. Much of the academic efficacy and performance information about our population of interest is anecdotal and generalized. Edwards-Joseph and Baker (2014) indicated that students who grew up in the Caribbean bring a strong sense of academic efficacy with them to U.S. universities. With this strong sense of academic efficacy, we were interested to see how their experiences contributed to their desire to remain within the United States. Our purpose was to gain greater understanding as to how international students from the Caribbean arrive at the decision to remain within the United States after attaining their highest degree.

LITERATURE REVIEW

International Students in the United States

International students who are studying in the United States contribute significantly to higher education, not only financially but also culturally, in terms of facilitating the development of intercultural competencies among all students and influencing the institution's internationalization efforts in positive ways (Urban & Palmer, 2014). Fostering meaningful engagement of international students with the rest of the university community, integrating intercultural perspectives into classrooms, and encouraging domestic students to operate in multicultural groups and teams can enhance the student experience and complement institutional recruitment and retention strategies (Urban & Palmer, 2014). In addition to the social and cultural contributions international students make to their institutions, they also help create jobs and add invaluable scientific innovation and technological improvements to the local community (Academic Credentials Evaluation Institute, 2017). With the plethora of contributions international students make to higher education settings, understanding their importance within the field is imperative for student affairs professionals because it will inform the work they do as it relates to serving this student population.

Theoretical Framework

Student affairs professionals can use Schlossberg's transition theory (1984) in the work they perform with international students. According to Schlossberg (1984), transition is viewed as a change in behavior or relations in response to an event or nonevent that affects one's beliefs about oneself or the world.

A major focus of Schlossberg's transition theory is on how students are *moving in, moving through,* and *moving out* of their transition, while also focusing on the individual and how that individual maneuvers their journey with the implementation of the four Ss (situation, self, support, and strategy). Kim (2012) stated that attending college is a critical time of transition in the life of a student. It signals the beginning of one's independence, because many students live away from home for the first time. It marks a transition to the assumption of adult responsibilities and serves as a time of reflection, when students begin to explore where they will fit into the world and what their future career will be.

Support for International Students

Departments, such as International Student Services, are put in place to provide support to the international student population as they move into university, move through university, and move out. The experiences international students have with those who work in such departments can contribute to their remaining within the United States. Likewise, student affairs professionals who work within Housing and Residence Life (HRL) play an important role in the process international students undergo as they arrive at their decision to remain within the United States postgraduation. This is because HRL staff assist the students in becoming acclimated to the institution through programming efforts and by recommending campus resources that aid in their professional and personal development. International students take all factors of their experiences into consideration while assessing their decision to remain after graduation. Ammigan (2019) reinforced the argument that support provided outside the academic setting, such as tutoring, study skills, career advice, counseling services, library resources, and physical space for learning, can be equally important to maintaining academic satisfaction and success on campus. All these interactions also come into play when the international student is determining whether to remain within the United States. Student affairs professionals might not understand the significance, but their actions and engagement with international students have a strong influence on how international students arrive at the decision of staying in the United States or returning to their home country or region.

Factors Influencing International Students' Decision to Remain in the United States

International students tend to consider certain factors in arriving at their decision to remain within the United States after completing their highest degree. Political, economic, and social conditions are cited frequently as factors pushing students to leave their home country (Altbach, 2004; Carr et al., 2005; Han & Appelbaum, 2016; Lee & Kim, 2010; Mazzarol & Soutar, 2002). These conditions can include lack of access to education and jobs, as well as concerns about political repression and academic freedom (Altbach, 2004). In most developing countries, access to higher education is still restricted, compared with high income countries, leading to reinforcement of existing social stratification (Dassin et al., 2014). As it pertains to economic factors, many students study abroad with the goal of staying in their host country to work and build a career, which makes the United States, with its large and diverse economy and high salaries, attractive (Altbach, 2004). Altbach (2004) stated that students seek education abroad because their home country's higher education systems lack space and a "world-class" (p. 21) reputation. This aligns with a perception that overseas education is better than local education (Li & Bray, 2007). Pertaining to political factors, students from some countries study abroad to escape political repression at home or to gain academic freedom (Altbach, 2004). They are looking for a congenial socioeconomic and political environment (Li & Bray, 2007). Finally, research has indicated that with social factors, the adjustment process for students can be a predictor of students' intent to stay in the host country (Baruch et al., 2007). During the adjustment process, students must choose how to balance their home culture with the host culture (Carr et al., 2005). This can be affected by support systems at the university and ties to family members in the host country.

METHOD

This study originated from a midsize public university in the southern

United States. The institution classifies an international student as a nonresident alien entering the United States on an F-1 or J-1 visa. Participants for this study were not enrolled students at the institution; rather, they had been students at various higher education institutions in the United States.

Sample and Procedure

Participants were six international students who had studied and remained in the United States after graduating with their highest earned degree. All participants were from various Caribbean countries. This was critical as we wanted to focus on developing countries within the Caribbean region, which is an underrepresented area in the literature, and also which is an international student population that pursues higher education degrees within the United States. The average age of participants was 28.67 years. Table 1 provides additional participant demographic information.

Table 1

Participant Demographics

Participant	Age	Gender	Country of origin	Highest degree earned
Participant 1	22	Female	St. Kitts & Nevis	Bachelors
Participant 2	34	Female	The Bahamas	Masters
Participant 3	33	Female	Jamaica	Doctorate
Participant 4	26	Male	Trinidad & Tobago	Bachelors
Participant 5	25	Male	St. Kitts & Nevis	Bachelors
Participant 6	32	Male	Trinidad & Tobago	Bachelors

After securing Institutional Review Board approval, we recruited participants from various institutions where Caribbean student organizations and alumni groups are present and were able to get individuals who remained within the United States after attaining their highest earned degree. We used snowball sampling to recruit participants who met the criteria for the study, which was that they were an international student from the Caribbean who remained within the United States after attaining their highest earned degree.

Data Collection

The first author scheduled semistructured interviews with each of the six participants. This semistructured protocol allows for researcher flexibility in the interview process and gives room for the "researcher to respond to the situation at hand" (Merriam, 2009, p. 90). Participants received the questions prior to their scheduled interview so they were aware of the questions the researcher would ask. Due to both the widespread geographical location of participants and COVID-19 restrictions, all interviews took place via the Zoom video conferencing platform. The purpose of these interviews was to gain a better understanding of how participants had arrived at their decision to remain in the United States, rather than returning to their homes, after completing their highest earned degree. Each interview lasted approximately 1 hour, and each was recorded with participant consent. To increase credibility and trustworthiness of the data collection process, the first author engaged in prolonged engagement (e.g., building rapport with participants), persistent observation (e.g., attention to participant emotions), and reflexivity (e.g., awareness of his own values, background, and experience with the topic under study). In addition, the first author engaged in a reflection memo bracketing technique prior to the beginning of our research. Gearing (2004) explained bracketing as a "scientific process in which a researcher suspends or holds in abeyance his or her presuppositions, biases, assumptions, theories, or previous experiences to see and describe the phenomenon" (p. 1430). As an international student who elected to remain in the United States after graduating with his bachelor's degree, the first author recognized the importance of examining his own experiences with, and perspectives on, the topic under investigation. Reflections continued throughout the data analysis process.

Data Analysis

At the conclusion of participant interviews, three of the four authors engaged in transcendental phenomenological data analysis. Transcendental phenomenology analysis focuses on one's ability to delve deeply into consciousness and uncover the underlying structures of a phenomenon (Moustakas, 1994). Merriam and Tisdell (2009) described phenomenology data analysis as the process of "focusing on experience itself and how experiencing something is transformed into consciousness" (pp. 25–26). We selected this approach because we wanted to focus and gain a deeper understanding of the experiences of the individuals as they navigated through their processes. Through the data analysis process, the first author engaged in bracketing, as well, to ensure his biases and assumptions were not a deciding factor in the way the data was coded.

We coded the data manually utilizing the inductive coding process. We broke the qualitative data set into smaller samples. We created codes for those samples and continued the process breaking the data into smaller samples and applying codes until we had coded all the data. After analyzing the data and summarizing the themes that emerged, we engaged in member checking procedures that provided participants the opportunity to validate whether we had interpreted the data accurately.

RESULTS

All themes that emerged from the data aligned with factors aligned with earlier research. Those factors were economic, social, and political. We provide examples of those themes from our research in the following subsections.

Table 2
Themes and Subthemes from the Data Analysis

Main theme	Subthemes
Economic	• Lack of jobs and expectations of receiving low salaries
Political	• Social injustices against different marginalized communities • Lack of accountability and urgency from the government
Social	• Full feeling of freedom and liberation • Support from close friends

Economic Factors

All participants emphasized that the lack of job opportunities and the expectation of receiving low salaries within their home country contributed to their decision to remain within the United States postgraduation as opposed to returning to their home country. One participant offered:

> A change in what I want to do… I wanted to work in social security back home, but while in college I decided I wanted to be a professor instead. That's not really an option back home, outside of the community colleges, there aren't many other opportunities. I know a lot of people have an unfortunate experience where, you know, they go off and they study and then they go back home…. then nobody wants to hire them because they're like, well, you're overqualified, and we can't afford to pay. I'm like, well, no, you just haven't tried yet. (Participant 5)

The lack of job opportunities was evident further in the narrative of additional participants as a main reason for remaining within the United States as opposed to going home. For example, Participant 1, a 22-year-old from St. Kitts and Nevis, shared that the career opportunities back home were not the same as they are in the United States and that people expect graduates to enter a traditional profession, such as a teacher, lawyer, or doctor. Knowing this was the stereotypical mindset of those in her home region, she decided to pursue and explore the abundant opportunities available in the United States because she did not want to limit herself in her home region.

Lower salaries for jobs in their home countries was a prime factor influencing students' decision to remain in the United States postgraduation. In particular, four participants emphasized how receiving more money for their job in the United States actually assists them to live a better life:

> So, I can make more money here. And as a result, I can think about sending my brothers to school, taking care of my family back home, sending extra money back home to, like, people in the community, all of that, like, I don't, I'm not yet at the stage where I can see myself making enough to do all that in Jamaica, if I were working in Jamaica, and I can definitely do that here. Also, there weren't, there aren't very many labs, where people are doing bench science research, and it just seems like I wouldn't be able to get a stable, reasonable income with just a bachelor's degree. So that made me decide to pursue higher education, even higher education and get the PhD with the understanding that with a PhD, I could at least go home or maybe continue to travel and get more research experience under my belt, and that, then, I could take that back home and, perhaps, get a professor position. (Participant 3)

Similarly, others discussed low salary expectations due to the inability of companies in their home regions to compensate them properly for their level of education or their expertise. For example, Participant 2, a 34-year-old from the Bahamas with a master's degree, stated she was receiving triple the amount of salary for her current job in the United States than she would have received in the Bahamas, especially given the fact that the exchange rate is 1:1. She knew she would never be able to receive that amount of pay in the Bahamas no matter how hard she tried. Finally, some participants stated the profession in which they earned their degree was not present in their home country so they would not be able to receive even the expected base pay for their degree area of knowledge.

Political Factors

Three participants spoke about some political factors that influenced their decision to remain within the United States post completion of their highest degree, as opposed to returning home. For example, three participants emphasized that social injustices against different marginalized communities within their home countries played heavily into their decision to remain in the United States. One participant commented,

> I know one thing for me was LGBTQ rights, like, in the Caribbean, it's still very taboo, and, like, my philosophy and thinking of those types of things have changed, as opposed to, like, some of my friends who I grew up with when I went to high school, etc. Like, their way of thinking, it's different... And I don't know if I can go back to a society full time where, like, not everyone has those types of rights and stuff like that. (Participant 6)

Other participants mentioned similar narratives about the issues and challenges members of various marginalized groups face in the home region of participants. Participant 3, who was from Jamaica, where a reputation of condemning same sex relationships is evident through some of its local artists' music, spoke about the existence of some views within her childhood community with which she was uncomfortable and how some of the conversations people engage in are violently homophobic. Likewise, Participant 1 expressed her appreciation for laws being in place in the United States that protect people from those types of injustices.

Three participants alluded to the lack of accountability and urgency from the government in following up on the completion of projects and communicating with students studying abroad who want to return home. Participant 4, who is from Trinidad and Tobago, stated:

> So there are instances where you have projects, millions of dollars spent on projects, they reach 90% completion, 95% completion, but when the government changes, so say the opposition wins the election, and they take over, they will discontinue projects that are 90%–95% complete, just because it was started by the other party, and they don't want the other party to look credible or look like they did something good. I'm seeing it right now because I'm at the Ministry of Education and we deal with maintenance and repairs and construction and new schools and stuff, and there are schools that are fairly recently built, 2015

or 2014, just a few years and these schools were at 95% completion and when you go to these schools, I have pictures, if you see the conditions of these schools are inhabitable and have overgrown vines and bushes all over.

Similarly, the narratives of other participants highlighted their experiences with inefficient and lackluster communication from officials within government organizations, especially given the fact participants were seeking ways to enhance that particular industry in the country. Participants also believed the government was not taking the high level of crime seriously. For example, Participant 3 described growing up in a crime-ridden neighborhood. She was married, and given that her partner did not come from that type of background and had little experience with high crime areas, she feared immensely for his safety and refused to return to a country with elevated crime.

Social Factors

Several participants highlighted how stifled and trapped they felt within their home countries. Participants described living independent lives in the United States, which allowed them to experience a full feeling of freedom and liberation. This was something they indicated they did not want to risk giving up by returning home. Participant 2 described this well:

> The Underground club we used to go there. We took the trains, to... I forget what that area is called, but it's called Underground. And they used to have these singers and stuff like that; they had the best barbecue wings. And we literally stayed up till 6 am in the morning listening to people singing, drinking, eating wings, and go home like nothing happened, and then when I am home in the Bahamas, I can't even do that, like my dad would be like, Miss, you need to be in by 12 o'clock. And I'd be like, look, how old I be, I'm 22, you don't know what you're talking about. Um, it was just a lot more freedom now. You know, like, you can make mistakes, people won't judge you, people aren't minding your business. You know, so I guess my social freedom, if you will, or liberation rather.

Other participants emphasized the differences in social culture between their countries and the United States and what it means to feel free and liberated. For example, Participant 5, hailing from St. Kitts and Nevis, stated that "for one, Americans mind their own business," insinuating that people in St. Kitts and Nevis tend to be involved in everyone else's affairs. This participant likened the involvement to a game of telephone, because whatever one does at home tends to get back to other people, as though everyone is relaying the information through telephone calls. However, this participant had greater freedom in the United States from the over involvement from others.

Participant 1 attributed the size of the country to the level of freedom and liberation she could feel. She stated, "I think because Nevis is so small, everybody knows everybody," highlighting that she preferred staying in the United States because there are so many people who do not know you and just continue going along their day.

The support from close friends made throughout their higher education journey within the United States was emphasized by four participants. They indicated they and their friends had been able to build close-knit communities and that these communities served as huge support systems throughout rough times when they felt lonely. Participant 1 articulated this well:

> I'm part of a business frat, Alpha Kappa Psi. When it comes to frats and sororities and stuff like that of course, your brothers and sisters, like that you went through something with you know, you just naturally will be close. So, I would actually say those people. So, I feel naturally close to these people and it's just, I think when you build like a family aspect when you're away at school. And you have these people who would do anything for you or vice versa, and because it was like a business frat, we have a lot of connections, we all have roles and all have different companies and organizations. So, if I express well, I don't know where I'm gonna work afterwards, like in terms of sponsorship and whatever. They're like, we're gonna help you do this and this and this and this; it's very encouraging.

Similar to comments from Participant 1, other participants spoke about being able to experience new things, such as carnival and football, with friends they had made within the United States and how those interactions played a big part in supporting their sense of belonging. Participant 2 mentioned that due to some of these relationships, she had even been given the opportunity to serve as a godparent to some of her friends' children. She also mentioned that she had been able to engage in activities with the parents of her godchildren, such as going to museums and clubs, which were things she would not have been able to do back in the Bahamas. On the other hand, Participant 4 spoke more about how using extracurricular activities, such as soccer, was a way to create those friendships. He mentioned that while in Miami, he was able to meet people from many different cultures, and that in spite of spoken language differences, he still appreciated the moment to develop and connect with someone new.

DISCUSSION

The purpose of this study was to gain a better understanding of how international students from the Caribbean arrive at their decision not to return home after completing their highest earned degree within the United States, which leads to a phenomenon known as brain drain. Similar studies have focused on international students from developed countries or leading places of origin, such as China, the United Kingdom, India, South Korea, or Saudi Arabia, for international students in the United States (IIE, 2019). Findings from this research add to the few existing studies that focus on international students from the Caribbean. The results of this study indicate that all six participants tied their decision to remain within the United States after completing their highest earned degree to three factors: economic, social, and political.

These results build upon existing evidence that international students take into deep consideration elements connected to these three categories and, based on those considerations, decide what is important for them to make that decision not to return home (Gensing 2017). As it relates to economic factors, participants spoke primarily to the lack of job opportunities and lower salaries if they were to go home. Participants spoke mainly about the lack or absence of job opportunities in their home regions' labor force, which were representative of the areas in which they had pursued their higher education degree; thus, finding gainful employment would be impossible. Participants believed they would have to find employment in professions for which they had not prepared or would have to create jobs themselves. Most job opportunities in Caribbean regions align with traditional careers pursued by most people in those regions. These include being a doctor, accountant, teacher, or lawyer. Although these occupations hold high prestige and might pay well in the United States, this is not necessarily the case in the Caribbean. Often, students who return to their home countries after studying in the United States return to diminished access to entry-level positions or face a lack of proper compensation for their credentials.

Pertaining to political factors, the lack of governmental protection for marginalized communities within their countries played a strong role in the participants' decision not to return. Although they did not identify as members of those communities, participants were aware of the narrative that exists among the citizens—a narrative that breeds violence—and the lack of protections afforded the very same citizens the government is elected to serve.

Most participants stated they enjoyed having that sense of freedom and liberation by remaining with the United States. This finding suggests participants experienced more restricted environments in their home regions. Some participants offered that perceived restrictions could be due to the geographical size of the country and the population size; thus, those participants were not able to do certain things or enjoy certain activities without being scrutinized and judged by either their family, peers, or strangers and without others sharing information with people they both knew. Participants stated they were able to do things in the United States without judgment because they were meeting so many different people each day, and that everyone tends to go about their lives without worrying about what the next person will think about what they are doing.

Implications

There are several ways in which the findings of this study inform student affairs practitioners in assisting all international students from the Caribbean with the conflicting ideas of remaining within the United States after attaining their highest earned degree. Mainly, participants in this study shed light on three key factors that played a significant role in their process—economic, political, and social. Participants spoke mostly about issues and challenges directly affecting their individual country of origin; however, it was evident that the issues were similar across the Caribbean.

In accordance with Schlossberg's (1984) description of transition, and highlighting that "transition is viewed as a change in behavior or relations in response to an event or non-event that affects one's beliefs about oneself or the world" (p. 65), these participants went through two transition processes—the first being their transition from their home country into the United States to begin their higher education journey, and the second being their transition out of their higher education institution.

Moving In

An overarching consideration that emerged from the study was economic reasons, meaning that students believed they would be able to gain better job opportunities within the United States. Upon a student entering the university, student affairs professionals within the International Student Services office can begin developing rapport with these students. Through the rapport-building process, the staff would be able to find out what considerations went into the students' process that led them to wanting to study abroad. Within these conversations these student affairs professionals, in collaboration with academic advisors, can begin developing a plan (e.g., providing career advice and development through connecting students to careers in the United States and focusing on salary negotiations) for students if they decide to remain within the United States after completing their highest degree.

Moving Through

Student affairs professionals employed in offices, such as International Student Services, can provide support to international students as they go through their transitions. With social factors, they can ensure that they are recommending students with organizations on campus that fit their interests so that they are able to socialize and develop relationships. Focusing on the economic factor, staff could conduct workshops that focus on tax preparation, financial literacy, improving credit scores, and money management, just to name a few. If international students are interested in exploring the political realm more, professionals in the International Student Services office can connect them to governmental organizations that align with their values and also provide workshops focused on gaining citizenship, applying for Optional Practical Training, and even attaining Social Security cards. These efforts would then translate into international students feeling like they belong due to the extra steps being taken to prepare them for when they transition out of university and work toward remaining within the United States.

Moving Out

As it relates to economic factors, participants shared that they are unable to return or refuse to return home, because their economic sector does not have space for their interest or work, or institutions are not able to pay them the equivalent of their degree so that they would be able to live comfortably. Politically, participants discussed that government entities are not taking social justice issues seriously and there are no laws in place that protect their citizens who identify as part of an underrepresented community or identity. Socially, participants indicated that at times they would feel trapped and they were not able to do as they pleased or live a life of freedom without ridicule due to individuals spreading information and passing judgment onto them.

Additionally, the universities in which the international students are currently studying and the International Student Services offices can work to build collaborative opportunities with the source countries through building strategies and creating policies to determine what would entice students to return after their studies

Limitations

This study produced important information in relation to understanding how international students from the Caribbean arrive at the decision to remain within the United States after completing their highest earned degree and that connection to the phenomenon known as brain drain. However, the study is not without limitations.

First, we conducted this research utilizing a phenomenological qualitative approach, and the results of the study cannot be generalized to an entire population (Lincoln & Guba, 1985; Wolcott, 2005). As someone who is currently living the experience of an individual from the Caribbean who is studying in the United States and facing the decision to remain in the United States or return home, the first author remained aware of the biases and personal views he holds. Although he engaged in bracketing practices to reduce biases, he recognized that his personal experience could have influenced research protocol.

A second limitation was the inability to conduct interviews face to face due to the coronavirus pandemic. Conducting the interviews via Zoom made it more difficult to notice nonverbal cues (e.g., response hesitancy, subtle emotional responses), which are important components to interviews (Ganguly, 2017). In addition, interruption to the flow of conversation is inherent in video telephony platforms due to lags in sound and other features. Further, lags in internet connections tend to add to disruptions or misunderstanding in communication.

Finally, we sought data from participants with varying highest levels of education, so as they progressed through their journey of higher education, participants might have had increased experiences that reinforced their decisions to remain in the United States versus those who at the time of the interview had attained an undergraduate degree more recently. Additionally, given the fact that each participant did not attend the same higher education institution, the services they received and interactions they might have had with people at these institutions plays a role in the portrayal of their experiences.

Recommendations for Future Research

This study focused heavily on the economic, political, and social considerations as to why international students from the Caribbean arrived at the decision to remain within the United States after completing their highest earned degree. Future research might include studying the psychological effects, such as homesickness and guilt of contributing to the brain effect, of students remaining after completing their studies. Additionally, future work could analyze the perspectives and the work of student affairs professionals in offices such as International Student Services and how they navigate the discussions with international students from the Caribbean who want to remain in the United States after completing their studies. Conducting a cross analysis with the results from this study with other studies that focus on international student populations might be useful. For example, studying the major differences and experiences leading to this population wanting to remain after their studies could be informative. Finally, research could be conducted on the governmental policies and procedures in place in different Caribbean countries to see what benefits or incentives are in place to entice students to return post completion of their studies.

CONCLUSION

The participants in this study emphasized similar experiences regarding the process they undertook toward arriving at the decision to remain within the United States after completing their highest earned degree. In conducting this study, our goal was to provide knowledge that will assist all stakeholders involved in assisting international students from the Caribbean with their transition process in, through, and out of the higher education system within the United States and to understand the role they play in helping international students arrive at the decision to remain within the United States post completion of their highest earned degree. In accordance with Schlossberg's transition theory (1984), the participants' experiences focused heavily on their moving in and moving out aspects, with only brief mention of the moving through. For example, regarding the moving in, prior to participants arriving to the United States, they took into consideration what factors (e.g., economic, political, and social) made them want to come, and as they moved through, the conversations they had with staff and faculty and the relationships that were developed with friends helped reassure them they were making the right decision. As they prepared to move out, these considerations were the determining factors for their remaining within the United States. It is imperative to note that this study contributes to expanding the limited research related to international students from the Caribbean and understanding how they arrive at their decision to remain within the United States. Knowing that this particular international student population is underrepresented within literature, our hope is that this study can serve as a critical foundation for deeper understanding and more intentional efforts aimed toward assisting international students from the Caribbean in arriving at this decision to the best of their ability.

REFERENCES

Altbach, P. G. (2004). Globalisation and the university: Myths and realities in an unequal world. *Tertiary Education and Management, 10*(1), 3–25. https://doi.org/10.1080/13583883.2004.9967114

Ammigan, R. (2019). Institutional satisfaction and recommendation: What really matters to international students? *Journal of International Students, 9*(1), 262–281.

Bailey, E. K. (2017). 'I am studying in the U.S. but': Observations and insights from Caribbean college students. *Social Identities, 23*(1), 87-103. https://doi.org/10.1080/13504630.2016.1179568

Baruch, Y., Budhwar, P. S., & Khatri, N. (2007). Brain drain: Inclination to stay abroad after studies. *Journal of World Business, 42*(1), 99–112. https://doi.org/10.1016/j.jwb.2006.11.004

Carr, S. C., Inkson, K., & Thorn, K. (2005). From global careers to talent flow: Reinterpreting 'brain drain'. *Journal of World Business, 40*(4), 386–398.

Creswell, J. W. (2008). *Educational research: Planning, conducting, and evaluating quantitative and qualitative research* (3rd ed.). Pearson Education.

Dassin, J., Enders, J., & Kottmann, A. (2014). Social inclusiveness, development, and student mobility in international higher education: The case of the Ford Foundation International Fellowships Program. In B. Streitweiser (Ed.), *Internationalisation of higher education and global mobility* (Vol. 23, pp. 73–86). Symposium Books.

Edwards-Joseph, A., & Baker, S. (2014). Factors Caribbean overseas students perceive influence their academic self-efficacy. *Journal of International Students, 4*(1), 48–59.

Ganguly, S. (2017). Understanding nonverbal cues: A key to success in interviews. *The IUP Journal of Soft Skills, 11*(2), 62–72.

Gensing, M. E. (2017). *Student global mobility: An analysis of international STEM student brain drain* [Unpublished doctoral dissertation]. Old Dominion University

Han, X., Stocking, G., Gebbie, M. A., & Appelbaum, R. P. (2015). Will they stay or will they go? International graduate students and their decisions to stay or leave the U.S. upon graduation. *PLoS ONE, 10*(3). doi: 10.1371/journal.pone.0118183

Hutchinson, D. (2018). *Overlooked and invisible: Student success among first-generation, foreign-born Caribbean Black immigrants* [Unpublished doctoral dissertation]. University of Nebraska.

Javed, B., Zainab, B., Zakai, S. N., & Malik, S. (2019). Perceptions of international student mobility: A qualitative case study. *Journal of Education and Educational Development, 6*(2), 269–287.

Johnson, N. (2009). Analysis and assessment of the "Brain Drain" phenomenon and its effects on Caribbean countries. *Florida Atlantic Comparative Studies Journal, 11,* 1–16. https://home.fau.edu/peralta/web/FACS/braindrain.pdf

Kim, E. (2012). An alternative theoretical model: Examining psychosocial identity development of international students in the United States. *College Student Journal, 46*(1), 99–113.

Li, M., & Bray, M. (2007). Cross-border flows of students for higher education: Push-pull factors and motivations of Mainland Chinese students in Hong Kong and Macau. *Higher Education, 53*(6), 791–818. https://doi.org/10.1007/s10734-005-5423-3

Lincoln, Y. S., & Guba, E. G. (1985). *Naturalistic inquiry* (Vol. 75). SAGE.

Mazzarol, T., & Soutar, G. N. (2002). "Push-pull" factors influencing international student destination choice. *International Journal of Educational Management, 16*(2), 82–90. https://doi.org/10.1108/09513540210418403

Merriam, S. B. (2009). *Qualitative research: A guide to design and implementation.* Jossey-Bass.

Moustakas, C. (1994). *Phenomenological research methods.* SAGE.

Authors Bios

TREVIS BELLE, MS, is from the twin-island nation of St. Kitts and Nevis in the West Indies. He earned his Master of Science in College Student Personnel Administration in 2021 from the University of Central Arkansas in the United States. His major research interests are international student experiences and student affairs practices. Email: trevisbelle@gmail.com

SUSAN R. BARCLAY is an Associate Professor at the University of Central Arkansas in the Department of Leadership Studies. Her research interests include student development and success, career transitions, use of career construction techniques in multiple settings, identity development, and life design. Email: srbarclay@uca.edu

THOMAS BRUICK, PhD, is an Assistant Professor and Program Coordinator for the College Student Personnel Administration program at the University of Central Arkansas in the United States. His research interests include graduation preparation within student affairs, higher education policy, and access. Email: tbruick@uca.edu

PHILLIP BAILEY, Associate Vice President for International Education and Engagement, is also a tenured Full Professor of French in the Department of Languages, Linguistics, Literatures and Cultures. Email: phillipb@uca.edu

© *Journal of International Students*
Volume 12, Issue 4 (2022), pp. 973-994
ISSN: 2162-3104 (Print), 2166-3750 (Online)
https://doi.org/10.32674/jis.v12i4.2563
ojed.org/jis

Exploring the Impact of the Academic Interactions and Social Relations of Graduate Black African Students on Their Learning Experiences in China

Raymond Agyenim-Boateng
Lingnan University, Hong Kong

ABSTRACT

Current research on international students has not particularly examined Black African students' experiences in Chinese universities. This study explores the challenges encountered by African international students in China. I used semi-structured interviews of 12 Black African graduate students studying in three different universities in Beijing, China. Results indicate Chinese language, limited interaction with Chinese lecturers, and discriminatory treatment as the major challenges. Although some were ambivalent about their experiences, in general, these experiences did not produce a negative impact on their learning rather Black African students reported their overall academic experiences as being positive. The study concludes by discussing the implications of the findings for practice and recommends specific interventions to enhance Black African students' learning experiences in Chinese universities.

Keywords*:* African students, China, academic experiences, international students

Know that many personal troubles cannot be solved merely as troubles, but must be understood in terms of public issues and know that the human meaning of public issues must be revealed by relating them to personal troubles and the problems of individual life (Mills, 2004, p. 226).

Since the late 1990s, Chinese higher education has experienced rapid development and has become increasingly open in terms of international exchange and cooperation. Chinese universities are filled with international students from around the world, including Asia, the Americas, Europe, and Oceania. In 2018, the Chinese Ministry of Education indicated that there were over 81,562 African students in China, as compared to fewer than 2,000 in 2003 (Ministry of Education, 2018). Li (2018) noted that African students are the second largest group of African diaspora in China. Similarly, Study International (2020) reported that African students in China outnumber African students in any other study-abroad destinations like the United States or United Kingdom. China's readiness for educational cooperation and favorable conditions provided has promoted the explosion of African students coming to China (see Bodomo, 2014; Haugen, 2013; Jack, 2020; Leudi, 2018).

Toward the end of the 20th century, the general mobility patterns of African students changed substantially, taking a new direction toward Asian countries, especially China (Ferdjani, 2012). The dramatic increase in students from Africa can be explained in part by the Chinese government's targeted focus on making education a key pillar of its engagements with Africa by offering scholarships and making it easy for African students to secure study visas (Breeze & Moore, 2017). As the figures above show, it is an undeniable fact that the number of African students studying in China has increased. Therefore, their academic interactions and social experiences are worth exploring. In contemporary Chinese universities, international students come from a broad range of learning and teaching cultures (e.g., Wen et al., 2018). This diversity demands that we pay attention to the unintended negative effects and potential problems that might arise. Thus, in the face of a diverse population of international students, highlighting approaches to working with others in an international university context in creating a harmonious campus environment is paramount.

Research on Africans in China is focused mainly on African traders. This nascent body of research, however, has largely been limited to the examination of African students. In the few instances when African students have entered the conversation, they remain relegated as an incidental consideration in studies that are primarily devoted to the African presence in China. Some authors have included African students engaged in trade in Guangzhou and Wuhan in their sample (e.g., see Haugen, 2013 Ho, 2017, 2018; Mulvey, 2019). These studies described the lived experiences of the African student as precarity. Nevertheless, this does not give the full picture of the African students' experiences. Despite the growing ambivalence toward African students, the literature portrays them under a wider category of "foreigner" or "migrant" without acknowledging the complexity of and nuances in their experiences. Beijing, where this study was conducted, is a major destination for international students in the Asia-Pacific region (Xinhua, 2020), yet there is no research dedicated solely to African students' presence in this region.

This highlights the importance of focusing on Black African students studying in Beijing. As a Black African student myself studying in Beijing, I "self-locate" and explore other Black African students' learning experiences to better understand my own academic and social experiences and those of other Black African students studying in China. To set the scene, the following anecdote presents a succinct summary of the issues that are interconnected with the larger issue that this study seeks to explore.

Anecdote

As a young man originating from West Africa of African ancestry studying in China, the challenges of lifestyle adjustments, cultural differences, skin color, and the acceptance of differences on many levels were not something one would consciously consider when pursuing education. Compared to the more or less smooth experience of internationalization at home (Beelen, 2011) where many international students from countries such as Nigeria, Zambia, Togo, and others, my arrival in China was jarring. The first change I encountered was the change of time zone and climate, both of which were quite different from my home country. I became disoriented and confused. I struggled with adjusting my body clock. As the days went by, I felt that I was living in the spotlight. Various identities were thrust upon me as I struggled to interact and communicate with the people. With time, the challenges mounted. I also became aware of the negative stereotypes some Chinese people hold of Africans, which I took to be somehow connected to our colonial history and our marginal position in the global economy.

My anecdotes represent a range of difficulties that I faced living and studying in China. Generally, I valued the educational experience in China; however, I felt isolated in the wider society. I acknowledge that my experiences are not fully reflective of all Black African students. Still, on a more general level, my experience has afforded me valuable insight into the possible challenges Black African students face living and studying in China.

Theoretical Justification

In connecting my personal experiences to those of other African students in China, I reason with Mills' (2000, p. 5) "sociological imagination." For Mills, sociological imagination "is the quality of mind" (p. 5) that enables an individual to understand how their troubles and inner life events are connected to the broader social context they inhabit. This suggests that the individual makes sense of their world, creates meaning, and relates this meaning to their personal experiences. Sociological imagination is a promising lens through which an individual views their experience by looking at what is going on and attributing such events to what has been established in the world around them.

In this study, I want to relate and contextualize my experiences as a Black African student in China to the experiences of other Black African students studying in Beijing. Accordingly, I "self-locate." Location as part of the research process validates and ensures that I am connected with and accountable to the entire Black African student population in China (Absolon & Willett, 2005). Location in this sense directs and guides my actions more responsibly, and it sets the grounds for knowledge transformation (Absolon & Willett, 2005, p.111). With that said, it is better to locate relevant and distinct aspects of oneself, rather than to make broad general statements. This research sits on the personal rationality of belief by offering insight into the background of the research and provides an understanding of my experiences and reasons for my actions. That way, knowing how this knowledge relates to the concepts and truth that has been justified in the anecdotes makes this research an epistemological problem that needs to be investigated (Steup, 2005).

The model or strategy I use to explore the academic interactions and social experiences of Black African graduate students in Beijing is guided by experiential knowledge. That is, the idea brought to this research emanates from my experiences. In doing so, I settle with Maxwell's (2005) notion that the researcher is the instrument of the research, and what makes them distinct is that their lives form part of their works (Maxwell, 2005). Thus, locating and detailing my personal experiences and identity through the lens of sociological imagination and exploring other students' experiences set the framework within which this study was designed and how the data was interpreted.

LITERATURE REVIEW

African International Students and their Experiences

In this section, I draw on studies undertaken in the United Kingdom, United States, and some international students' destinations. Integrating literature from these contexts provides a helpful overview of African student experiences, and establishes familiarity with and provides a holistic understanding on the topic. The experiences of international African students may of course not be unique in what is a highly diverse multicultural environment, as all students must adjust to and develop new ways of living and studying. Studies have shown that international African students easily adapt to their new learning environments, despite the adjustment challenges that the students may face in transitioning into a new environment (Jones et al., 2002). Aside from the feelings of alienation and isolation many international students are exposed to (Boafo-Arthur, 2014), it is also documented that the experiences of the international African student are coupled with discriminatory and prejudicial treatment that predisposes them to stress-related acculturation (Boafo-Arthur, 2014; Hashim & Zhiliang, 2003). A qualitative study involving 21 postgraduate African students revealed that African students experience social exclusion and unwelcome attitudes from local students (Hyams-Ssekasi et al., 2014). These authors reported that isolation and feeling unwelcome impacted the ability of African students to work together with the local students, making the integration process more difficult (Hyams-Ssekasi et al., 2014).

African students face several unfamiliar situations in an unfamiliar social and institutional context. The degree of such a situation depends on the differences in individual personality, race/ethnicity, sex roles, and stigma or prejudice experienced (Hayes & Lin, 1994). Issues due to hostile relationships with host nationals as a result of culture shock (Bochner, 2013; Luo & Jamieson-Drake, 2013), discrimination and racism (Brown & Jones, 2013), and unfamiliar academic standards and teaching approaches (Robertson et al., 2000) are not uncommon among African students' experiences. Concerning this, Evivie (2009) posited that all these challenges are a result of differences in educational systems, culture, and norms described as an educational shock (Eng & Manthei, 1984) between host countries and the students' countries of origin. Lastly, African students often lack knowledge of the language of their host countries, which inhibits their social interaction and eventually poses a challenge (Yang et al., 2006). Collectively, problems within the academic and social environment challenge students' well-being and their ability to adjust to new academic settings resulting in negative consequences such as regrets, emotional conflicts, and self-devaluation (Moores & Popadiuk, 2011). Despite the handful of studies on this topic, there is a paucity of research critically reflecting on the impact academic interactions and social relations have on the learning experiences of Black African students.

African Students in China and Their Experiences

In spite of a large number of studies surrounding international student experiences abroad, relatively few have focused on the experiences of Black African students in China. To some extent, Black African students are included in studies of international students more generally where they are considered under a broader spectrum of "African students." It should be noted, however, that the racial identification of African students is not always homogenous as it seems to appear, but rather a mixture of races. Although the dominant racial group within the African student population is likely to be Black, the plethora of research available (see, for example, Dong & Chapman, 2008; Haugen, 2013) has failed to capture the diversity or emphasize the racial makeup of the African student population represented in China. Since race, identity, and physical differences in our everyday interaction influence social relations, the experiences of a Black African might differ from a White African or multiracial African or may depend on the different ethnic group the student identifies with. Various studies within the context of the United Kingdom and the United States have indicated that Black students compared with other racial groups, experience significant racism and alienation as part of their study abroad experiences (Brown & Jones, 2013; Karkouti, 2016; Torres, 2009). This evidence affords the exploration of the Black experience within the context of China.

Until recently, the earliest work was done by Hevi (1963) who had personal experience of studying in China. Other scholars (e.g., Dong & Chapman, 2008; Haugen, 2013; Tian & Lowe, 2018) have also focused on African students' cultural adaptation, China-Africa cooperation, educational experiences, and students' opinions toward the experiences in China. Studies on African students' experiences in China over the years have focused on matters of stress perceptions and cross-cultural adaptation (Hashim & Zhiliang, 2003) with little on their academic interactions and social experiences. Racial discrimination and stereotypes are among the many challenges that international students face, particularly with students from racially homogenous countries (Sandhul & Asrabadi, 1994, as cited in Evivie, 2009). African students in China generally report experiences of discrimination based on race in China (Mulvey, 2019). Ho (2017) noted that African students' experiences of living in China only reproduce racial prejudice. Racial discrimination based on color and "neo-racism" form part of the stereotypes African students face in their host society, particularly stereotypes that are somehow connected to the larger structural issue of Africa's colonial history, and lower standards in the global economy (Lee & Rice, 2007). In examining the transnational connections of African student migrants and their experiences in Chinese cities, Ho (2017) argued that "the social differentiation and everyday sociality that the African student experiences in Chinese cities reinforce racial coding and development asymmetries" (p. 15). This implies that the everyday life challenges and problems African students encounter in Chinese cities are rooted in racial prejudice and cultural dominance. The overall consequences of social differentiation create the impression that racial discrimination is consciously practiced by Chinese people (Hevi as cited in Liu, 2013). Haugen (2013) argued that the conflicts between African students and Chinese students in Chinese university campuses are rooted in racial identification on both sides, yet there is a lacuna in the literature critically exploring the Black learning experience. Together, the extent of how these experiences impact the learning experience of the student has not been much explored. In this light, I explored how Black African students' academic interactions and social relations have an impact on their learning experiences in Beijing.

METHOD

The study was conducted in Beijing. At the time of undertaking this study, there was not a single identified published study dedicated to the experiences of Black African students living in Beijing (Bodomo, 2020). Beijing serves as the political capital of China and is an educational hub for several prestigious universities, ranking among the world's top 40 cities for international students and listed as the leading city with the highest number of international students in China (Shuo, 2019).

Participants

Twelve African graduate students identified as Black (seven females, five males), enrolled in English-taught programs, studying in Chinese universities in Beijing for at least a year, were recruited for participation. Participants profiles are presented in Table 1. I advertised the study on various African students' social media platforms of which I was a member, inviting students to participate in the study. Participants gladly agreed to partake. I employed a purposive sampling method in recruiting students from three universities located in Beijing. My positionality as a Black

African student, enrolled in an English-taught program at the time informed the sample selection. I purposively recruited and engaged participants who identified as Black Africans. This sampling approach was necessary to ensure that the interviews explored participants' experiences consistent with the research aim, and more so to contextualize participants' experiences in line with my anecdotes outlined above.

Data Collection

I used semistructured interviews for data collection as they allowed the exploration of participants' experiences on specific issues and further assisted me to access realistic experiences that were hidden (Peräkylä & Ruusuvuori, 2008). This approach also enabled me to capture the meaning and structure of these experiences that are not easily quantified (Lin, 2013). I conducted interviews at places of convenience chosen by participants. This allowed each interview to progress well in a comfortable setting. Interview sessions ranged from 30 to 45 minutes. Participation in the study was voluntary, and participants read and signed an informed consent document before the interviews. I engaged my respondents in chat to collect some background information on my participants. The first set of questions captured students' perceptions on the academic and learning practices in China, perceived benefits of studying in Chinese universities, and how students engaged and coped in their learning environment. I also explored problems and challenges students perceived and encountered in their academic environment. During the interviews, other questions emerged. In addition, I asked participants to provide critical, constructive feedback for improving practices, programs, and services for Black Africans and other international students at their universities. None of the students alerted me to any distress they may have experienced during the interviews, nor did any of them express a desire to discontinue participation in the study. All the interviews were audiorecorded for precision and notes were taken for easier transcription with participants' permission.

Analytic Strategy

All interviews were audio recorded and transcribed for line-by-line analysis. To obtain a general sense of the data, I did a preliminary exploratory analysis by reading through all the transcriptions for insights into specific comments. First, I read the transcripts without attempts at coding. In the second reading, I did an open-coding process and noted individual words, phrases, and sentences relevant to the research objectives. As I read each transcript, I examined and compared similarities and differences. I then developed themes from the transcriptions before analyzing the data inductively, beginning with the raw data consisting of multiple sources of information and then broadening to several specific themes (Johnson & Christensen, 2012). I closely examined frequent and outstanding words, phrases, and sentences that emerged from the transcripts.

Ethical Considerations

As a Black African graduate student studying in China, I had several concerns about conducting this study and presenting the data collected. During the interviews, I avoided imposing my values on the students. I had to deal with matters of subjectivity by ensuring that the interview protocol was unbiased and subjective. The interview protocol was face validated by non-African experts interested in identity-related research and went through an ethical review for approval. These concerns were continually acknowledged. The advantages of having a shared African origin with the student participants allowed for a greater rapport, which in turn resulted in a high level of comfort and honesty in the interviews. It should be noted that the findings might not be generalizable and may not resonate with other universities in China. Meanwhile, my values and understanding as a Black African student at the time might be unconsciously imposed upon the study findings; however, I tried not to impose my interpretation on the problems shared by the participants. Further, after transcribing all the audio recorded interviews, I did a member check by providing each participant with their recording and coded transcripts containing highlighted words, phrases, and sentences intended for the analysis. Triangulation took the form of cross-checking the data with the literature that I had and reflecting on my own experiences and observations as a Black African student to validate the congruency of the data. Member checking and triangulation helped to deal with inaccurate transcription, my own biases, and errors. To protect the confidentiality and anonymity of participants' names and other recognizable data, the recordings and transcripts from the interviews were not made available to anyone not directly involved in the study. During the member checks, no other participant had access to the data of other participants. Participants were assigned numbers (e.g., Participant 1, Participant 2) to protect their identities.

Table 1

Demographic Characteristics of Study Participants

Participant ID	Nationality	Gender	Major	Years in China
1	Liberia	F	Education	1 y 5 mo
2	Malawi	M	Education	1 y 5 mo
3	Ghana	M	Communication	3 y 5 mo
4	Cameroon	F	International trade	1 y 5 mo
5	Uganda	F	Social policy	1 y 5 mo
6	Rwanda	M	Natural science	1 y 5 mo
7	Zimbabwe	F	Master's, business admin	1 y 5 mo
8	Malawi	M	Social policy	1 y 5 mo
9	Tanzania	M	Finance	1 y 5 mo
10	Liberia	F	Economics	1 y 5 mo
11	Tanzania	F	Higher education	1 y 5 mo
12	Zambia	F	Education	3 y 5 mo

RESULTS AND DISCUSSION

Several issues emerged from the qualitative analyses, which were categorized into two broad themes: rewarding experiences and exclusion, discrimination, and the language barrier.

Rewarding Experiences

The majority of students described their experiences with and within their university with stories worth noting. Participants touched on the academic requirements of their various programs, emphasizing research work, the feeling of studying in a diverse classroom, and a better system of education. Students noted how well-resourced Chinese universities are and how this positively impacted their learning experiences. Participants 10 outlined that "the education system in China is outstanding and equipped with resources for best learning." Similarly, the diverse nature of the staff and student body enhanced their learning experiences, helped their career growth, and knowledge expansion. Participants reported:

I think China is a very good country to study economically because most of its universities are well equipped with resources, facilities, and staff. Compared to my country I am positively impressed with the quality of education provided by this university. I had never been to any foreign country apart from China so I can say I like overseas experience. (Participant 10)

I have had a nice experience so far and I enjoyed my studies…I have been getting all the resources and materials to study and also communication between students and teachers is much better. Studying in a class with a diversity of students and professors all over the world has enriched my experience and knowledge… I am well equipped to go home and make an impact. (Participant 12)

Students seemed pleased with the education they were receiving in China, compared to their home universities. Moreover, participants were impressed with the internationalization of their various universities and appreciated the international visiting professors they got to interact with occasionally. Educational infrastructure as mentioned by participants did play a huge role in their learning. This observation is not entirely surprising considering that participants had come from geographical regions mostly in the global south that still have developmental issues to deal with. Essentially, concerning educational infrastructure, China (one of the largest economies in the world) certainly has high-quality infrastructure as compared to their home countries. Indeed, high-quality educational infrastructure improves international students' learning. To a large extent, all participants concurred that the knowledge acquired will put them in a better position when they get back home.

On the whole, teaching and learning ran more efficiently than they had ever experienced before. For example, Participant 7 mentioned that the "stress of being a student was manageable." Participants also detailed the experiences of being able to participate in class discussion, giving presentations and interacting with their classmates. To participants, the various teaching strategies they have been exposed to were more student-centered, which optimized their learning experiences.

Methods of teaching are all on point. So, I think it is a great opportunity to study here. The stress is manageable. We're allowed to make presentations, talk, and discuss issues among ourselves in class. Even the course outline will state clearly that you should participate in class. So, I think all of them encourage you to be expressive enough in class and you are also allowed to teach to your peers in terms of presentation and stuff. (Participant 7)

To a certain extent, excerpts like the above point to the discrepancies related to participants' home learning experiences in comparison to their experiences in Chinese universities. It is quite fascinating that the differences in the educational system did not result in educational shock as previously described (Eng & Manthei, 1984; Evivie, 2009). Even though the study did not seek to dichotomize between participants' home learning experiences and that of China, it appears that participants reflected on their previous (home university) learning experiences in drawing inferences from their learning experiences in China.

Probing further, participants explained that the atmosphere within a Chinese classroom was relaxed and friendlier against that of the formal-authoritative classroom in their home universities. Participant 8 described: "It's like here, students are made not to be afraid of teachers at all, the aura around here gives room for students to approach professors and ask for assistance, materials, and they deliver easily." Likewise, Participant 12 reported that "communication between students and teachers was much better." Along with this evidence, with my 4-year experience in Ghana as an undergraduate student, I couldn't recall a moment when teachers disclosed their contact details in a class. As a researcher listening to participants' stories, I understood their experiences relating to their professors in Chinese universities. All of the students interviewed mentioned the competencies they had acquired through research, teaching, and professional development opportunities and were optimistic. Equally, studying in China, I attained international experience and developed competencies through conducting research. These findings given here enable the study to draw a firm linkage with Zha's (2015) assertion that Chinese education is perceived as excellent, strives for uniformity and standardization, and follows consistent practices. Thus, Chinese universities are highly regarded by Black African students, and I should point out that participants were appreciative of Chinese education despite some challenges in the learning process. To wrap up on this theme, it is important to emphasize that participants being appreciative of their learning in China, in terms of the well-resourced education infrastructure and quality content of learning, were not hesitant in pointing out the challenges of being a student, particularly being a Black African student. I will discuss further these challenges students outlined in the next section.

Exclusion and Discrimination in Classroom Spaces

Against the rewarding experiences participants outlined above, they further reported experiences of discrimination and exclusion based on their skin color within classroom spaces and other spaces on campus. This observation appears to contradict the earlier findings related to the rewarding experience detailed above. However, it stands to reason that the experiences of Black African students evidenced from this research are double-edged. Thus, both positives and negatives form part of the academic interactions and social experiences of the Black African students' experiences in Beijing. Moreover, reporting these opposing views provides a more nuanced understanding of the Black African student experiences in China. That being said, what made the learning process frustrating was the discriminatory practices from Chinese professors and instructional materials that depicted negative stereotypes about Black people. Some excerpts are below:

> The people I come into contact with in this university make me feel some way. Chinese people are good and very helpful but sometimes they shy away when you want to talk to them, giving excuses that they do not understand, or do not know. (Participant 3)

> Life has not been bad neither is it rosy… We had issues; I have talked about issues of attitude… from the books that we have been reading; there is this label given to people. They have categorized that White man is more intelligent seconded by Asian then they say Black people are dull to some extent. I will be frank with you that, I have seen that attitude from some professors basically from China. The way they treat us Africans …. You could see that they always direct every question to students from western countries. (Participant 2)

Clearly, stereotypes about Africans discussed in the literature were acted out and these form part of the Black African students' experience. The broader historical narratives about Black Africans that perpetuate stereotypes about them lend support to this evidence. Along this line of reasoning, it is important to recognize how the individual experiences are a consequence of both the historical context in which they sit and the everyday immediate environment in which the individual exists (Mills, 2000/1959). On top of this, the preferential treatment given to White students was mostly reported by respondents. Students were more inclined to attribute discriminatory practices meted against them due to their black skin color. Likewise, in my case, I noticed how discrimination and feeling of alienation influenced my lived experiences and identity as a Black African student. Respondents narrated:

> There is this particular professor whom I won't mention his name, anytime he asked a question straight away he points to the student

from the UK... like hey, you, what happens in the UK or how it is like in the UK. An incident happens when he asks for a meaning of a word and an African student wanted to answer, but this man said no I want this particular guy to answer. Everybody was like why? We are in the same class and everyone has the same opportunity to participate... There is a kind of segregation, preference of students I do not know whether it is based on skin color, on country or continent I don't know. (Participant 5)

> My only problem is with attitude in the context of some Chinese lecturers. How they look at people whom they think looks different from them. The entire thing, I have said deals with attitude... it's about perception. My experience in China tells me that there is a mindset about African students. I see that the first choice is always for western students. Personally, sometimes when a teacher says something and I want to contribute, I withdraw because I know that my contribution is far less and not needed. Discrimination is there, it is coming but that's how they were brought up. Chinese do not trust Africans. (Participant 8)

As evidenced in the above quotes, discriminatory treatment was most often mentioned as challenging. Black African students reported being treated unfairly as compared with international students from western countries. Incidences of discrimination reported by students were as a result of some classroom practices and attitudinal dispositions students received from faculty members, local students, and other people they came into contact with within their daily scholastic activities. To participants, "Chinese people have a mindset about Africa, and that has resulted in exclusionary practices with white preference over black" and they do not know the origin of such attitudes (Participants 4). Similar experiences were reported outside the classroom also:

> I think there is some form of discrimination against Blacks. Say like in the dormitory if you are having a program or having a meeting, the porters will come and say you can't hold a meeting here and all that. But you won't see that when White people or other people are having such. (Participant 4)

Stories from participants resonate with some of the issues I found problematic within classroom spaces. In one of my classes in which the majority of students were Africans, we were trying to compare educational systems across different countries, but only the handful of students originating from outside the continent of Africa were asked to share their opinions. This was particularly surprising. The repetition of such incidents in which identifiable groups of students were consistently given opportunities to share their ideas in the name of "familiarity with the material" and, what's more, whatever they said and delivered was positively evaluated, created the impression of differential treatment and explicit exclusion. These findings and my observations converge to indirectly support the notion that racial inequalities and discrimination form part of the international Black student experiences (Brown & Jones, 2013). Students mostly attributed these events to their race. They asserted that "it could be because they are from Africa." Then again, it reflects the stereotypical challenges African students face as a result of racial discrimination based on color and neo-racism as described by Lee and Rice (2007). Essentially, the issue of preferential treatment given to Whites and color discrimination against Blacks is not surprising as this evidence provides a nuanced understanding of the positive prejudice toward White skin in all areas of Asia as well as China (Saito, 1996). However, on a slight contrast, findings and my own observations did not document any issue of extreme racism as the literature has it (Liu, 2013). Nevertheless, this substantiates the claim that racial identity generation and social differentiation generates conflicts, thus affecting the relationship between the Africans and Chinese students on university campuses (Dikötter, 1994).

Language Barrier

Another challenge that was very often mentioned was difficulties with the language. Although participants were all enrolled in programs taught in English, Chinese language was their biggest challenge. Concerns on how zero knowledge in Mandarin affects daily activities on campus were common. From the dormitory where it is hard to communicate with the porters, orientation sessions and international students' activities conducted in Mandarin without any translations, electronic kiosks and other machines that lack dual-language functions, were considered challenging. As a Participant 11 put it, "My first challenge was the Chinese language… I struggle with the language and service providers. For instance, when I go to the library it becomes difficult to talk to the librarian for assistance."

Participants' experiences with language difficulty are consistent with several findings from the literature (Hashim & Zhiliang, 2003; Haugen, 2013), implying that the difficulty in understanding the Chinese language poses a challenge to the Black African student, and eventually inhibits their social interaction among host countries as revealed by Yang et al. (2006). Indeed, language difficulty is part of the dilemma most international students faced. Particularly, international students who lack knowledge of the language of their host country experience challenges (Yang et al., 2006). On a more serious note, the issue of language barrier frequently appearing in the literature is more convoluted than it seems. On the one hand, host institutions need to ensure that they have the necessary infrastructure in place to host a diverse body of students. On the other hand, the international students must equally endeavor to acquire some basic language skills before embarking on the international journey and continue to perfect their language skills on arrival. All the same, institutions responsible for recruiting and hosting Black African students are highly recommended to implement strategies to negotiate this language conundrum.

Largely, participants talked about the difficulty of having to adapt to the new culture, weather, climate, food, etc., which is a common challenge for international students (Hendrickson et al., 2011; O'Reilly et al., 2010). Despite the challenges identified by almost all the participants, one participant stated unequivocally that "there are no challenges largely because he sees nothing that is out of place" (Participant 7). This finding appeared as a counternarrative and tended to downplay the challenges identified by 99% of the sample. It should be noted, however, that out of the 12 Black African students, it was just a single participant who expressed such sentiments. Essentially, concerning the fraction of the sample, the challenges identified still hold. Nevertheless, this incongruence points to the fact that regardless of the situation, participants' experiences might not be homogenous, more so this incongruence opens an avenue for future research.

CONCLUSION

In this study, I examined the academic interactions and social relations of 12 Black African students in Beijing through the lens of "sociological imagination" and "self-location." I established a normative position and drew on my personal experiences to explore salient features and events that were similar to other Black African students. This approach enabled an in-depth understanding of the Black African student experiences that surpasses my limited subjective experiences. It was necessary to focus on the Black African students' experiences, in particular, to bring to light the nuances in racial perspectives that have been ignored in the literature. I sought to provide evidence to make connections between the social process and my biography. My experiences were not different from those of the stories told by participants. Participants' stories substantiated my claims. Sociological imagination was central to this study as my experiences as a Black African student afforded me the methodological perspective in pulling away from my situation as a Black African student to reconcile two different and abstract concepts ("I and other Black African students") of my social reality in China. As a researcher, listening to participants' stories helped to better situate my understanding of the Black African student experience.

Generally, participants appreciated the educational benefits they received in China. The diverse classroom environment, student-centered learning, and the emphasis on cooperative learning within the Chinese educational system were considered rewarding. However, this does not preclude the issues of subtle discriminatory treatments with and within the universities, alongside the language barrier and other frustrations in the educational process. Discrimination was the code of practice among some professors in classroom dynamics. My experiences and those of the respondents chronicled are somewhat homogenous. From a historical perspective, the effects of colonization and subsequent degeneration of the African continent is fundamental to understanding the adverse attitudes and behavioral disposition meted against Black Africans today. Beginning my inquiry from my lived experiences provided me with the methodological lens to reflect on the broader social issue, question the situated issue, and explore this issue with participants. Thus, reflecting on my individual experiences concerning differential treatments and explicit exclusion during classroom interactions, it is evident that these weren't isolated incidences, as reports from participants support and validate my observations. For example, what I experienced as "personal trouble" like being ignored as a Black African student in classroom interactions were issues affecting my fellow Black African students too. Overall participants' experiences are a toss-up between rewards and challenges; however, the dichotomy between rewarding experiences and the experiences of discrimination did not mar the learning experiences of the Black African student. However, my impressions and frustrations in China did not deter me from enjoying the positives and the advantages of studying in China on the prestigious Chinese government scholarship. Indeed, African students easily adapt to their learning environment despite the challenges with adjustment (Jones et al., 2002).

Implications

Findings from the study may have significant practical implications. First, the study recommends that universities provide intercultural competence training and training on antiracism, color consciousness, and critical race theory to help staff identify their implicit biases. This will better help staff to work with Black African students and any diverse student population. Instructors are also encouraged to be more inclusive of diverse perspectives and to develop strategies to counter stereotypes and biases particularly about Blacks and Africans present in teaching materials. Moreover, universities are recommended to provide language training for nonacademic staff who deal with Black African students as well as international students on a regular basis. Likewise, there should be avenues for Black African students as well as international students, in general, to acquire basic Mandarin skills as part of their learning. Collectively, this will help alleviate students' challenges and improve the overall experiences of Black African students in China.

Limitations and Future Directions

This study is of course not without limitations. First, given that all the study participants were largely from English-taught programs with zero knowledge in Mandarin, language barrier might have strongly influenced the academic interaction and social relations of the Black African student. Future research is suggested to explore the experiences of this population utilizing a sample with proficiency in Mandarin. Second, the sample drew exclusively on the experiences of Black African students in three Universities in Beijing. Hence, this is an incomplete description of the Black African student experience in China. Future research should apply a more robust methodology by studying students from a wide range of disciplines and locations across China to optimize our understanding of the African student experience more effectively.

Despite these limitations, this study provides empirical evidence of a range of difficulties faced in my life as a Black African student and fellow Black African students living and studying in China. Largely, I valued the educational experiences, as did the participants; however, I felt isolated in the wider society. I acknowledge that my experience is not fully reflective of all Black African students. Still, on a more general level, connecting my experiences with fellow Black African students has afforded me valuable insight into the experiences of Black African students living and studying in China.

Acknowledgments

I want to thank Dr. Lorin G. Yochim (Concordia University of Edmonton) for his intellectual guidance. Without his support this paper would not have materialized. I would also like to thank the anonymous reviewers for their thoughtful comments towards improving the manuscript.

REFERENCES

Absolon, K., & Willett, C. (2005). Putting ourselves forward: Location in Aboriginal research. In L. Brown & S. Strega (Eds.), *Research as resistance: Critical, Indigenous, and anti-oppressive approaches* (pp. 97–126). Canadian Scholars Press.

Beelen, J. (2011). First steps in internationalization at home. *Educación Global, 15*, 59–67.

Boafo-Arthur, S. (2014). Acculturative experiences of Black-African international students. *International Journal for the Advancement of Counselling, 36*(2), 115–124. https://doi.org/10.1007/s10447-013-9194-8

Bochner, S. (Ed.). (2013). *Cultures in contact: Studies in cross-cultural interaction* (Vol. 1). Elsevier.

Bodomo, A. (2014, September). *Africans in China: The experiences from education and training* [Paper presentation]. The International Conference of China and Africa Media, Communications and Public Diplomacy, Beijing, China.

Bodomo, A. (2020). Historical and contemporary perspectives on inequalities and well-being of Africans in China. *Asian Ethnicity, 21*(4), 526–541. https://doi.org/10.1080/14631369.2020.1761246

Breeze, V., & Moore, N. (2017, June 30). China has overtaken the US and UK as the top destination for Anglophone African students. *Quartz Africa*. https://qz.com/africa/1017926/china-has-overtaken-the-us-and-uk-as-the-top-destination-for-anglophone-african-students

Brown, L., & Jones, I. (2013). Encounters with racism and the international student experience. *Studies in Higher Education, 38*(7), 1004–1019. https://doi.org/10.1080/03075079.2011.614940

Dikötter, F. (1994). Racial identities in China: Context and meaning. *The China Quarterly, 138*, 404–412. https://doi.org/10.1017/S0305741000035815

Dong, L., & Chapman, D. W. (2008). The Chinese government scholarship program: An effective form of foreign assistance? *International Review of Education, 54*(2), 155–173. https://doi.org/10.1007/s11159-007-9075-7

Eng, L. L., & Manthei, R. J. (1984). Malaysian and New Zealand students' self-reported adjustment and academic performance. *New Zealand Journal of Educational Studies, 19*(2), 179–184.

Evivie, L. G. (2009). *Challenges faced by African international students at a metropolitan research university: A phenomenological case study* [Doctoral dissertation]. The University of North Carolina at Charlotte. libres.uncg.edu/ir/uncc/f/Evivie_uncc_0694D_10077.pdf

Ferdjani, H. (2012). *African students in China: An exploration of increasing numbers and their motivations in Beijing.* SUNScholar.

Hashim, I. H., & Zhiliang, Y. (2003). Cultural and gender differences in perceiving stressors: A cross-cultural investigation of African and Western students in Chinese colleges. *Stress and Health, 19*(4), 217–225. https://doi.org/10.1002/smi.978

Haugen, H. Ø. (2013). China's recruitment of African university students: Policy efficacy and unintended outcomes. *Globalisation, Societies and Education, 11*(3), 315–334. https://doi.org/10.1080/14767724.2012.750492

Hayes, R. L., & Lin, H. R. (1994). Coming to America: Developing social support systems for international students. *Journal of Multicultural Counselling and Development, 22*(1), 7–16. https://doi.org/10.1002/j.2161-1912.1994.tb00238.x

Hendrickson, B., Rosen, D., & Aune, R. K. (2011). An analysis of friendship networks, social connectedness, homesickness, and satisfaction levels of international students. *International Journal of Intercultural Relations, 35*(3), 281–295. https://doi.org/10.1016/j.ijintrel.2010.08.001

Hevi, E. (1963). *An African student in China.* Pall Mall Press

Ho, E. L.-H. (2017). The geo-social and global geographies of power: Urban aspirations of 'worlding' African students in China. *Geopolitics, 22*(1), 15–33. https://doi.org/10.1080/14650045.2016.1149697

Ho, E. L.-H. (2018). African student migrants in China: Negotiating the global geographies of power through gastronomic practices and culture. *Food, Culture & Society, 21*(1), 9–24. https://doi.org/10.1080/15528014.2017.1398468

Hyams-Ssekasi, D., Mushibwe, C. P., & Caldwell, E. F. (2014). International education in the United Kingdom: The challenges of the golden opportunity for Black-African students. *SAGE Open, 4*(4). https://doi.org/10.1177/2158244014562386

Jack, A. (2020). China surpasses western government African university scholarships. *Financial Times.* https://www.ft.com/content/4b2e6c1c-83cf-448a-9112-477be01d2eee

Johnson, R. B., & Christensen, L. (2012). *Educational research: Quantitative, qualitative, and mixed approaches.* SAGE.

Jones, L., Castellanos, J., & Cole, D. (2002). Examining the ethnic minority student experience at predominantly White institutions: A case study. *Journal of Hispanic Higher Education, 1*(1), 19–39. https://doi.org/10.1177/1538192702001001003

Karkouti, I. M. (2016). Black students' educational experiences in predominantly white universities: A review of the related literature. *College Student Journal, 50*(1), 59–70.

Lee, J., & Rice, C. (2007). Welcome to America? International student perceptions of discrimination. *Higher Education, 53*(3), 381–409. https://doi.org/10.1007/s10734-005-4508-3

Leudi, J. (2018). *Why African students are choosing China over the West.* Asia by Africa. https://www.asiabyafrica.com/point-a-to-a/african-international-students-study-in-china

Li, A. (2018). African students in China: Research, reality, and reflection. *African Studies Quarterly, 17*(4), 5–44.

Lin, C. S. (2013). Revealing the "essence" of things: Using phenomenology in LIS research. *Qualitative and Quantitative Methods in Libraries, 4*, 469–478.

Liu, P. H. (2013). Petty annoyances? Revisiting John Emmanuel Hevi's *An African Student in China* after 50 Years. *China: An International Journal, 11*(1), 131–145. https://www.muse.jhu.edu/article/505522.

Luo, J., & Jamieson-Drake, D. (2013). Examining the educational benefits of interacting with international students. *Journal of International Students, 3*(2), 85–101.

Maxwell, J. A. (2005). Conceptual framework: What do you think is going on? In J. A. Maxwell (Ed.), *Qualitative research design: An interactive approach* (pp. 39-72). SAGE.

Mills, C. W. (2000). *The sociological imagination.* Oxford University Press. (Original printed 1959)

Mills, C. W. (2004). On intellectual craftsmanship. In W. K. Carroll (Ed.), *Critical strategies for social research* (pp. 54–66). Canadian Scholars' Press.

Ministry of Education. (2018). *Statistical report on international students in China for 2018.* http://en.moe.gov.cn/documents/reports/201904/t20190418_378692.html

Moores, L., & Popadiuk, N. (2011). Positive aspects of international student transitions: A qualitative inquiry. *Journal of College Student Development, 52*(3), 291–306. https://doi:10.1353/csd.2011.0040.

Mulvey, B. (2019). International higher education and public diplomacy: A case study of Ugandan graduates from Chinese universities. *Higher Education Policy, 33*, 459–477. https://doi.org/10.1057/s41307-019-00174-w

O'Reilly, A., Ryan, D., & Hickey, T. (2010). The psychological well-being and sociocultural adaptation of short-term international students in Ireland. *Journal of College Student Development,* 51(5), 584-598. https://doi:10.1353/csd.2010.0011.

Peräkylä, A., & Ruusuvuori, J. (2008). Analyzing talk and text. In N. K. Denzin & Y. S. Lincoln (Eds.), *Collecting and interpreting qualitative materials* (3rd ed., pp. 351–374). SAGE.

Robertson, M., Line, M., Jones, S., & Thomas, S. (2000). International students, learning environments and perceptions: A case study using the Delphi technique. *Higher educationresearch&development,*19(1),89-102. https://doi.org/10.1080/07294360050020499

Saito, M. (1996). Comparative studies on color preference in Japan and other Asian regions, with special emphasis on the preference for white. *Color Research & Application,* 21(1), 35–49.

Shuo, Z. (2019, July 31). Beijing and Shanghai among 40 top cities for international students. *China Daily.* http://www.chinadaily.com.cn/a/201907/31/WS5d415e1da310d830564020ab.html

Steup, M., & Neta, R. (2005). Epistemology. In E. N. Zalta (Ed.), *Stanford Encyclopedia of Philosophy* (Spring 2014 ed.). https://plato.stanford.edu/archives/fall2020/entries/epistemology/

Study International. (2020, January 20). *There are more African students than ever in China. Why are they still alienated?* https://www.studyinternational.com/news/african-students-china-alienated/

Tian, M., & Lowe, J. (2018). International student recruitment as an exercise in soft power: A case study of undergraduate medical students at a Chinese university. In *International students in China* (pp. 221–248). Palgrave Macmillan. https://doi.org/10.1007/978-3-319-78120-4_10

Torres, K. (2009). 'Culture shock': Black students account for their distinctiveness at an elite college. *Ethnic and Racial Studies, 32*(5), 883–905. https://doi.org/10.1080/01419870701710914

Wen, W., Hu, D., & Hao, J. (2018). International students' experiences in China: Does the planned reverse mobility work? *International Journal of Educational Development, 61*, 204–212. https://doi.org/10.1016/j.ijedudev.2017.03.004

Xinhua. (2020). *More foreign students come to study in Beijing.* http://www.xinhuanet.com/english/2020-09/06/c_139347503.htm

Yang, H., Harlow, S., Maddux, C., & Smaby, M. (2006). The impact of cross-cultural experiences on the worldviews of Chinese international students. *Counselling and Values, 51*(1), 21–38. https://doi.org/10.1002/j.2161-007X.2006.tb00063.x

Zha, Q. (2015, August 16). The good, bad, and ugly dimensions of Chinese Education. *Inside Higher Ed.* https://www.insidehighered.com/blogs/worldview/good-bad-and-ugly-dimensions-Chinese-education

Author Bio

RAYMOND AGYENIM-BOATENG is a PhD candidate at the Department of Applied Psychology at Lingnan University, pursuing research at the intersection of social cognition and intergroup relations for his PhD. He is also interested in research on diversity and inclusion in global higher education and the experiences of African international students in China. Email: raymondowusubaoteng@ln.hk

Article

© *Journal of International Students*
Volume 12, Issue 4 (2022), pp. 995-1018
ISSN: 2162-3104 (Print), 2166-3750 (Online)
https://doi.org/10.32674/jis.v12i4.2193
ojed.org/jis

Conflict Resolution Skills of Chinese International Students in the United States

Zhiwei Wang
Shenzhen Polytechnic, China

Qijun Zhu
St. Thomas University, USA

Ke Dong
University College London, UK

ABSTRACT

The number of Chinese international students in the United States has dramatically been increasing for the past two decades, while little is known about how these Chinese students handle campus conflicts in the United States. With an interpretative phenomenological research methodology, we invited 10 Chinese students at three different universities in the United States to share their experiences and strategies in resolving campus disputes. Five themes emerged based on the experiences of research participants. The findings strongly indicate that conflict management strategies and styles of Chinese students are significantly shaped by Chinese culture, and Chinese international students are less likely to express their needs and negative feelings. According to findings, this study suggests that more attention and resources of student help centers should be allocated to Chinese international students in the United States for improving their learning experiences.

Keywords: Chinese international students, conflict resolution skills, qualitative study

American universities have a much more diverse student body than at any previous time (Urban & Palmer, 2016). An increasing number of international students are studying at thousands of colleges in all 50 U.S. states, greatly contributing to the diversity and internationalization of classrooms, campuses, and communities (Altbach & Knight, 2007; Wu et al., 2015). According to data released by Institute of International Education (IIE, 2021), for the past decade, the total number of international students in the United States increased from 690,923 in 2009 to 1,075,496 in the academic year 2019–2020, almost doubling. The increasing number of international students has cultural influences on the United States. Not only can international students greatly contribute to the diversity and academic prestige of American universities, but domestic students are also able to take advantage of the diversity of their campuses (Carnevale, 1999). For example, American domestic students can have a deeper understanding of cultural sensitivities and acquire communication skills through working with international students (Calleja, 2000; Perry, 2016).

The number of Chinese students made up the largest portion of all international students studying in the United States and accounted for 32.5% of the total population in the academic year 2016–2017 (IIE, 2017). The passion and enthusiasm of Chinese students for pursuing their overseas education can in part be understood from the competitive job market, as data show that over 98% of Chinese workers aspire to gain a higher level of education for improving their professional skills and becoming more competitive in the Chinese job market (Wenting, 2017). Among many different choices, the United States is one of the most ideal countries for pursuing quality education as many Chinese students are deeply attracted by American culture and the American education system, which offers international students many different academic programs at all levels (Chen & Jordan, 2016). However, earning a degree as an international student is surely not an easy endeavor. It is more so for many Chinese students studying in the United States, where they have to overcome many challenges such as cultural differences, language barriers, and homesickness. Many researchers (e.g., McClure, 2007; Msengi, 2003; Poyrazli & Lopez, 2007; Wadsworth et al., 2008; Unruh, 2015) have studied a series of serious challenges often encountered by international students. Among empirical work on challenges faced by international students, the cultural adaptation experiences of Chinese international students have been extensively explored (see Gill, 2007; Li, 2016; Yuan, 2011), but few research studies look at how Chinese students deal with disputes and conflict at American institutions to achieve their academic success.

Campus conflict plays a critical role in influencing students' learning experiences. When Chinese students do not get along with domestic students or their professors, it diminishes the potential for their success. Not only are the Chinese students involved often unable to concentrate on their coursework, but teachers must spend extra time and energies dealing with those in conflict (Johnson, 2005). Holzinger (2004) distinguished three different types of conflict according to the substance of conflict, which respectively is conflict over facts, over values, and over interests. The last two types are often faced by Chinese students in the United States as their cultural backgrounds lead them to have different value systems from the Americans. Although campus conflict is ubiquitous among Chinese students, American domestic students, and American professors, it can be effectively managed through conflict resolution skills and strategies. Any attempt to resolve a conflict or to terminate a dispute will usually be accompanied by communication skills wherein involved parties learn from their past experiences and their culture. The absence of studying conflict resolution skills of Chinese students in the United States makes understandings inadequate of how to better drive Chinese students to succeed in the United States. The goal of this study was to fill this literature gap with an interpretative phenomenological research approach, so a more comprehensive understanding of how Chinese students at American universities resolve classroom conflict with peers and faculty could be built.

LITERATURE REVIEW

There are four components in the following literature review. First, we discuss general challenges for international students in the United States. We introduce some empirical research findings on the difficulties of international students in the United States. We then analyze the unique challenges for Chinese students studying in the United States, considering the distinctive challenges Chinese students face based on their cultural backgrounds, as well as general challenges faced by all international students such as language barriers. We also present the features of Chinese culture and how it shapes Chinese students' behaviors. Then, we review the conflict management styles developed by Thomas and Kilmann (1974) and further examine how to understand the conflict resolution behaviors of Chinese students in the United States. Last, we address the campus conflict resolution systems of some American universities. The literature review section covers the causes of campus conflict for international students and generalizes conflict resolution strategies and resources of which Chinese students may take advantage.

Challenges for International Students

Many research studies have addressed the academic cross-cultural adjustment of international students (e.g., Barratt & Huba, 1994; Bauer & Picciotto, 2013; Bochner, 1985; Briguglio, 2000; Paez, 1985; Unruh, 2015). Barratt and Huba (1994) argued that international students who were less fluent in English normally experienced greater challenges in adapting to American higher education. The results of this study were repeated by the findings of many other scholars such as Liu (2011), Paze (1985), Poyrazli and Lopez (2007), and Probertson et al. (2000), who all argued that international students with weak English language skills were more likely to encounter social and academic problems. For example, they hardly made local American friends but more easily got involved in unexpected conflict with local students because of misunderstandings caused by language barriers. In addition, lack of English proficiency is one of the main sources of conflict between international students and their advisors and instructors (Liu, 2011; Probertson et al., 2000; Terui, 2011). Liu (2011) examined her personal experiences to discuss the negative effects that the language barrier caused in hampering relationships between her and her instructors during her learning journey as an international student in an English-speaking country. Some scholars (e.g., Brigulio, 2000; Habib et al., 2014) further argued that different educational styles also play an important role in causing misunderstandings between international students and their instructors. For example, in western universities, instructors often encourage students to express their thoughts in class while many international students feel uncomfortable speaking and discussing their opinions in the classroom (Brigulio, 2000). Some international students, with their cultural concerns, even believed that they may cause negative feelings of other classmates if they answered questions in the classroom too often (Brigulio, 2000). Based on their qualitative study, Wu et al. (2015) argued that transition difficulties and cultural difference present a major problem that many international students in the United States have to solve for achieving better learning experiences, but at the same time, they also believed that these difficulties have some positive effects on international students, such as motivating them to integrate themselves into American culture.

Unique Challenges for Chinese Students

Chinese students in American universities often face difficulties and challenges that they have to skillfully resolve to achieve academic success. Lack of English proficiency, cultural differences, and unfamiliarity with the American classroom environment often catch them in unpleasant situations, even conflict, with their classmates and faculty members

(Hsieh, 2007; Y. Huang, 2012; Sun & Chen, 1999;). Based on a case study exploring a Chinese student's experiences in the United Statets, Hsieh (2007) argued that some Chinese students were isolated and often felt ignored by American students because of cultural differences. Indeed, many Chinese students in the United States suffer significantly from a high level of academic stress due to ineffective interactions with American professors and academic advisors (Yan & Berliner, 2009). Valdez (2015) found, with the qualitative double consciousness approach, that many Chinese students in the United States believed that American faculty members, advisors, and students had negative perceptions and bias against Chinese students. Moreover, the problem of English listening is especially a huge obstacle in making some Chinese students less confident and thus negatively influences the use of their conflict resolution skills at American universities, discouraging them from seeking resources offered by American universities to resolve their classroom conflicts (J. Huang, 2006).

Chinese culture is a distinctive type of high contextual culture in which the traditional value systems along with collectivism have tremendously shaped the Chinese society where being humble is always promoted (Hanzan & Shi, 2009; Hofstede, 1991), so Chinese students are more likely to show agreement at the thoughts of others and avoid arguing with peers and instructors in the classroom. Also, during the conflict resolution process, Chinese people are always encouraged to conduct self-criticism and apologize first to earn others' respect (Fei, 1993; Perkovich, 1996). Conducting self-criticism is one of the central ideas promoted by Confucianism that has had a long-lasting influence on Chinese culture. Confucianism stresses the harmony of the community. The essence of self-criticism is to educate disputants to not think about other's mistakes, but to focus only on what they have done wrong. In contrast, American students are encouraged to express their thoughts in public and firmly defend their stances (Hofstede, 1991). Also, self-criticism is not a common practice in the American conflict resolution process, which pays great attention to fair procedures to identify a mutually acceptable outcome (Moore, 2003). Hence, when Chinese students in the United States encounter classroom disputes with American classmates or instructors, their conflict resolution experiences acquired in China may not be effective.

Conflict Management Styles

One of the most widely cited definitions of conflict given by Rubin et al. (1994) describes conflict as "perceived divergence of interests, or a belief that parties' current aspirations can not be achieved simultaneously" (p. 5). Conflict is unavoidable and inherent in any interpersonal relationship, but it can be managed with decreased odds of nonproductive escalation (Katz & Lawyer, 1993). Thomas and Kilmann (1974) developed a conflict-handling model that used two parameters, cooperation and assertiveness, to create five distinct styles: avoiding, competing, collaborating, accommodating, and compromising. The following is the figure of the model.

Figure 1. The Conflict-Handling Style (Thomas & Kilmann, 1974).

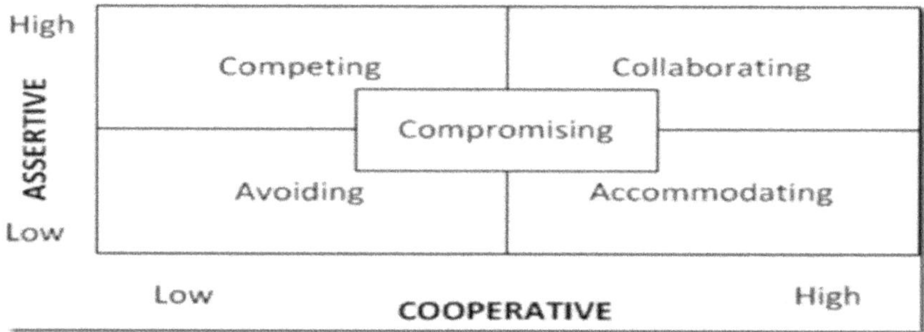

According to Thomas and Kilmann (1974), the avoiding style is when people just simply avoid the issue. People in this style do not help the other party reach their goals, and they do not assertively pursue their own goals. The accommodating style refers to people who cooperate to a high degree at the cost of sacrificing their own goals and desired outcomes. The collaborating style means that people partner with the other party to achieve both of their goals. The competing style is the "win-lose" approach. People with this style normally act in a very assertive way to achieve their goals and they do not cooperate with others. The compromising style is the "lose-lose" scenario where neither party really achieves what they want.

When applying the conflict managing styles of Chinese students in the United States to the conflict handling model, there are some salient features. Culturally, Chinese students pay greater attention to long-term relationships, so their styles, arguably, tend to be more cooperating and accommodating. However, culture is not a fixed thing attaching people forever, and people can change their cultural predisposition over time. . If Chinese students in the United States learn that being more assertive and tougher to their classmates and professors may result in a better outcome in practice, they may gradually adjust their conflict managing strategies. Thus, their experiences of handling campus conflict in the United States along with their cultural background are critical in forming their conflict styles that guide their behaviors and strategies in resolving conflicts.

Campus Conflict Resolution Systems

Although classroom conflict is a natural occurrence on college campuses, some American universities have started providing mediation and consulting services to decrease the number of campus dispute cases for the past several decades (Katz, 2016; Warters, 2011). However, many international students do not take advantage of these campus services and the underutilization of conflict resolution services by international students has been studied in some academic reports (e.g., Russell et al., 2008). When it comes to Asian students in the United States, the situation gets worse. In terms of the nature of high-context culture in the conflict resolution process, Asian people are more likely to solve problems independently to maintain a strong and positive self-image (Augsburger, 1995; Heggins & Jackon, 2003). Compared with other international students, Chinese international students have fewer experiences in seeking help from various service centers as mediation and counseling services at school are highly unpopular in China (Hou & Zhang, 2007). Lack of experience with campus counseling services may further make Chinese students less likely to seek resources of American universities to deal with their classroom conflicts, while seeking help from mediation centers can benefit Chinese students in many ways. On one hand, Chinese students can learn and improve conflict resolution skills at these mediation centers. On the other hand, by interacting with the staff of mediation centers, Chinese students can have a deeper understanding of American culture and may further integrate themselves into the American learning community.

Research Questions

Previous research studies on Chinese international students have mainly aimed at their psychological stress, English deficiency, cultural transition, and academic difficulties, focusing on the negative experiences of Chinese students, while there is a clear research gap of understanding the conflict resolution skills of Chinese international students in American universities. The ability to resolve disputes for Chinese students in the United States is crucial because it can play a decisive role in influencing their academic performance in many cases. The goal of this study intended to fill the academic gap by examining both the positive and negative experiences of Chinese students in applying conflict resolution skills to achieve their academic success. Thus, the research questions of this study are as follows:

- RQ1: What conflict resolution skills do Chinese students use in the United States?
- RQ2: What kind of conflict resolution resources do Chinese students seek in the United States?

METHOD

In order to achieve a deeper understanding of what conflict resolution skills and strategies Chinese international students at American universities use for cross-cultural adjustment and academic achievement, we used an interpretative phenomenological research approach to allow Chinese students in the United States to give meanings of their lived experiences. Certain conditions regarding the experiences of Chinese students require the use of a qualitatively interpretative phenomenological methodology. First, phenomenological research methods help stitch together diverse perspectives on a single phenomenon to transfer the meaning of an experience to others (Moustakas, 1994), so it is fitting for the research questions of this study which examine the dispute resolution skills and experiences of Chinese students in the United States. Additionally, an interpretative phenomenological analysis allows us to explore the subjective interpersonal experiences of Chinese students in the United States (Pietkiewicz & Smith, 2014), increasing substantial understandings of researching subjects.

Participants

Following the requirement of the interpretative phenomenological analysis that samples should be small and homogenous, we recruited 10 Chinese students. The participants in this study were identified as Chinese students currently studying at American universities. Chinese international students who had graduated from an American university before December 2018 were not qualified. We chose these Chinese participants purposefully, recruiting them through the our personal networks. We sent an informed consent agreement to each participant at a preliminary stage so all participants were well informed of the purpose of this study. All participants were from three different universities in South Florida—one public university and two private universities. All three universities are research universities that offer doctoral programs. The student size of each of the three universities is over 10,000 people, which means that participants were more likely to experience a bigger class size and had more chances to interact with American domestic students. Eight participants were from graduate programs and two were undergraduates. Although all participants were in their 20s, the oldest participant was 9 years older than the youngest one. The rationale for the sampling is that the 20s age group takes the largest proportion of Chinese students in the United States among all age groups. Also, the number of Chinese students studying for a degree at the graduate level is much more than the number pursuing a bachelor's degree in the United States. Participants' majors ranged from social sciences to technology. The gender ratio of participants was seven women and three men. Almost all participants were from big cities in China. Their names are anonymous in this study for confidentiality.

Table 1. Demographic Characteristics of Study Participants

Name	Gender	Age	Years in the U.S.	Major	Interview length (minutes)
Participant A	Female	Late 20s	3	Mathematics	52
Participant B	Female	Mid 20s	4	Conflict Resolution	53
Participant C	Male	Mid 20s	6	Business	72
Participant D	Female	Early 20s	1	Biology	55
Participant E	Male	Early 20s	2	Engineering	63
Participant F	Female	Mid 20s	4	Accounting	56
Participant G	Female	Mid 20s	4	Business	54
Participant H	Female	Early 20s	5	Psychology	55
Participant I	Male	Early 20s	5	Oceanology	58
Participant J	Female	Late 20s	3	Family therapy	52

Procedure

There were three steps for data collection. The first stage was a preliminary stage at which we sent informed consent agreement to all 10 participants, so they were able to learn the purpose, importance, and benefits of this study. We also held several informal, face-to-face meetings at the preliminary stage to build rapport with the participants in a cafe or a conference room, based on participants' requests. We also learned more detailed background information during this preliminary stage. These informal and face-to-face meetings served as an ice-breaking process for helping participants to have a better understanding of this study, allowing more productive conversations to take place at coming formal interviews.

In the second stage we used semistructured, open-ended interviews from January to March 2019 that were 50–60 minutes long. We interviewed five participants at their home, four participants in a classroom, and one participant at a café. Although the planned time for each interview was 1 hour, we gave extra time if participants wanted to share more information. Thus, one interview was 72 minutes long. To secure the accuracy of data, we conducted all interviews in Chinese, which made participants more comfortable. We recorded all interviews with the participants' permission.

At the last stage, we conducted follow-up interviews with all participants through either phone calls or face-to-face meetings to verify the accuracy of the data, depending on the availability of participants. The follow-up interviews were relatively short, about 10 to 15 minutes long. The subsequent interviews allowed us to produce more detailed explanations from participants, and we discussed anything that was not clear from the previous discussions. Through a three-stage data collection process, we secured richness and validity of data.

Analysis

We read all interviews carefully to make sure that the meanings of participants were 100% understood and fully interpreted before we translated from Chinese to English verbatim. The 10 interviews produced over 100 pages of research data. Following the rules of coding of the interpretative phenomenological analysis process (Smith et al., 2009), each researcher first put words having the same meanings in groups independently and we then met to discuss findings together. We discarded low frequency groups or combined them into superordinate themes. As all the researchers in this study are Chinese native speakers, we were able to catch the covered meanings hidden in words with our own explanations.

Credibility and Subjectivity

To ensure this study's credibility, we used triangulation involving cross-checking of both the transcribed interview data and the audio-recorded data. Two of three researchers checked the similar data generated across both sources, as both measures are integral to corroborating what the research participants had contributed to this study. Also, as all three researchers have a Chinese cultural background, it is impossible to be completely objective. However, we made concerted efforts to keep our thoughts and biases hidden, not negatively influencing the interview and data analysis process. Nevertheless, we may have still interpreted research data with our personal experiences. Thus, after the data analysis process, we shared the research findings with participants to see if we misinterpreted their meanings and thoughts. Participants confirmed that the transcripts had accurately captured their opinions, and the essence of their discussions has been effectively depicted.

Positionality

Positionality is integral to qualitative research, as it can impact all aspects and stages of the research process (Holmes, 2020). In this study, we played both insider and outsider roles from the data collection to the data interpretation. As all three researchers of this study are Chinese, as insiders, our cultural background allows us to ask more meaningful and insightful questions. We could better find nonverbal cues and the hidden meaning of some Chinese words that "outsiders" of the culture may have difficulty perceiving. However, we fully realized the disadvantages of being "insiders" to the research study, so we manipulated our positionality with some strategies. For example, in the process of designing the questionnaire for interviewees, we double-checked questions for latent biased possibility. For another example, during the interview, when participants answered questions like "you are Chinese, and you were an international student before, so you should know how it feels," we reminded the research participants of the goals and tasks of the study. Thus, information that the participants thought obvious to "insiders" was still explained and discussed. Although we tried to straddle both positions with strategies, the joint knowledge-producing process of this study leans toward the "insider" position. Thus, the findings of this study may fall more in the lens of the Chinese culture.

RESULTS

In this section, we present five themes identified in this study: managing conflict at an earlier stage; seeking suggestions from older Chinese people; keeping distances from American peers, advisers, and instructors; bringing gifts to develop relations; and apologizing first to earn others' respect.

Managing Conflict at an Earlier Stage

We found that all Chinese participants believed that conflict should be managed at an earlier stage before escalation and eruption. However, as to how to skillfully avoid or manage a classroom conflict, different participants have applied different strategies in terms of their different personalities and gender. Two outgoing, talkative, male participants shared their past experiences in actively seeking a chance to discuss with their peers in a polite but cautious way to avoid the escalation of the conflict. They believed that the earlier people address problems, the less likely people would be bothered by latent conflict.

> You have to tell them your feelings at the very beginning. If you do not tell them and just hide your anger, your anger will outbreak one day and put you in trouble. I got experiences. I am from Chongqing and you know people from Chongqing are simple and

straight. Thus, my experiences tell me if I am not happy with something, I have to tell my American classmates or friends directly. Let me take an example for you. One of my classmates joked about my name in a way that I dislike in front of several other classmates, so I immediately told him how I felt like in private. He said sorry and he never did it again. (Participant C)

Yes, I did have few minor problems with American classmates which had been solved. You know I am good at Mathematics, so some classmates just wanted to plagiarize my homework. I knew their heavy pressures, but it is dangerous. I do not want to be expelled from my university. Thus, now I tell those friends who want to take advantage of my assignments very clearly, I would not lend them my assignments. But instead, I can teach them, so they can learn mathematics from me and I can improve my English by teaching them. Hence, my experiences are that you have to tell your rules to American friends when you just know them. You can express it jokingly, but make them realize where your bottom-line is. I think that it can help avoid latent conflict. (Participant E)

In contrast, several Chinese participants would not actively seek a straightforward conversation to address problems with their peers and instructors, but they all discussed their experiences and concluded that escaping from a latent conflict at an earlier stage is a good strategy that can save them from any possible hurt. In the case of Participants B, F, and G, their experiences showed that avoidance or stopping further contact with American peers at an earlier stage of conflict helped them deescalate the fuses of conflict.

One of my classmates got biases on me. She thought she got stronger English writing and speaking skills so she would not partner me on an assignment when a professor put her and me in a team randomly. She cared about her grades, so did I. Then, she started asking the progress on my part of the assignment by texting messages to me a couple of times. I quickly replied to her that we should not be on the same team and I proposed that we should re-choose our partners. She was happy with that, as I made my decision very fast and helped her save enough time to choose a new partner. You have to do it fast and react appropriately when something bad comes to you (Participant B)

> I knew my ex-classmate was mean and I could tell it at the beginning. He was a lazy guy and when we were on the same team, he did nothing. As I knew his personality was just like that, I avoided talking to him as much as possible at the beginning and just smiled at him. If you did not provoke them, they would not argue with you. Thus, at the very beginning, I told myself that I needed to handle the assignment by myself. When I told myself so and adjusted my moods, everything was better. (Participant G)

Participant D even expressed the importance of the first impression. She believed that classroom conflict is a cultural concept to her. On a few occasions, she experienced misunderstandings either caused by cultural differences between the United States and China or the language barrier, but she immediately explained or apologized to comfort others.

> Believe or not, I know who can be my friends at first glance. Some Americans like Chinese culture, some do not like and it is common. I always smile to other classmates and instructors first so they can feel my politeness at our first meeting. As an international Chinese student in their country, you also have to care about their feelings. I know a Chinese girl in our major. She often asked Americans some private stuff that was not supposed to ask in terms of American culture. I dislike her. When I made the same mistake and caused their resentment, I explained it immediately. It is always good to eliminate misunderstandings as soon as possible. (Participant D)

Keeping Distance from American Peers, Advisers, and Instructors.
Of All 10 participants, only one (Participant E) clearly explained that he had high self-confidence in his English proficiency and spent more time with American peers than Chinese students at school and was able to build good relationships with American peers and instructors. All other Chinese participants viewed keeping distance with American peers and instructors as a good strategy to avoid conflict, and they illustrated this idea with different experiences in detail. Participants A and B believed that studying in the United States was merely a step of their whole life, so by keeping distance from Americans, the possibility of getting involved in conflict was lower.

> I do not think our lives are closely related. I mean, me and my American classmates. Once I finish this program and earn my degree, I will go back to China and get a job in Beijing. There were

no many common topics among me and Americans. If something happens between me and an American classmates, it must be something bad. Thus, I believe that I should not get closer to American classmates. My goal is to get a job in China after graduation. I just study here and I would not bother them and I hope they do not bother me either. (Participant A)

You got bored and stereotyping people all around the world, not just in the U.S. There are many boring and mean people in China too, so my understandings and experiences of conflict resolution are, do not even talk to them. Especially in the U.S., keeping distance and being cautious with Americans are always good. Look at what happened to other Chinese international students, Zhangyingying, for example. They should not trust strangers. If you do not talk to them, they got no chance to hurt you. (Participant B)

Zhangyingying was a young Chinese scholar at the University of Illinois at Urbana who was abducted and killed by Brendt Allen Christensen in 2017 (Rhodes et al., 2017). Participants D, F, and H had negative experiences with a few American advisers and professors with some academic issues, but in their understanding, American advisers and professors were at higher social rankings than they were, so they thought that getting out of touch with those problematic advisers and professors was a better choice for deescalating disputes and conflicts. Participants D and H even stressed repeatedly how important an American degree was to them, and they did not want to mess with academic professors and advisers and just wanted to study and earn their degree quietly.

Many professors at this institution got problems. They were bad at teaching but good at researching. This institution was classified as a research university, so I felt like professors were more interested into researching than teaching. One professor even used the wrong materials on Blackboard. When I told our program coordinator, the professor said it was his TA's fault. What was worst, he knew that it was me to rat him out. I could feel he treated me a little bit differently. Therefore, I would not say any more to our program adviser and I did not want to get trouble and I just wanted to get my degree. My strategy was simple, keep distance and being invisible. (Participant D)

One of my instructors got attitude problems. Whenever I asked her questions, she thought that was my problem. She thought I was too stupid to understand her course, but actually, she did not explain everything clearly in her course. I was not the only one in her class who got this feeling. She even insulted me. I mean, not every openly, but I could tell her contempt. However, what can I do? I just avoided taking her course again. I knew irresponsible teachers like her exist in many universities and I was just not lucky. I wanted to graduate and I did not want to get involved in trouble. (Participant H)

Apologizing First to Earn Others' Respect and Understanding

Findings showed that when the participants were involved in an argument or experienced an unpleasant quarrel with their classmates or instructors, apologizing first was one of the most frequent conflict resolution skills that they were likely to use. Seven out of 10 participants shared their experiences of applying apology first to handle the difficult conversations with American classmates or instructors. Although participants who regarded apologizing first as a conflict resolution strategy had different opinions on how effective the strategy is in resolving conflicts, they all believed that apologizing first could at least build a bridge for resolutions. Participant D stated her points as follows:

Before I left China, my mom told me to be polite and nice to American classmates. Thus, I believe that if I say sorry first, it delivers a sign of good faith to my classmates...from my experiences, I know when people are in a quarrel, they are emotional and angry, so an apology may help ease their emotion.

One participant shared his personal experiences to explain the effectiveness of apology first.

I borrowed my classmate's notebook and took it home, but I did not know she so cared about it and wanted me to give it back to her on the next day. We did not have class the next day and that was why I kept it for a few days. When other classmates mentioned that she was not happy with that, I immediately apologized to her first and returned her notebook. I think that if you sincerely apologize first, they can feel it. Now, we are still friends, it is a good way to get you out of some embarrassing situations. (Participant I)

The other participant discussed why she chose to apologize first to her classmates from a different angle. She believed that apologizing first could help build a good self-image and earn others' respect and support.

> We can never win from a quarrel with local students, as English is not our native language. Thus, apologizing first and say something that they want to hear to end the conversation is a smarter choice, is not it? If you have different issues and opinions, you do not have to speak it out. You can keep it in your heart and do things in your way. However, in the classroom, you should be nice and most importantly, make them realize that you are nice and polite. Apologizing first to the person who emotionally roars at you can beautify your own image and earn others' respect and support. (Participant J)

Seeking Suggestions from Older Chinese People in the United States

When we asked Chinese participants what kind of resources they relied on for resolving conflict, all participants mentioned their connections with other Chinese people and the Chinese community with different evaluations on the effectiveness of support and suggestions provided by the Chinese community. Some participants (Participants B, D, F, H, and G) relied highly on support and suggestions from the Chinese community in the United States, and they not only sought suggestions for resolving disputes, but they also learned other information, experiences, and knowledge from other older Chinese people such as housing and insurance information.

> Of course, I have to ask for help from a Chinese schoolmate if I am involved in a dispute with my American peers or professors. It is nothing wrong to learn about their experiences. I trusted the Chinese more, because they can understand me better. Their suggestions were helpful and they introduced new friends to me. For example, before I took courses, I always asked other Chinese people who had taken those courses, listening to their feedback on the academic performance of professors teaching those courses. For another example, I got my package lost and I was very angry and I asked other Chinese people for help. They accompanied me to the post office and I got my compensation for the lost package. Thus, it is good to live with Chinese people and listen to their suggestions which can help you save time and money. (Participant B)

Participants F and G would not share bad news with their families in

China as they did not want their family to worry about them. Thus, when they were involved in school conflict with American classmates and/or instructors, asking help from the Chinese community in their eyes seemed to be the only possible resource that they could use.

> My mother always thought too much. She texted me almost every day, so I would not let her know my unhappiness. Last time I got a quarrel with my American roommate. She did not like me and she often went to night clubs in the middle of the night. Then, I asked how other Chinese people handle situations like this and I learned a lot. I mean, although their suggestions may not all be good, some were helpful. In the end, I moved out and lived with a Chinese girl who is a hard working student. That was good. See, although their suggestions may not be useful, you still learned other information that helped you. For some people, you do not need to resolve your issues, but just keep some distance with them. You can choose to live with the people whom you like. (Participant F).

Other Chinese participants (Participants A, C, and E) believed that although support from Chinese people may have only played a minor role in helping them resolve classroom conflict, it was better than nothing. Their experiences of seeking help from other Chinese people were all positive, but not effective in dealing with causes of conflict.

> Yes, I asked other Chinese when I got a quarrel with other Americans. I guess that every Chinese international student did the same. It was normal. We are foreigners and are not familiar with American culture and regulations. The reason why I did ask for help from program advisers, but from other Chinese was because I was worried if the conflict got escalated if program advisors handled it. I wanted to put it down, but not heat it up. (Participant A).

Bringing Gifts to Develop Relationships

Interestingly, this theme in the research study explored the fact that most Chinese participants are naturally born diplomats who would like to spend time and money to build relationships with their classmates and professors who are important or have negative views on them. Eight out of 10 research participants admitted that they had offered gifts to either their classmates or professors to develop good relationships. The participants believed that bringing gifts changed the attitude of people who did not like them, so it was a good strategy in conflict resolution.

> I used to give a box of Chinese tea to a professor who did not like me. I submitted his assignment late once so he thought that I am a lazy student and he kept one eye on me and got a stricter requirement. Then, I stopped by his office with a box of Chinese tea before thanksgiving and we talked a little bit. It worked. I can feel that he changed his attitude a little bit to me after that. For example, the words he used in his feedback on my assignment were more encouraging. (Participant C)

> Giving a gift is one of the fastest ways to make you closer to the people and eliminate misunderstandings, so I did use this stunt to re-develop relationships. I had given lots of gifts to my advisers, professors, classmates, schoolmates. Just like the old Chinese sayings, people like you when you give gifts to them. (Participant I)

DISCUSSION

The findings of this study are relatively rich. On one hand, the findings repeated the patterns of previous studies analyzing negative factors of Chinese students in handling campus conflict in the United States. On the other hand, this study explores new facts that previous scholars in the field have not paid attention to. Previous studies (e.g., Mitchell et al., 2007) have found that international students at American universities were less likely to seek suggestions and consulting services when getting involved in school conflict, compared with American students. This pattern was also confirmed repeatedly in this study. The pattern of conflict resolution skills and experiences of Chinese students in the United States could be understood through a cultural lens where Markus and Kitayama (1991) argued that in collective cultures such as the Chinese culture, people are not encouraged to directly ask for help but are encouraged to imagine what another might want. Chinese students thus prefer to express their feelings and emotion in a more indirect way, and as the findings reveal, they prefer to give gifts to show their goodwill, but not speak out. In contrast, American students have the freedom to seek help in American culture . Therefore, Chinese students at American universities are more likely in a disadvantageous position in a conflict resolution process, as they may not express themselves very clearly.

However, Chinese students in the United States, according to the stories and experiences of participants in this study, have distinctively effective strategies in solving campus disputes with American peers and professors, such as resolving conflict at an earlier stage and bringing gifts to build relationships. Resolving conflict at an earlier stage means that Chinese students have to identify the source of the conflict and look beyond the incident to the essence of the conflict. Identifying the causing factors of conflict is hard, but the identities of Chinese students in the United States have helped make them more culturally sensitive to latent factors that may lead to unexpected situations. Apologizing first as a strategy in the conflict resolution toolbox of Chinese students could be explained through cultural differences, as keeping the harmony of the community has always been an important concept in Chinese culture (Hanzan & Shi, 2009). Interestingly, Chinese people are always encouraged to apologize first by Confucianism, so it also reveals that Confucianism still plays a role in guiding the behaviors of Chinese students in the United States. Additionally, giving gifts to develop relationships is a soft and flexible strategy in dealing with conflict. It again shows that Chinese students prefer to apply relatively soft strategies in managing unpleasant situations.

The findings of this study also describe the conflict managing styles of Chinese students in the United States. Overall, the conflict managing styles of Chinese students were less competitive, as there was no theme falling into the competing category. Facing campus disputes, some Chinese students used the avoiding style, as they wanted to keep a distance from their peers, and even from instructors in some cases. Other Chinese students had more positive styles such as the collaborating style, as they cared about long-term relationships with their peers and wanted to maintain the relationships by giving gifts. Interestingly, the "win-lose" model is always criticized and discouraged in the Chinese traditional culture, so the conflict styles of Chinese students were highly similar to the norms and strategies promoted by Chinese culture. For example, a famous Chinese old saying says "avoiding is always better than fighting." Thus, it may in part explain why some Chinese students like to use the avoiding style when having a campus conflict.

The findings of this study strongly indicate that more resources and attention to mediation and consulting centers at American universities need to be given to international students, especially for Chinese students who are less likely to express their needs, stress, and other negative personal feelings. Stronger relationships among Chinese students and their academic program advisers need to be further developed, so these consulting centers and mediation service systems at American universities could really work for help. Working with Chinese students requires rich cultural sensitivity of university staff and instructors. Seeking suggestions and information from older Chinese people as a conflict resolution skill could be understood through uncertainty reduction theory (Berger & Calabrese, 1975; Kramer, 1999; Redmond, 2015), which assumes if people face much uncertainty, they have to seek information more actively to reduce their questions and uncertainty. The findings also suggest that more mediators, advisers, and consultants with Asian/Chinese background may be recruited into various service centers and international offices of American universities so Chinese students are more willing to share their concerns with the staff of these service centers.

In the present study, the lack of interaction with American peers has been addressed as a conflict resolution skill, but it is *de facto* extremely negative for Chinese students' cultural integration. One Chinese participant even thought that her lifestyle in the United States was somewhat similar to studying in China as all people around her were Chinese and she barely got a chance to speak English on a daily basis. Thus, how to skillfully help the large number of Chinese students get integrated into the American learning community remains a difficult question for many American universities and urgently calls for a course of effective actions. At the same time, there is some good news in this study. Some Chinese participants realized that a conflict resolution process could be a good chance to redevelop their relationships with American peers, advisers, and professors, as they learned in practice that apologizing first and bringing gifts to their classmates and professors who used to have problems with them can help change the relationships. Some strategies learned from Chinese culture do help them resolve campus conflict in the United States.

Limitations and Future Research

While this study was confined to Chinese students at three American universities in Florida, it provides direction and insight for future research to build upon. The sample size can be accepted as a good number for an interpretative phenomenological research study, as an overlarge sample size can hinder phenomenological studies and should normally be avoided (Smith et al., 2009).

Due to the issues addressed in this study, we believe that additional issues related to the school conflict resolution experiences of Chinese international students at American universities need to be further investigated. Unfortunately, the number of both qualitatively and quantitatively academic research studies on the lived experiences of Chinese international students on American campuses is still small (Bertram et al., 2014; Lertora et al., 2017; Yan & Berliner, 2013). More surveys regarding learning and the conflict resolution experiences of Chinese students in the United States should be collected to have a broader and deeper understanding of Chinese students.

To date, there are not many research studies focusing on the unique experiences and strategies of Chinese international students in resolving conflicts. We believe that the findings of this study begin to fill this research gap and allow researchers and educators to better understand both the experiences and the strategies of Chinese students in overcoming campus conflicts to reach their academic success. We also anticipate that this study will help shed a light on studying conflict resolution experiences of international students, so more international students in the United States can be better helped.

REFERENCES

Altbach, P. G., & Knight, J. (2007). The internationalization of higher education: motivation and realities. *Journal of Studies in International Education, 11*(3–4), 290–305.

Augsburger, D. W. (1995). *Conflict mediation across cultures: Pathways and patterns*. Westminster John Knox.

Barratt, M. F., & Huba, M. E. (1994). Factors related to international undergraduate student adjustment in an American community. *The College Student Journal, 28,* 424–436.

Bauer, H., & Picciotto, M. (2013). Writing in America: International students and first-year composition. *Writing on the Edge, 23*(2), 75–86.

Berger, C. R., & Calabrese, R. J. (1975). Some explanations in initial interaction and beyond: Toward a development theory of interpersonal communication. *Human Communication Research, 1*(2), 99–112.

Bertram, D. M., Poulakis, M., Elsasser, B. S., & Kumar, E. (2014). Social support and acculturation in Chinese international students. *Journal Multicultural Counseling & Development, 42*(2), 107–124.

Bochner, S. (1985). The friendship patterns of overseas and host students in Oxford student residence. *Journal of Social Psychology, 125,* 689–694.

Briguglio, C. (2000). Language and cultural issues for English-as-a-second/foreign language students in transnational educational settings. *Higher Education in Europe, 25*(3), 425-434.

Calleja, D. (2000). The world at your door. *Canadian Business, 73*(20), 108–111.

Carnevale, A. P. (1999). Diversity in higher education: Why corporate American cares. *Diversity Digest.* Association of American Colleges and Universities.

Chen, T., & Jordan, M. (2016). Why so many Chinese students come to the US? *The Wall Street Journal.* https://www.wsj.com/articles/why-so-many-chinese-students-come-to-the-u-s-1462123552

Fei, X. (1993). *Rural China and its restoration.* Feng Yun Shi Dai Publisher.

Gill, S. (2007). Overseas students' intercultural adaptation as intercultural learning: A transformative framework. *Compare, 37*(2), 167-183.

Habib, L., Johannesen, M., & Ogrim, L. (2014). Experiences and challenges of international students in technology-rich learning environments. *Journal of Educational Technology & Society, 17*(2), 196–206.

Hanzan, M. D., & Shi, R. (2009). Argument processes, harmony and conflict in Chinese societies. *China Media Research 5*(2), 75–88.

Heggins, W. J., & Jackson, J. F. L. (2003). Understanding the collegiate experience for Asian international students at a Midwestern research university. *College Student Journal, 37,* 379–391.

Hofstede, G. (1991). *Cultures and organizations.* McGraw-Hill.

Holmes, A.G.D. (2020). Researcher positionality, a consideration of its influence and place in qualitative research, a new researcher guide. *Shanlax International Journal of Education, 8*(4), 1–10.

Holzinger, K. (2004). Bargaining through arguing: An empirical analysis based on speech art theory. *Political Communication, 21,* 195–222.

Hou, Z. J., & Zhang, N. (2007). Counseling psychology in China. *Applied Psychology, 56,* 33–50.

Hsieh, M. (2007). Challenges for international students in higher education: One student's narrated story of invisibility and struggle. *College Student Journal, 41*(2), 379–391.

Huang, J. (2006). English abilities for academic listening: How confident are Chinese students? *College Student Journal, 40*(1), 218–226.

Huang, Y. (2012). Transitioning challenges faced by Chinese graduate students. *Adult Learning, 23*(3), 138–147.

Institute of International Education. (2021). *Open Doors Report.* Retrieved March 16, 2022, from https://opendoorsdata.org/data/international-students/enrollment-trends/

Johnson, D. W. (2005). *Teaching students to be peacemakers.* Interaction Book.

Katz, N. H. (2016). Mediation and dispute resolution services in higher education. In A. Georgakopoulos (Ed.), *The mediation handbook: Research, theory, and practice* (pp.176–184). Routledge.

Katz, N. H., & Lawyer, J. W. (1993). *Conflict resolution: Building bridges.* Crowin.

Kramer, M. (1999). Motivation to reduce uncertainty, a reconceptualization of uncertainty reduction theory. *Management Communication Quarterly, 13*(2), 305–316.

Lertora, I. M., Sullivan, J. M., & Croffie, A. L. (2017). They are here, now what do we do? Recommendations for supporting international student transitions. *VISTAS.* https://bit.ly/3AYcC41

Li, Z. (2016). *Chinese international students attending American universities: How can we help you? A qualitative study on Chinese international students' acculturation experiences* [Unpublished doctoral dissertation]. BYU.

Liu, L. (2011). An international graduate student's ESL learning experience beyond the classroom. *TESL Canada Journal, 29*(1), 77–92.

Markus, H. R., & Kitayama, S. (1991). Culture and the self: Implications for cognition, emotion, And motivation. *Psychological Review, 98*(2), 224–253.

McClure, J. W. (2007). International graduates' cross-cultural adjustment: Experiences, coping Strategies, and suggested programmatic responses. *Teaching in Higher Education, 12*(2), 199–217.

Mitchell,S., Greenwood, A., & Guglielmi, M.C. (2007). Utilization of Counseling Services: Comparing International and U.S. College Students. *Journal of College Counseling,10*(2), 117-129.

Moore, C. W. (2003). *The mediation process: practical strategies for resolving conflict.* Jossey-Bass.

Moustakas, C. (1994). *Phenomenological research methods.* SAGE.

Msengi, I. G. (2003). Sources of stress and its impact on health behaviors and academic performance of international students at a comprehensive Midwestern university. *International Journal of Global Health and Health Disparities, 5*(1), 55–69.

Paez, G. S. (1985). *The student service related problems of international and English as a second language students in a selected community college* [Unpublished doctoral dissertation]. University of North Texas.

Perkovich, R. (1996). a comparative analysis of community mediation in the United States and the People's Republic of China. *Temple International and Comparative Law Journal, 10*(2), 313–328.

Perry, C. (2016). Comparing international and American students' challenges: A literature review. *Journal of International Students, 6*(3), 712–721.

Pietkiewicz, I., & Smith, J. A. (2014). A practical guide to using interpretative phenomenological analysis in qualitative research psychology. *Czasopismo Psychologiczne –Psychological Journal, 20*(1), 7–14.

Poyrazli, S., & Lopez, M. D. (2007). An exploratory study of perceived discrimination and homesickness: A comparison of international students and American students. *Journal of Psychology, 141*(3), 263–280.

Probertson, M., Line, M., Jones, S., & Thomas, S. (2000). International students, learning environments and perceptions: a case study using the Delphi technique. *Higher Education Research and Development, 19*(1), 89–102.

Redmond, M. (2015). *Uncertainty reduction theory.* Iowa State University. https://lib.dr.iastate.edu/cgi/

Rhodes, D., Wong, G., & Mccoppin, R. (2017, July 1). Nobody saw this coming: Arrest in Chinese scholar's disappearance stuns U. of I community. *The Chicago Tribune.*

Rubin, D., Pruitt, D., & Kim, S. (1994). *Social conflict: Escalation, stalemate, and settlement.* McGraw-Hill.

Russell, J., Thomson, G., & Rosenthal, D. (2008). International student use of university health and counseling services. *Higher Education, 56,* 59–75.

Smith, J. A., Flower, P., & Larkin, M. (2009). *Interpretative phenomenological analysis: Theory, method and research.* SAGE.

Sun, W., & Chen, G. (1999). Dimensions of difficulties Mainland Chinese students encounter in the United States. *Intercultural Communication Studies, 9*(1), 19–30.

Terui, S. (2011). Second language learners' coping strategy in conversations with native speakers. *Journal of International Students, 2*(2), 168–183.

Thomas, S. W., & Kilmann, R. H. (1974). *Thomas-Kilmann conflict mode instrument.* Mters-Briggs Company.

Unruh, S. (2015). Struggling international students in the United States: Do university faculty know how to help? *Athens Journal of Education, 2*(2), 99–110.

Urban, E., & Palmer, L. (2016). International students' perception of the value of U.S. higher education. *Journal of International Students, 6*(1), 153–174.

Valdez, G. (2016). U.S. higher education classroom experiences of undergraduate Chinese international students. *Journal of International Students, 5*(2), 188-200.

Wadsworth, B. C., Hecht, L. M., & Jung, E. (2008). The role of identity gaps, discrimination, and acculturation in international students' educational satisfaction in American classrooms. *Communication Education, 57*(1), 64–87.

Warters, W. (2011). *Timeline of major events in higher education dispute resolution.* http://www.campus-adr.org/CR_Services_Center/con/

Wenting, Z. (2017, June 16). Survey: Most Chinese want more education. *The China Daily*, P.3.

Wu, H., Garza, E., & Guzman, N. (2015). International students' challenge and adjustment to college. *Education Research International,* https://www.hindawi.com/journals/edri/2015/202753/

Yan, K., & Berliner, D. C. (2009). Chinese international students' academic stressors in the United States. *College Student Journal, 43*(3), 939–960.

Yan, K., & Berliner, D. C. (2013). Chinese international students' personal and sociocultural stressors in the United States. *Journal of College Student Development, 54*(1), 62–84.

Yuan, W. (2011). Academic and cultural experiences of Chinese students at an American University: A qualitative study. *Intercultural Communication Studies, 20*(1), 141–157.

Authors Bios

ZHIWEI WANG, PhD, is an Assistant Professor in the Department of Communication at Shenzhen Polytechnic, China. Email: zw44@mynsu.nova.edu

QIJUN ZHU is a graduate student in the College of Business at St. Thomas University. Email: vv962464@hotmail.com

KE DONG is a graduate student in the Institute of Education at the University College London. Email: 292338297@qq.com

© *Journal of International Students*
Volume 12, Issue 4 (2022), pp. 1019-1025
ISSN: 2162-3104 (Print), 2166-3750 (Online)
ojed.org/jis

Reimagining a Model for International Students' College Readiness and Transition

Michelle L. Trimpe
Johns Hopkins University, USA

ABSTRACT

Existing literature reveals that international students' contextual awareness of social networks, academic culture, logistics, and the host country's culture influence college readiness and transitions. As international students' experience navigating U.S. colleges and universities differs from domestic students, college readiness models should reflect the differences between the two populations. This article explores the implications of Conley's (2007) facets of college readiness model and the contextual skills and awareness element related to international students' experience transitioning to U.S. institutions. Additionally, existing literature reveals a need for higher education institutions to take greater ownership in supporting international students' college readiness and transition. By reimagining a college readiness model inclusive of international students' experiences and the responsibility of higher education institutions, educators can improve understanding of international students' experiences, enhance support, and work toward more equitable practice, both in the United States and other contexts.

Keywords: college readiness, educational responsibility, foreign students, hidden curriculum, international education, student development

---

Recent data emphasize the growth of international students applying to higher education institutions (HEIs) in the United States and other contexts. In 2020–2021, 1,075,496 international students enrolled in U.S. HEIs, nearly double from 547,867 in 2000–2001 (Institute of International Education [IIE], 2020). As international student enrollment has grown to comprise 5.5% of total U.S. college enrollment, educators increasingly focus on students' transition to college, a critical milestone influencing degree attainment (IIE, 2020; Moores & Popadiuk, 2011). While prior research has revealed important findings related to international students' college transitions, few frameworks exist to explain this phenomenon, except for Conley's (2007) facets of college readiness model focused on U.S. domestic students. Aligning with Conley's (2007) model, existing literature on college readiness additionally emphasizes the student's role in their transition, with minimal responsibility for HEIs to clarify the hidden curriculum within institutions (Wink, 2011). Using Conley's (2007) model as a starting point, this article explores elements important to a college readiness and transition model for international students. By reimagining a college readiness model inclusive of international students' experiences and the responsibility of HEIs, educators can develop a foundation to improve understanding of international students' experiences, enhance support, and work toward more equitable practice in U.S. higher education and beyond.

Conceptual Framework

College readiness models explain how students transition to new academic environments. Conley (2007) described college readiness as students' prior preparation impacting their potential to transition and succeed within a college or university. Within the facets of college readiness model depicted in Figure 1, Conley asserts that students need to have appropriate readiness levels across four areas or facets. Key cognitive strategies refer to students' ability to leverage cognitive strategies to navigate an academic environment within the model. Key content refers to students' specific subject matter knowledge necessary to succeed. Additionally, academic behaviors refer to students' non-cognitive strengths, including motivation, resilience, and time management. Finally, *contextual skills and awareness* include students' access to information and resources specific to navigating HEIs (Conley, 2007). This article will explore international students' college readiness related to contextual skills and awareness. Additionally, this article will address the role of institutions in supporting international students' transitions through demystifying the hidden curriculum found within HEIs.

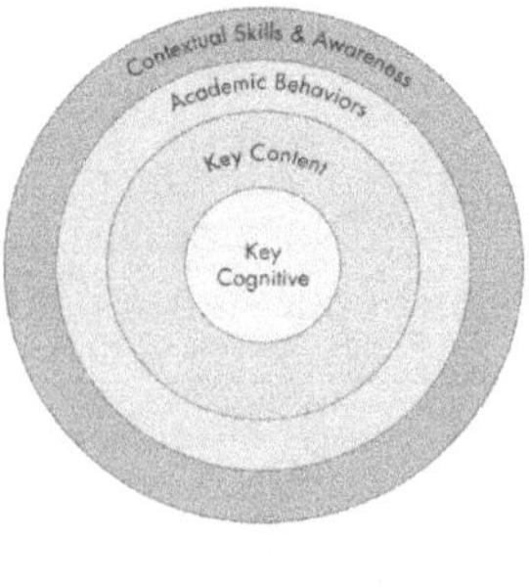

Figure 1

Conley's (2007) Facets of College Readiness Model. Adopted from *Toward a more comprehensive conception of college readiness,* ©EPIC

LITERATURE REVIEW

Literature on international students' college readiness and transition reveals that students' contextual skills and awareness impact their transition to U.S. HEIs. Additionally, international students' contextual skills and awareness impact their navigation of the institution's hidden curriculum, which includes information students need to succeed in their transition, but is not explicitly taught (Conley, 2007; Moores & Popadiuk, 2011; Wink, 2011). Within the literature, four themes related to international students' contextual awareness emerged, including knowledge of social networks, academic culture, logistics, and host country culture (Gautam et al., 2016; Luo et al., 2019; Mohamed, 2020; Moores & Popadiuk, 2011). Exploring these themes within Conley's (2007) model and the contextual skills and awareness facet further supports understanding international students' experiences transitioning to U.S. HEIs.

Social Networks

Conley's (2007) model emphasizes that students' success in navigating social relationships and communicating effectively with individuals of diverse backgrounds influences their transition to HEIs. Across the literature, international students cited that contextual awareness related to the availability of social networks impacted their transition to college. For example, Moores and Popadiuk (2011) conducted a qualitative study with seven international students from Asia, Europe, and Central America. The authors identified eight themes that positively impacted international students' transitions, including students' prior knowledge of social support networks, the presence of supportive peers, and strengths in relationship building (Moores & Popadiuk, 2011).

These findings align with Gautam et al.'s (2016) study on international student transitions in which the authors conducted qualitative interviews with six students following their transition to U.S. HEIs. The authors found that international students' experiences navigating a new social environment influenced their transition. Luo et al. (2019) additionally conducted a study with 216 international students in the United States on factors influencing their well-being. Similarly, the authors found that students' perception of domestic student social support influenced their well-being and transition (Luo et al., 2019). Ultimately, international students' contextual awareness of social support networks within the host institution impacts college readiness and experiences when transitioning to HEIs.

Academic Culture

Aligning with Conley's (2007) model, international students' contextual awareness of the institution's academic culture influences college readiness and transition. Moores and Popadiuk (2011) found that international students frequently engaged in research to support their knowledge of the host institution's academic culture, which positively impacted their transition. Moreover, students expressed that their personal development and confidence grew alongside increasing their knowledge of the academic culture, thus supporting their positive transition (Moores & Popadiuk, 2011). Similarly, Luo et al. (2019) found that students' prior contextual awareness of the academic culture impacted their transition. Consequently, international students' contextual awareness of the academic culture within the host institution and environment supports students' college readiness and transition to college.

Logistics

Logistical readiness expands Conley's (2007) college readiness framework to include an additional theme within contextual awareness that impacts international students' transitions. When transitioning to a U.S. HEI, international students frequently navigate logistics, including setting up a bank account, securing housing, and navigating transportation, often in a new cultural context (Gautam et al., 2016; Mohamed, 2020; Moores & Popadiuk, 2011). Consequently, international students may have different experiences than domestic students when navigating logistics while transitioning to college. In Mohamed (2020)'s study with 25 international students across 17 countries, students articulated that logistical considerations, such as food adjustment, influenced their transition. Furthermore, Gautam et al. (2016) found that international students cited navigating public transportation and the on-campus job application process as logistical knowledge impacting their transition. Consequently, international students' contextual awareness of logistics influences college readiness and transitions.

Host Country Culture

Conley's (2007) model does not reflect contextual awareness of the host country's culture. However, international students indicated that awareness of the host country's culture impacted their transition (Gautam et al., 2016; Mohamed, 2020). For example, in Mohamed's (2020) study on international students' perception of their transition, students' prior knowledge of the host country's culture improved their transition. Additionally, international students in Moores and Popadiuk's (2011) study cited that learning about the host culture through a guide or course improved their transition. These studies emphasize the need for institutions to recognize the role of students' contextual awareness on their experience navigating the hidden curriculum and interacting within a new cultural environment. Additionally, these findings confirm the importance of a college readiness model inclusive of international students' experiences to explore the influence of contextual awareness of the host country's culture.

DISCUSSION

International students' contextual awareness of social networks, academic culture, logistics, and the host country's culture may influence their college readiness and transitions. Aligning with Conley's (2007) framework, literature on international students' college readiness identifies contextual awareness of social networks and academic culture as influencing student transitions. However, themes including contextual awareness of logistics and the host country's culture do not appear in the framework. Consequently, Conley's (2007) model and contextual awareness facet reflect some, but not all, of the elements that international students shared as important in their college transitions.

Across the four themes, contextual awareness of the host country's culture requires additional emphasis within a college readiness model reflecting the experience of international students. Awareness of a host country's culture is critical, as cultural knowledge may impact contextual awareness of other domains, including social networks, academic culture, and logistics (Gautam et al., 2016; Mohamed, 2020; Moores & Popadiuk, 2011). However, although contextual awareness of the host country's culture emerged as a factor influencing college readiness and transitions in the literature, it is important to recognize that international students are not a monolithic group. International students' individual characteristics, cultural backgrounds, and prior experience may influence if and how important this element is in their transition. Thus, a college readiness framework for international students should balance emphasizing the potential impact of contextual awareness of the host country's culture with recognizing the role of individuals' unique experiences and backgrounds on their transition.

Regarding the model's structure itself, Conley's (2007) framework includes "contextual skills and awareness" as a facet impacting college readiness. However, upon reviewing the literature, nuances between contextual skills and contextual awareness appeared. For example, international students frequently cited that their existing skills influenced their successful transition (Moores & Popadiuk, 2011). Additionally, international students described the role of contextual awareness related to the hidden curriculum separately from their skills (Gautam et al., 2016; Mohamed, 2020; Moores & Popadiuk, 2011). As a result, a college readiness framework should emphasize the differences between contextual awareness and contextual skills.

Finally, a college readiness model reflective of international students' experiences should reflect the impact and responsibility of HEIs on students' transitions to college. Conley's (2007) framework places agency on the student, with no responsibility on HEIs. Given the hidden curriculum within colleges and universities that is challenging for both domestic and international students, institutions should take greater ownership of supporting students' transitions (Moores & Popadiuk, 2011; Wink, 2011). Although Conley (2007) called institutions to simplify students' admissions and financial aid processes to support college readiness, administrators need to do more to reveal the hidden curriculum and support international students' transition (Wink, 2011). In sum, a college readiness model for international students should reflect the role of HEIs in supporting students' contextual awareness across the four themes.

Implications for Practice and Research

Existing literature emphasizes that institutional policies, practices, and climate influence international students' transition to college (Gautam et al., 2016; Luo et al., 2019). Consequently, HEIs should consider further opportunities to improve policy and institutional structures to support international students' college readiness and transitions. For example, a more collaborative approach between campus partners who serve international students may improve the clarity and consistency of information shared with international students throughout their transition. Moreover, HEIs should proactively address challenges impacting campus climate and culture to support international students' inclusion and sense of belonging on campus, both before and after their arrival. On a smaller scale, college admissions offices within HEIs can further improve practice to support international students' transition to college. Opportunities to support students' contextual awareness of social networks, academic culture, logistics, and the host country's culture occur during all admissions cycle phases, including recruitment outreach, the application process, and predeparture support. For example, admissions offices can develop predeparture programming and conduct individualized outreach to understand international students' individual experiences and provide tailored support during their transition.

Future research should explore the role of international students' contextual awareness of social networks, academic culture, logistics, and host country culture on college readiness and transitions to college, both within U.S. HEIs and other countries around the world. Moreover, researchers may also consider if international students' college readiness and transitions differ based on country of origin and their selected host country. Additionally, future research may consider how institutional policies and practices create the hidden curriculum and influence international students' transitions to college. Together, these implications for practice and research can place more ownership on institutions at multiple levels and support theory and practice related to international students' college readiness and transitions.

REFERENCES

Conley, D. T. (2007). *Toward a more comprehensive conception of college readiness*. Educational Policy Improvement Center.

Gautam, C., Lowery, C. L., Mays, C., & Durant, D. (2016). Challenges for global learners: A qualitative study of the concerns and difficulties of international students. *Journal of International Students, 6*(2), 501–526. https://doi.org/10.32674/jis.v6i2.368

Institute of International Education. (2020). Open Doors Report. Retrieved June 19, 2021, from https://www.iie.org/Research-and-Insights/Open-Doors

Luo, Z., Wu, S., Fang, X., & Brunsting, N. C. (2019). International students' perceived language competence, domestic student support, and psychological well-being at a U.S. university. *Journal of International Students, 9*(4), 954–971. https://www.doi.org/10.32674/jis.v0i0.605

Mohamed, A. M. (2020). Challenges and adjustment of international students in Malaysia: Pre-departure factors and post-arrival strategies. *Asian Journal of Multidisciplinary Studies, 8*(10), 43–52.

Moores, L., & Popadiuk, N. (2011). Positive aspects of international student transitions: A qualitative inquiry. *Journal of College Student Development, 52*(3), 291–306. https://doi.org/10.1353/csd.2011.0040

Wink, J. (2011). *Critical pedagogy: Notes from the real world*. Pearson.

Author Bio

MICHELLE TRIMPE, MA, is a doctoral student in the School of Education at Johns Hopkins University in the United States, and the Director of International Admissions within the Office of College Admissions at the University of Chicago. Her major research interests lie in the areas of international student enrollment, student development, and international student inclusion. Email: mtrimpe@uchicago.edu

Research in Context

© *Journal of International Students*
Volume 12, Issue 4 (2022), pp. 1026-1031
ISSN: 2162-3104 (Print), 2166-3750 (Online)
ojed.org/jis

Pluralizing Mobility:
Women Pilgrims and Wandering Bodhisattvas

Kalyani Unkule
O.P. Jindal Global University, India

ABSTRACT

In higher education internationalization literature, mobility has almost exclusively been analyzed with reference to study abroad for academic and professional development purposes. The cost incurred is an impoverishment of frames to guide the exchange student, to converse with the nomad scholar, and to make sense of knowledge from the borderlands. Not only has the COVID-19 pandemic been a shock to conventional expectations about mobility, but it has also presented an opportunity to engage with the justifications, ethics, and limits of travel, anew. This essay centers experiences of women's pilgrimages in medieval Europe and wandering Asian seeker scholars in the ancient world to invite inquiry into mobility as a complex, normative paradigm and an imaginative reengagement with its multifaceted implications for learning.

Keywords: internationalization, knowledge creation, mobility, pilgrimage, spiritual learning, wandering

In higher education internationalization literature, mobility has almost exclusively been analyzed with reference to study abroad for academic and professional development purposes. The reasons for this inward-gaze are two-fold: The first stems from internationalization practice in universities that has progressively "educationalized" study abroad by relying on interuniversity partnership agreements as the chief operative modality. The second is the thrust toward empiricism in research, triggered by the vogue of evidence-based educational policymaking. Critical internationalization discourse has commendably broached questions about directions of flows and their hegemonizing and colonizing predilections, yet underlying assumptions about the place of travel in learning and self-realization remain unexamined. Mobility has been reduced to an epiphenomenon because of such approaches, and rigorous, ongoing investigation into the human motivations behind its occurrence has not, somewhat counterintuitively, been a prime concern for practitioners and researchers alike. Not only has the COVID-19 pandemic been a shock to conventional expectations about mobility, but it has also presented an opportunity to engage with the justifications, ethics, and limits of travel, anew.

In this essay, I aim to expand ideas about mobility and its relationship to learning by revisiting the wanderings of women pilgrims in medieval Europe and scholars motivated by spiritual learning journeying throughout Asia in ancient times. These instances of wandering take us back to an epoch when mobility was far less "expected" and as such the pilgrim and the seeker scholar were pathbreakers and norm setters. Wandering evokes a more open-ended quest, marked by curiosity, but intentional nonetheless. Wandering presupposes that traveling is learning, thereby alleviating the burden of educationalizing the experience further. And yet, due regard must be paid to the kind of knowledge creation that such wandering brought to fruition if we are to upend the simplistic assumptions about "experiential learning" that pervade study abroad discourse.

WOMEN UNDERTAKING PILGRIMAGE

In "Wandering Women and Holy Matrons: Women as Pilgrims in the Later Middle Ages," Craig (2009) explained that "Pilgrimage is a broad term, which, for medieval Christians, embraced a variety of activities" including "devotional prayer, short trips to local churches, long journeys to the Holy Land, and the process of human life itself" (p. 79). The parallel between pilgrimage and the journey of life spotlights openness to experience as a learning tool inherent to human nature. Pilgrimage as a "marvellously flexible kind of ritual, with meanings that suit many needs" (Craig, 2009, p. 9) caters to the varied motivations behind travel, even in educational contexts. Craig surveyed a whole range of circumstances informing medieval women's pilgrimages—seeking healing and changes of fortune, escaping difficult domestic environments, and unwillingly accompanying the husband or family among them.

As a practice shared by many cultures, pilgrimage denotes shared meaning amid diverse and dynamic ritual enactment. Focusing on women's experiences as pilgrims yields insights into how travel might disrupt established norms. Prevailing misogynistic tropes surrounding the wandering woman reflect the ways in which social norms governing mobility have dictated who is allowed to be mobile. The medieval European female pilgrim was thus a pathbreaker, and her stories are a reminder that mobility is often at odds with conformity and therefore has the potential to drive meaningful change. Her experiences represent continuity across the many ages of globalization, including the current neoliberal variant, where the right to freedom of movement is always disproportionately enjoyed by some and beyond the reach of others.

An important source of historical accounts about wandering women are the miracle stories that served as the basis for canonization. Miracle stories represent a form of knowledge production where the visitor and the local co-create a record of events, involving "at least one intermediary, usually a clergyman, who recorded her story in a collection of similar stories" (Craig, 2009, p 79). This process of co-creating an account for posterity decimates the hierarchy between the traveller, the seeker, the researcher as the subject and the destination or the host society as the "knowable" object—a familiar feature of the colonial epistemic paradigm.

For internationalization practitioners, the miracle stories open an avenue for reimagining study abroad and reorient participants from "competence" to "receptivity," from "deficit" to "pluriversality" and from "analyzing the other" to "reflecting on the self." The idea of study abroad as setting out in search of a miracle counters ethnocentric othering and hierarchizing impulses and infuses educational mobility with curiosity and intention. Craig (2009) viewed miracle stories as representing "a community's consensus memory of a series of events, which, as best it could, met the varying needs of belief, individual memory, promotion, and legal scrutiny" (p. 87), pointing to a framework of inductive social study based on firsthand observation and a reaching across the abyssal line (see Unkule, 2021) of subject object to co-create. Miracle stories exemplify "learning with" local social actors and making space for other ways of knowing (see Wane et al., 2019), testing, and validating. As a form of historical record, the stories embody a dynamic of responsibility and are testament to the values based on which legitimacy and respectability (sainthood) is ascribed in society. Upon return to the home institution, the miracle stories thus co-created during study abroad might be used to test theoretical abstractions in academic literature.

ASIAN SEEKERS IN ANCIENT TIMES

In the ancient world, many a wandering scholar from East and Southeast Asia visited India, often as part of delegations of merchants and diplomats, over time becoming the mode of transmission of Buddhist philosophy and

Hindu mythology and contributing to a civilizational consciousness. The records of these journeys vividly document how ideas intermingle with local specificities and morph as they travel. The wanderings themselves were grounded in the counterhegemonic and learner-centric beliefs that "spiritual practice of enlightened beings is not to be found in any one place or embodied in any single individual" (Shashibala, 2015, p. 243) and that "there are no shortcuts to enlightenment" (p. 237). Drawing on depictions in Indonesian and Chinese art, Shashibala described the pilgrimage of Sudhana whose teachers known as "kalyanamitras" included laypersons, monks, and divine beings. Sudhana's is an education achieved through contact with a broad cross-section of society and a two-eyed seeing that invests not only the intellect but also the spirit in learning (see Bartlett et al., 2012). As a knowledge creator, the seeker scholar's practice was to return to the homeland with Buddhist texts and translate them in the local language. The art of translation—not to be confused with uncritical assimilation and wholesale transplantation—allows the wanderer to seamlessly blend the global/universal with the local. It is thus that principles such as *"tathagathagarbha"*—meaning Buddha nature is the essence of all beings and attainable by all—become unifying ideals of a region with a formidable cultural and geo-political sprawl (see Ahn 2013). *Tathagathagarbha* serves as the axiological prior of an Asian concept of learning as knowing oneself. Frost (2011, p. 11) found this ideal still resonant in the age of European empire among Asian intellectuals who believed that "the human intercourse of the wandering Indian Ascetic and the Japanese peasant traveller, whose cultural contributions were born out of harmonious interaction with nature and their fellow man, was what made Asia distinct."

In the early twentieth century, Asian thought leaders like Rabindranath Tagore, Kakuzo Okakura, and Ananda K. Coomaraswamy drew heavily on the spread of Buddhism throughout Asia to arrive at a conception of Asiatic modes of discovery and dialogue from which to further derive grounds for solidarity. Thinkers of this generation had to contend with the fact that India, which once was the core of this ideational sphere of influence, was in their time a colony of the British empire. Their sensitivity to the mutual interplay of the local, national, and global and their express concerns about ascendence and assertion of one over the other, strike as prescient—notwithstanding the test of the essentializing proclivities of orientalism and occidentalism that their legacy has subsequently endured.

CONCLUSION

It is hoped that the above examples will inspire interest in the phenomenon of mobility and the nature of knowledge created through travel among studies concerning international students. The Asian experience of ancient cultural links has been discussed as a counterpoint to the European mission civilisatrice that presupposes superiority and universality of the western worldview. Probing deeper we find, however, that the desire to make one's own beliefs influential is corollary to the very idea of civilization and mobility, indispensable to the venture.

Conceptualization of mobility in existing research heavily relies on the ideal type of the European male explorer. The experiences of female pilgrims in medieval Europe and Asians traversing the continent on journeys of spirituality and solidarity challenge the embeddedness of a singular narrative, its selective portrayals, and its constricted conceptual and practical potential. Research on internationalization and international students has shied away from investigating the ethics of mobility. Craig (2009, p. 9) noted that by the later Middle Ages, the image of pilgrims was tarnished, and they were accused of "using a purportedly penitential practice in order to escape the tedium of home rather than bring themselves closer to God." Similarly, the spread of Buddhism across East and Southeast Asia demonstrates that while mobility yields hybridity, it could also conspire in the destruction of pre-existing local ways and practices. Within the structural parameters of neoliberal globalization, mobility is a foregone conclusion with an aspirational gleam—assumptions that bypass considerations of relationality, responsibility, and reasonable restrictions. Education and research have appropriated this myth of mobility as commonplace to further the ends of commerce and expedience, but the cost incurred is an impoverishment of frames to guide the exchange student, to converse with the nomad scholar (Lock et al., 2022), and to make sense of knowledge from the borderlands. The examples used in this article invite inquiry into mobility as a complex, normative paradigm and an imaginative reengagement with its multifaceted implications for learning.

REFERENCES

Ahn, S. D. (2013). Reception and assimilation of the 'Buddha-nature' idea in east Asian Buddhism. In A. Sharma (Ed.), *Civilizational dialogue: Asian interconnections and cross-cultural exchanges*. Manohar Books.

Bartlett, C., Marshall, M., & Marshall, A. (2012). Two-Eyed Seeing and other lessons learned within a co-learning journey of bringing together indigenous and mainstream knowledges and ways of knowing. *Journal of Environmental Studies and Sciences, 2*(4), 331–340.

Craig, L. A. (2009). *Wandering women and holy matrons: Women as pilgrims in the later middle ages*. Brill.

Frost, M. R. (2011). *That great ocean of idealism: Calcutta, the Tagore Circle and the idea of Asia, 1900-1920* (Nalanda-Sriwijaya Centre Working Paper No 3). Nalanda-Sriwijaya Centre Institute of Southeast Asian Studies.

Lock, D., Caputo, A., Igwe, P., & Hack-Polay, D. (Eds.). (2022). *Borderlands: The internationalisation of higher education teaching practices*. Springer.

Shashibala. (2015). Ten stages of enlightenment (Daśabhūmi) in the journey of Sudhana in Indonesian and Chinese art. In D. Qin & J. Yuan (Eds.), *Ancient silk trade routes: Selected works from Symposium on Cross Cultural Exchanges and Their Legacies in Asia*. World Scientific.

Unkule, K. (2021). Homogenise and rule: Empires of the mind in 21st century higher education. *Empires of the mind: (Post)colonialism and decolonizing education abroad* (No. 9). CAPA Global Education Network.

Wane, N. N., Todorova, M., & Todd, K. L. (2019). *Decolonizing the spirit in education and beyond: Resistance and solidarity*. Palgrave Macmillan.

Author Bio

KALYANI UNKULE is an Associate Professor at O.P. Jindal Global University, India. Her research complements her practice in intercultural dialogue and impact-driven projects in higher education internationalisation and spiritual learning. Email: kalyani.u7@gmail.com.

© *Journal of International Students*
Volume 12, Issue 4 (2022), pp. 1020-1025
ISSN: 2162-3104 (Print), 2166-3750 (Online)
ojed.org/jis

International Doctoral Student Experience: Compassion, Connection, Commitment, and Creativity

Jing Mao
University of Victoria, Canada

ABSTRACT

International doctoral students live with more uncertainty than most academic populations. In this essay, I attempt to provide a framework for living an international doctoral life by reflecting on my academic studies and personal living practices, drawing on van Lier's (2008) notion of learner agency. Living a rhythm of life through compassion, connection, commitment, and creativity could holistically benefit the academic studies and wellbeing of international doctoral students.

Keywords: doctoral students, learner agency, international students

I THOUGHT I COULD THRIVE, BUT I BARELY SURVIVED

I enrolled in a PhD program in the Faculty of Education at a western Canadian university in 2015. Despite some delays caused by the pandemic in my research process, I managed to complete my degree by the end of August 2021. Before studying in Canada as an international student, I was an English instructor in a Sino-U.S. cooperative college in China for almost 8 years. Being familiar with the campus environment, but I still felt challenged as an international student in a western country. Like many mature and devoted graduate students who have to navigate childcare, a part-time job, and family chores, I also faced the similar situation of navigating family responsibilities and my academic studies.

In retrospect, I found two primary challenges in the long journey of my academic studies: one was figuring out what I am truly passionate about. Although locating a research topic could be difficult for anyone at the doctoral level, it was particularly challenging for me to discover what

I love to do and how to do it with sustained efforts. Another issue that I confronted was how to communicate in a scholarly way efficiently. For a long time, I struggled with communicating my ideas clearly with my supervisor and negotiating the differences in our interactions. I also felt struck by the misunderstandings or conflicts and how to ask for help appropriately. For example, when my supervisor declined my request to meet once a month, I only chose to passively accept it and tried to manage everything on my own rather than seeking ways to communicate my concern.

Gradually, I realized the need to take initiative and to be responsible for my academic studies. In addition, I learned not to take things personally when things did not occur as I expected. While composing my dissertation, I positioned myself as a novice researcher and completed the first draft with two kids at home during the pandemic year 2020. Meanwhile, I also managed to compose some research manuscripts aiming for publication. Nevertheless, the lockdown time unexpectedly served me: I began to reflect on how to live an academic life as an international doctoral student while navigating my academic life on a daily basis. I was attracted by an ecological perspective since it does not focus on linear relations of reason and effect, but attends to the dynamic interactions between individuals and their environments. Personally, I found resonance of van Lier's (2008) notion of learner agency in the process of negotiating with uncertainties and challenges in my doctoral studies.

ENACTMENT OF LEARNER AGENCY

Learner agency is an important notion to holistically understand how learning agents interact with their surrounding environment. According to van Lier (2008), learner agency is the capacity to act "mediated by social, interactional, cultural, institutional and other contextual factors" (p. 171). Additionally, van Lier proposed three core features of learner agency: (a) initiative or self-regulation, (b) contextual interdependence, and (c) an awareness of the responsibility for one's actions vis-à-vis the environment. Inspired by van Lier's ideas, Dufva (2013) further placed the dynamic and interactive relations between agents and their environment at the central stage. According to Dufva, such a learning process is called "appropriation," which emphasizes the sociocultural feature of the learning process as participatory and communicative (p. 10).

The notion of leaner agency can be applied to understand international students' experiences. Generally, studying abroad provides both opportunity and challenges for international students. Previous studies have shown that international students exhibit learner agency in response to their academic challenges (Anderson, 2017; Haggerty, 2019; Zhang & Zhou, 2010). For instance, Haggerty's (2019) empirical studies showed most international English as an Additional Language (EAL) participants succeeded in their first-year academic program despite their initial confusion and frustration toward the unfamiliar design features of academic courses. Similarly, Anderson (2017) emphasized international graduates strategically seeking both internal and external resources to achieve their academic goals. In navigating my doctoral studies and personal life in a Canadian university, I have experienced transformational changes through an enactment of learner agency. Given the limited learning affordances due to campus lockdown during the pandemic, especially, I have learned to explore new opportunities for keeping momentum and persisting in my learning. By bringing agency in my learning process, I empower myself to interact with the supportive resources around me. From an ecological perspective, this reflection summarizes four critical factors: compassion, connection, commitment, and creativity, which featured the rhythm of my doctoral experiences. These four aspects reflect how my learner agency was enacted and strengthened by drawing both internal and external resources from the context of studying abroad.

INTERNATIONAL DOCTORAL STUDENT'S ACADEMIC LIFE

Compassion

Compassion is a gateway and inner sources for me to build a sense of learner agency. In navigating my doctoral studies and life, I gradually recognize the importance of compassion and began to cultivate it, both to others and to myself. Compassion literally means "to suffer together." Psychologist Dr. Christine Neff (2013) has categorized three components of self-compassion: being kind to yourself, understanding common humanity, and being mindful toward your experiences. For international students at graduate level, it is hard to go through the challenges, such as adapting to new academic conventions, establishing a sense of belonging, or develop a researcher identity, without being kind and caring toward themselves. In my case, in addition to my academic studies, I sometimes teach as sessional instructors or do a part-time job while taking care of my young kids; self-compassion used to be the last thing on my list. Although I tried hard to manage various roles, most of the time, I was still haunted by self-criticism, guilt and shame to claim myself as a Ph.D. student or a qualified mom. Only until I started practicing self-compassion with awareness, did I realize I could be the one that cared about myself with acceptance without judgements. When I attune to my needs, rather than ignore them, I also become more present to others' needs and concerns. In some critical occasions, such as taking Candidacy exams, I prioritized my need to focus on writing papers and invited my mom to be a helping hand. By drawing on my inner source of compassion and cultivating it in my academic and life environment, I gained a solid sense of agency.

Connection

An ecological perspective focuses on relations between people and their living environment, which is interactive and reciprocal (van Lier, 2004, 2008). As human beings, we are wired to connect with others. However, having authentic and intimate connections with others may be challenging. Although social media and technology have become popular, you can talk online all day without truly being connected. International students may also face the challenges of connecting with others both socially and academically. Investigating the socialization process of Mexican international students in a Canadian university, Zappa-Hollman and Duff (2015) found students managed their academic learning challenges by building their individual network of practice. In their study, EAL students were observed to seek support from helpful others by exercising learner agency in classrooms and beyond. As an international student who occasionally felt marginalized and isolated in my learning community, I learned to build meaningful connections with supportive people and resources in my surrounding environment. Given the constraints of campus shutdown during the COVID-19 period, I navigated my challenges of academic writing by meeting online with a tutor at the writing center in my university for a whole year, despite my responsibilities of taking care of my kids at home. During the process of interacting with helping specialists and engaging with various supportive resources, my learner agency was actualized and further strengthened.

Commitment

Making a commitment to a long-term goal and taking efficient action toward it is also an enactment of leaner agency. I practiced making and honoring my commitment to my doctoral studies by rooting my research interests in my learning community. Committing involves dedicating yourself to a cause. I would recommend careful decision-making for anyone who commits to the challenging journey of entering a PhD program. According to recent statistics, which are pre-COVID 19 numbers, almost 50% of graduate students will not complete their PhD (Cassuto & Weisbuch, 2021). Some students may withdraw from their program because of life transitions or changing goals of academic pursuits.

This is understandable and the earlier they could make informed decisions, the better for their overall life. However, if their reasons lie in the challenges, such as writing a dissertation or negotiating a relationship with your supervisor, I would suggest clarifying their commitment. A professor who impacted me a lot asked questions during class time: How do you define academia? What kind of academic do you want to be? These questions reminded me to continuously reflect on my purpose of pursuing my PhD studies. Although I kicked off my study without a clear picture in my mind, I gradually learned to integrate a goal with my lifelong commitment: Learning knowledge and skills in a way to serve people who need help. Accordingly, I exerted my learner agency by committing to a meaningful long-term goal and identifying myself as an emerging scholar who exerts efforts in academic pursuit.

Creativity

Learning agency can also be exhibited through creative interactions with a surrounding environment and engagement with various activities. Being creative is also part of human nature and a source for seeking purpose for our life. In PhD studies, being creative is a natural flow of energy, the full expression on a topic or a project you spend 4 or 5 years on. To be creative is the core for being energetic and engaged with research activity. However, being creative in academia does not mean crafting a project from the original, doing an experiment, or writing a journal article from scratch. We are finding ways to enter into a conversation by connecting with the existing literature and building on others' contributions. As such, it is a process of co-creation with expert others within a research community, in which learner agency is manifested as being creative and cooperative. If we focus too much attention on creating the original idea or project, it is easier to be trapped by perfectionism and procrastination, which may prevent us from enjoying the process and being resilient in navigating challenges, setbacks, and uncertainties. Coupled with commitment, creativity means finding meaning and purpose in both academic and personal life. If doctoral students could find ways to enjoy the process of crafting their research journey, at least trying to find some rewards on the way, such as a relief after composing a strong argument or a sense of fulfillment after submitting an article for publishing, they could creatively integrate their efforts into long-term committed goals.

CONCLUSION

In a study abroad context, my involvement with doctoral studies has been characterized by four factors: compassion, connection, commitment, and creativity. In this reflection, I called the interrelatedness of these factors the rhythm of a doctoral student's academic life since I have acted on them and modified my practices ongoingly in my daily academic studies. However, the achievement of agency is also a complex and nonlinear process involving an interplay of individual efforts, available resources, and contextual factors. This reflection encourages discussion and insights into how international doctoral students can live their academic and personal life in a holistic manner, especially now when we seem to be stuck in collective anxiety and uncertainties, and how to be ready for returning to the new normal during and after the pandemic.

REFERENCES

Anderson, T. (2017). The doctoral gaze: Foreign PhD students' internal and external academic discourse socialization. *Linguistics and Education, 37*, 1–10. https://doi.org/10.1016/j.linged.2016.12.001

Cassuto, L., & Weisbuch, R. (2021). The Ph.D. isn't working right now. *The Chronicle of Higher Education.* https://www.chronicle.com/article/the-ph-d-isnt-working-right-now?

Dufva, H. (2013). Language learning as dialogue and participation. In E. Christensen, L. Kuure, A. Mörch, & B. Lindström (Eds.), *Problem-based learning for the 21st century. New Practices and Learning Environments* (pp. 51–72). Aalborg University Press.

Haggerty, J. (2019). *Multilingual undergraduate writers' discourse socialization in a sheltered academic English Program* [Unpublished doctoral dissertation]. University of British Columbia.

Neff, K. (2013). *Self-compassion.* Hodder & Stoughton.

van Lier, L. (2004). *The ecology and semiotics of language learning: A sociocultural perspective.* Kluwer Academic.

van Lier, L. (2008). Agency in the classroom. In J. P. Lantolf, & M. E. Poehner (Eds.), *Sociocultural theory and the teaching of second languages* (pp. 163–186). London: Equinox.

Zappa-Hollman, S., & Duff, P. A. (2015). Academic English socialization through individual networks of practice. *TESOL Quarterly, 49*(2), 333-368. doi:10.1002/tesq.188

Zhang, Z., & Zhou, G. (2010). Understanding Chinese international students at a Canadian university: Perspectives, expectations, and experiences. *Comparative and International Education, 39*(3), 43–58. https://doi.org/10.5206/cie-eci.v39i3.9162

JING MAO, PhD, is a recent graduate from the University of Victoria, Canada. Her research focuses on internationalization of higher education and academic writing. Email: mao.l.jing@gmail.com

© *Journal of International Students*
Volume 12, Issue 4 (2022), pp. 1026-1034
ISSN: 2162-3104 (Print), 2166-3750 (Online)
ojed.org/jis

The Madman and Psychotherapy in the Neoliberal Academy: A Chinese Doctoral Student's Experience in the United States

Jing Zhang
West Virginia University, USA

ABSTRACT

This self-reflective essay examines my experience as a Chinese doctoral student while studying in a large research university in America. Through my self-reflection, with Foucault's analysis on power, I hope to shed some light on my experience with the neoliberal academy, which caused much discomfort and created my fragmented identities. Instead of questioning the problematic neoliberal power relations that caused my discomfort in the first place, as the *madman* of higher ed, I was directed to psychotherapy to treat my symptoms, which only caused more confusion. Through my story, I hope to reveal how social context, neoliberalism in this case, and social discourse of psychotherapy, work hand in hand in the higher education space, which have exercised intangible power and created fragmented identities among many international doctoral students in America. At the end of the article, I provide suggestions for graduate students to navigate the neoliberal academy.

Keywords: competitive individualism, higher education, international doctoral student, madness, neoliberalism, power relations, psychotherapy

---

This self-reflective article examines my experience as a Chinese doctoral student while studying for my doctoral degree in education at an American university. As a Chinese student, on many occasions during my study, I have felt that my presence has disturbed the norms of my department because of my different cultural background, which has prevented me from producing the desired "right" output.

No one has ever explicitly described to me who the most desired doctoral students are. However, the secret message passing around in my department daily led me to the understanding that to fit into the polished class of higher ed, one must constantly talk up one's ability and always be on the go seeking out new challenges and avoiding vulnerability.

THE *OTHER* STUDENT

To put my frustration in context, there was one time I made a light joke about how the assigned articles were hard to read in a meeting with my peers, mentor, and another professor. After the meeting, my mentor kindly told me in private that words like those made me look bad in front of others. I was perplexed about her comment at the time since academic reading is different from other forms of reading because it is complex and discipline-specific (Sohail, 2015). And the same thought about academic reading was shared in private among a cohort of doctoral students, but why couldn't I bring it up in the meeting?

Other similar experiences made me extremely anxious for all the classes, meetings, and gatherings I attended within my department. I was so nervous about saying the wrong words, and I had to write down things such as: "Don't ask stupid questions" or "Think carefully before you talk," as a reminder to conduct myself properly in front of my colleagues.

I started to observe those doctoral students who were the "golden children" of my department. I found that they acted and talked quite differently with and without their professors' presence. They often shared their frustrations about their work in private but presented an entirely different picture in a highly positive manner in public and often spoke in a way that highlighted their achievements compared to their peers. However, as a Chinese student, I have been taught to be modest and downplay my achievement. My communal background also plays a role in how I speak about myself—one's success is achieved as a group with the assistance of many people.

My body became a massive site of struggles because I felt the need to discard part of who I am and take up an identity that was alien to me, to be seen as intelligent as my colleagues. The official discourse on campus claims it values diversity; however, the secret message passing around in my department states otherwise. One must be "alike" to be accepted. It seemed like everyone knew the secret codes of conduct, and I was clueless.

I searched extensively on the internet for stories of similar kinds and came across many psychological terms such as "imposter syndrome" or "social anxiety disorder". Road signs about the on-campus counseling center were placed all over my university back then. Altogether, they sent out a message to me suggesting that I didn't fit in because of my mental issues and I needed help. By the end of my first year of doctoral study, I started my counseling journey.

The act of talking helped relieve some of the stress I had, but it did little with my situation at my department. I was convinced that I would be cured eventually if I kept up with my counseling sessions. Two years passed and my counselor suggested that I join a summer counseling group since students in this group all shared similar experiences. From this experience, I have learned many similar stories from a variety of colleagues across different disciplines of studies, and each of them was positioned differently in the "matrix of domination" (Angelucci, 2017) and experienced disadvantages in various ways.

I still remember a girl who was always in tears during our group counseling sessions. As the only two female members in her department, she and her professor were under tremendous pressure to bring external research funds to show they were valuable to the university. The stressful working environment also led to a troubled relationship between her and her professor. She was often verbally abused when she could not meet her professor's expectations. However, by the end of each group session, all the suggestions we could give her were to go back home and clean her room. Those moments made me start questioning these on-campus counseling services. It was clear that this student's problems were rooted in the unhealthy power dynamics in higher education. Suggesting that she should go back and clean her room does little to address the troubling power relationships within her department, which had caused all her discomforts in the first place.

I stopped going to the counseling sessions after that. Instead, I started to read extensively on the culture of higher education institutions. It seems like current research on international graduate students' experiences mainly focuses on documenting our negative perceptions and difficulties when studying at American universities. Little research has critically examined the underlying reasons for their struggles in higher education. As a result, most research focuses on socializing international students with the host culture rather than considering the inadequacies of the host societies, which should be resisted and changed rather than accommodated.

For me, the moment of enlightenment finally came when I came across Michel Foucault and his work on *Madmen* (1988). As Foucault (1988) explained in his writing, madmen were disobedient; they were physically and mentally excluded by society. The formula of exclusion was established with the lazar house (historically a place to quarantine people with leprosy); leprosy was the madman's disease, which suspended him from society. Through the segregated practices used on the lepers, the number of lazar houses decreased over time; hence the formulas of exclusion were validated, and they continued to be carried out ritually (Foucault, 1988).

Foucauldian analyses and power have found their way through modernity into the present (e.g., Ball & Olmedo, 2013; Holloway & Brass, 2018). In the neoliberal age of reason, all sorts of people who are unwilling to be structured into the economic model of competition (Metcalf, 2017) are deemed irregular and abnormal and are confined and treated in "asylums." The ancient organization and disciplining of the bodies and then souls has provided the basis for the rejection and exclusion of the madmen in the field of higher education in the modern days.

In the next section of this article, I hope to share some of my understanding of the neoliberal higher education institutions based on Foucault's work. Specifically, I hope to highlight how the neoliberal culture and the on-campus counseling center work hand in hand, exercising power and marginalizing the nonconformists. It is by no means my intention to claim that I have found a definite answer for all the problems graduate students face in higher education. Instead, I hope to contribute to the existing scholarly works on graduate students' lives by sharing some of my findings of the field.

NEOLIBERALISM AND ITS IMPACTS ON INTERNATIONAL GRADUATE STUDENTS

Neoliberal assumptions consider a college education as a personal financial investment; hence higher education is no longer viewed as a public sector, contributing to the defunding of universities across the United States (Mintz, 2021).With reduced funding from the states, colleges in the United States have been engaged in recruiting international students as a source of revenue while paying little attention to these students' desires and requirements (Alfattal, 2016). International students are defined as those who have crossed a national or territorial border for the purpose of education and are now enrolled outside their country of origin (UNESCO, 2021). The United States hosted more than 1 million international students in 2019–2020 (Moody, 2020).

Under neoliberalism, public institutions are remodeled along commercial lines as corporations, which have been encouraged to pursue entrepreneurial qualities (Peters, 2001). Accordingly, a new type of personality is needed to navigate neoliberal relations. As I mentioned earlier in this article, I used to constantly feel the need to talk up my capacity as much as possible so that I could stand out among my peers in my department. I was also expected to continually seek out risks and challenges and embrace competition to align with the entrepreneurial qualities perpetuated by the neoliberal culture (Verhaeghe, 2014). However, at home, Chinese people are often taught to be modest and keep a low profile regarding their achievements and status when interacting with others ("Proper Character and Behavior, 2013). As a result, I have had to adopt behaviors that were inauthentic for me to fit in while working for the neoliberal academy. This chronic phoniness has created much discomfort inside me and eventually has led to much psychological distress.

THE MADMAN AND PSYCHOTHERAPY IN HIGHER EDUCATION

What made things worse is that my epistemological concerns and internal conflicts are framed as madness through the official psychotherapeutic discourse that flows on American campuses. I have been in and out of the mental treatment facility provided by my university for years while studying for my doctoral degree. However, the on-campus service of psychotherapy only treats the symptom of my madness instead of helping me to understand the conditions through which my madness is formed.

As the madman (Foucault, 1988) of higher education, doctoral students' experiences are often shaped by the discourse of the neoliberal enterprise culture, such as competitiveness and efficiency, and they tend to experience more issues and are usually directed to counseling services provided on campus (Benshoff et al., 2015; Brunila, 2014). Neoliberal ideology denies the inherited interdependence of human beings, and we are taught to manage ourselves as an enterprise; we take sole responsibility for our own mental and physical well-being (Sugarman, 2015).

Psychotherapeutic technologies work as influential vehicles in the process of producing highly individualized, self-monitoring, and governing consumer citizens (Bondi, 2005). They govern and control the soul not by crushing the subjectivity of the individual but by harnessing the whole personality through the alignment of neoliberal political, social, and institutional pleasures and desires (Bondi, 2005; Brunila, 2014). As shown through the stories I shared in the first part of this article, it was through these therapeutic spaces that graduate students' oppressive experiences are replayed (Reeve, 2002), and the victimhood of international students and their status as the madman in higher education is established (McLaughlin, 2012, as cited in Brunila, 2014).

The positions of graduate students' victimhood and their status as the survivalists of higher education are closely tied to the idea that through therapeutic interventions, one can get rid of psychic and emotional chains and vulnerabilities as they eventually become self-autonomous and disciplined individuals (Brunila, 2014). In this sense, therapeutic discourse and neoliberal ideology work hand in hand to create the illusion of self-autonomy that can be realized only "in the right way" (Brunila, 2014), which is the hidden norm of academia.

As the madmen of higher ed, graduate students can only be released from these mental treatment facilities when they can imitate all the formal requirements of social existence in the neoliberal academy and display such behaviors in a congruent and orderly manner (Foucault, 1988). In other words, they must be the "alike" in order to be accepted.

Psychotherapy and counseling are often criticized for ignoring and depoliticizing questions of power relations such as racism, sexism, etc., and focusing on fostering the universality of experiences of the oppressed to build social connections with other graduate students through shared victimhood on college campuses (Benshoff et al., 2015; Brunila, 2014; Moodley, 2007). The act of speaking offers the possibility of shifting power dynamics. The words of the madmen, however, are interpreted by their counselors. In this process, the madman becomes the object of experts' analyses (Zhang, 2020). Their experiences are described with abstract diagnostic language without troubling these simple categorizations used to describe complex human experiences shaped within relations and context (Brunila, 2014; Foucault, 1988).

CONCLUSION

Through my story, I hope to shed some light on how the neoliberal systems mark certain people, which results in some graduate students' vulnerabilities while studying in the neoliberal academy (Montoya et al., 2000; Phoenix, 2006). Instead of challenging the neoliberal power relations that created the adversaries the graduate students face daily, our vulnerabilities are treated as mental disorders in different psychotherapy spaces provided on campus as a quick fix.

The concept of competitive individualism is central to the neoliberal system. There is a prevailing attitude that the individual is responsible for taking care of their own needs (Verret, 2012). To combat the individualist attitude as perpetuated by the neoliberal culture and to improve international graduate students' experience in higher education, I believe that students of communal backgrounds would benefit both emotionally and academically from more peer interactions. For example, departments within higher education could assign new graduate students more advanced peers as their mentors at the beginning of their doctoral studies, who might help them navigate their program of study and guide some of their research and teaching practices (Zhang, 2020)

Moreover, I believe that pushing for students' unions is another way for graduate students in general to resist the neoliberal agenda in higher education (Zhang, 2020). On the national level, neoliberalism has profound effects on education overall (Kuehn, 2008). Under the globalized neoliberal education movement, teachers' unions have been playing a leading role in terms of protecting public education from being destroyed by neoliberal policy (Kuehn, 2008). In the field of higher education, graduate students have fought hard to establish unions that allow them to bargain collectively related to pay and working conditions with their universities and at the same time provide them with protection against unfair or arbitrary treatment by supervisors and other detrimental situations where they currently lack power (Benderly, 2018).

Lastly, this article has its limitations. My reflection focuses primarily on the drawbacks of neoliberal education institutions in general. I wonder if I could achieve a more layered and thorough understanding of the neoliberal culture should I examine my intersectional identities more carefully (Chung et al., 2018)? For instance, as a female, first-generation Chinese college student, how does each of my identities interact with the neoliberal culture and position me differently within the higher education institution? These are some of the questions I will continue to explore as I move forward.

REFERENCES

Alfattal, E. (2016). A new conceptual model for understanding international students' college needs. *Journal of International Students, 6*(4), 920–932. https://doi.org/10.32674/jis.v6i4.326

Angelucci, A. (2017). *From theory to practice: The Intersectionality Theory as a research strategy.* https://www.urbandivercities.eu/

Ball, S. J., & Olmedo, A. (2013). Care of the self, resistance and subjectivity under neoliberal governmentalities. *Critical Studies in Education, 54*(1), 85–96. https://doi.org/10.1080/17508487.2013.740678

Benderly, B. L. (2018, June). *The push for graduate student unions signals a deep structural shift in academia.* Science. https://www.sciencemag.org/careers/2018/06/push-graduate-student-unions-signals-deep-structural-shift-academia

Benshoff, J. M., Cashwell, C. S., & Rowell, P. C. (2015). Graduate Students on Campus: Needs and Implications for College Counselors. *Journal of*

College Counseling, 18(1), 82–94. https://doi.org/10.1002/j.2161-1882.2015.00070.x

Bondi. (2005). Working the spaces of neoliberal subjectivity. *Antipode, 37*, 497–514. https://doi.org/10.1111/j.0066-4812.2005.00503.x

Brunila, K. (2014). The rise of the survival discourse in an era of therapisation and neoliberalism. *Education Inquiry, 5*(1), 24044. https://doi.org/10.3402/edui.v5.24044

Chung, A. Y., Chen, K., Jung, G., & Li, M. (2018). Thinking outside the box: The national context for educational preparation and adaptation among Chinese and Korean international students. *Research in Comparative and International Education, 13*(3), 418–438. https://doi.org/10.1177/1745499918791364

Foucault, M. (1988). *Madness & Civilization: A history of insanity in the age of reason.* Vitage Books.

Holloway, J., & Brass, J. (2018). Making accountable teachers: The terrors and pleasures of performativity. *Journal of Education Policy, 33*(3), 361–382. https://doi.org/10.1080/02680939.2017.1372636

International or internationally mobile students. (2021). UNESCO Institute of Statistics. http://uis.unesco.org/en/glossary-term/international-or-internationally-mobile-students

Kuehn, L. (2008). The education world is not flat neoliberalism's global project and teacher unions' transnational resistance. *The Global Assault on Teaching, Teachers, and Their Unions: Stories for Resistance,* 53–72. https://doi.org/10.1057/9780230611702

Metcalf, S. (2017). *Neocolonialism: The idea that swallowed the world.* The Guardian. https://www.theguardian.com/news/2017/aug/18/neoliberalism-the-idea-that-changed-the-world

Mintz, B. (2021). Neoliberalism and the crisis in higher education: The cost of ideology. *American Journal of Economics and Sociology, 80*(1), 79–112. https://doi.org/10.1111/AJES.12370

Montoya, L. J., Hardy Fanta, C., & Garcia, S. (2000). Am I a black woman or a woman who Is black? A few thoughts on the meaning of intersectionality. *PS: Political Science and Politics, 33*(1), 315–353. https://doi.org/10.1017/S1743923X07000074

Moodley, R. (2007). (Re)placing multiculturalism in counselling and psychotherapy. *British Journal of Guidance & Counselling, 35*(1), 1–22. https://doi.org/10.1080/03069880601106740

Moody, J. (2020, November 16). *Annual study: International student numbers in U.S. Drop* . U.S. News & Word Report. https://www.usnews.com/education/best-colleges/articles/annual-study-international-student-numbers-in-us-drop

Peters, M. (2001). Education, Enterprise Culture and the Entrepreneurial Self: A Foucauldian Perspective. *Journal of Educational Enquiry, 2*(2). https://ojs.unisa.edu.au/index.php/EDEQ/article/viewFile/558/428

Phoenix, A. A. (2006). Interrogating intersectionality: Productive ways of theorising multiple positioning. *Kvinder, Køn & Forskning, 2–3,* 21–30. https://doi.org/10.7146/kkf.v0i2-3.28082

Reeve, D. (2002). Oppression within the counselling room. *Counselling and Psychotherapy Research, 2*(1), 11–19. https://doi.org/10.1080/14733140212331384948

Sohail, S. (2015). Academic reading strategies used by Leeds Metropolitan University graduates: A case study. *Journal of Education and Educational Development, 2*(2), 115–133.

Sugarman, J. (2015). Neoliberalism and psychological ethics. *Journal of Theoretical and Philosophical Psychology, 35*(2), 103–116. https://doi.org/10.1037/a0038960

Verhaeghe, P. (2014). *Neoliberalism has brought out the worst in us.* The Guadian. https://www.theguardian.com/commentisfree/2014/sep/29/neoliberalism-economic-system-ethics-personality-psychopathicsthic

Verret, C. (2012, March). *Competitive individualism.* PB Works. http://neoliberalismeducation.pbworks.com/w/page/50829895/Competitive Individualism

Zhang, J. (2020). *The "other" teacher: Understanding the experience of graduate teaching assistants in neoliberal teacher education settings* [West Virginia University]. https://doi.org/https://doi.org/10.33915/etd.7725

JING ZHANG earned her EdD in curriculum and instruction, with a minor in instructional design and technology. Her primary research interests lie in neoliberalism, instructional design and technology, teacher education, diversity and equity in education, Foucault's analysis of power, and narrative analysis. Email: jnzhang1@mix.wvu.edu

© *Journal of International Students*
Volume 12, Issue 4 (2022), pp. 1047-1051
ISSN: 2162-3104 (Print), 2166-3750 (Online)
ojed.org/jis

Sustaining Indigenous Weapons to Defeat Indigenous Monsters

Amanda R. Tachine. Sustaining Indigenous Weapons to Defeat Indigenous Monsters. Teachers College Press, 2022. 209 pp. $39.95 (paperback). ISBN 9780807779965.

Reviewed by
Bhavika Sicka, Old Dominion University, USA

In *Sustaining Indigenous Weapons to Defeat Indigenous Monsters*, Amanda Tachine delineates the barriers that hinder the personal and academic goals of Navajo students, and what sources of strength and comfort these students channel to guide them toward college. Tachine stresses the importance of story-sharing and world-making, which she herself employs. She uses a story rug technique, weaving together the narratives of ten Navajo students as they journey to and through college, bringing together their experiences of belonging in educational settings and offering us lessons gleaned. The storylines serve as threads, which she connects to construct collective themes as part of a larger tapestry. In particular, she unmasks the insidious workings of White supremacy, settler colonialism, and cisheteropatriarchy in American education (pre-K through university) and society at large, forces which systematically disadvantage Indigenous and Other non-White populations in their efforts toward college attainment. Ultimately, she suggests ways to confront White privilege in education and to center and nourish the voices, perspectives, aspirations, and needs of Indigenous students.

Being Navajo herself, Tachine is intimately connected to Navajo lived experiences and effectively able to articulate her community's desires and dilemmas. She opens with the Twin Warriors tale, an origin myth following two brothers who use powerful tools and prayers to save their people from monsters (naayéé'). By beginning with Diné storytelling, she centers Diné ways of being in the world and highlights the importance of harnessing ancestral and memory knowledge. She stresses, in her introduction, that belonging, while desired and needed, is a deeply contested concept and shows how Western universities are exclusionary and elitist sites that maintain the status quo of whiteness. She recounts ways in which Black, Brown, and non-cisgender bodies are policed, harassed, or pushed out simply for existing as different in White spaces such as college campuses, dispossessions and removals that upset the victims' personhoods and fracture their ideas and practices of self-acceptance. She poses the questions: Who belongs in college settings? And who defines and sets the terms of belonging?

She defines systemic monsters as "interlocking structures of power rooted in White supremacy" (p. 7) that are disruptive to harmony, balance, and goodness. For example, while COVID-19 was detrimental to Native communities, the virus was not the real monster but rather the larger structural preconditions that exacerbated health disparities. Tachine explains that normative constructions of everyday logics and behaviors delegitimize, devalue, and decenter non-White ways of acting, thinking, and being and reinforce the nation state's control over Native bodies, lands, and minds, thereby reproducing harm and trauma. Hauntings are described as vestiges of colonialism, genocide, slavery, and disinheritance, which Navajo and more broadly Black and Brown peoples encounter on a daily basis. She offers weapons to defeat monsters, describing these as knowledges and ethical engagements rooted in Navajo place-based knowing, that sustain Navajo students and ignite their power, presence, and persistence.

This book commences with a concise foreword by Django Paris and is divided into three parts. In the first part, Tachine introduces the financial hardship monster, anchored in settler colonialism. She provides a historical overview of the devastating hardships that Native peoples underwent at the hands of settlers, and laments that even today, Native lands are occupied and controlled by a government that has failed to adequately acknowledge and provide for Native interests. Many Navajo students come from low-income livelihoods, with limited access to basic sustenance needs and preparatory educational pathways, which in turn threatens their chances of college attainment, diminishing their agency and ultimately survival. The financial hardship monster manifests as limited scholarships and high tuition and living costs for Native students and can, the author argues, be resisted if students tap into Diné values to enact the weapon of resurgence, described as generative and love-centered.

In part two, Tachine covers the deficit monster, born of assimilation to Whiteness, and recounts how conceptions of deficiency were historically employed to legitimize the civilization and taming of Natives by Europeans. She elucidates how assimilationist practices to educate Native children and youth through special programs fostered damaging perspectives of Native identity and self-worth. The deficit monster manifests as measurements, achievement gaps, and outcomes based on non-Native notions of success and is internalized as feelings of being unaccepted and unloved, responses to historical trauma. It can be overcome by deploying the weapon of continuance, grounded in matrilineal teachings of birth and life. Tachine encourages readers to revisit narratives of meritocracy and disrupt settler ideologies in curriculum.

In the third part, Tachine elaborates on the failure monster, which stems from capitalism, and informs that while meritocracy poses as a fair system, it breeds entitlement and disprivileges the disempowered. Native students are often cash-strapped and food insecure, and when grades and money determine belonging, these students internalize a fear of failing that is not an individualized problem but rather a collective burden. Tachine is critical of the neoliberal model of education, which prizes individual over communal achievement, and reminds that education can be used to strengthen Tribal sovereignty and wellbeing instead of priming students for hierarchy and maintaining White standards of belonging that are cloaked in the language of "success." To vanquish the failure monster, Tachine recommends activating reverence, which is sacredness-centered and grounded in a connection with divinity.

The final monster mentioned by Tachine is the (in)visibility monster, which recreates centuries of harm by dehumanizing and pathologizing Indigenous peoples, dimming their intellect, unsettling their connection to home(lands), and perpetuating erasure. She offers, as an example, the writing out of Indigenous peoples from the Morrill Act. She explains that Natives have been both invisibilized as unimportant and hypervisibilized as flawed, misrepresentations that serve the interests of White domination and are based on the White gaze through which "Indianness" is constructed as inferior. As a result of this manipulation, many Native students internalize inadequacy and second-guess their identities. To ward off this monster, Tachine urges actuating the sovereignty-centered weapon of refusal, a discarding of the White gaze.

Tachine wraps up by reiterating the importance of examining hegemonic frameworks and disengaging from colonial thinking. She invokes la paperson's (2017) call to theorize in the break, recommending that we detach from constructions of belonging that serve the interests of White patriarchy and capitalism. Her advocacy brings to mind Mignolo's (2020) definition of decolonial thought and action as an attempt at delinking from the epistemological foundations of colonialism. Mignolo further described a second stage, which he termed as re-existence: "a sustained effort to reorient our human communal praxis of living" (p. 106), and this is echoed by Tachine's demand for rematriation, a call to upend the heteropatriarchal underpinnings of settler colonialism. Tachine also asks that we reconceptualize belonging from our ethical engagements and land-based sensibilities, which she terms as a peoplehood sense of belonging.

Since this book employs Diné thought to interrupt colonial practices in education, it bridges theory and practice. It upholds and champions Native epistemes, a crucial endeavor considering that non-White forms of knowledge production have historically been invalidated and peripheralized in settler dominated spaces. It adds to a growing body of literature on Native student persistence and provokes us to reimagine education in ways that affirm Indigenous stories, myths, and worldviews without setting them in opposition to Western knowledges. Moreover, it celebrates hope and survivance and exemplifies what Tuck (2009) has referred to as desire-centered research. Though the lessons offered are centered toward Navajo students and their lands, languages, lifestyles, and futures, they can pave educational pathways for Black, Latinx, Asian, Pacific Islander, Arab, and Other marginalized students.

This book is a beneficial resource for educational practitioners and policymakers who wish to address equity gaps in education, particularly with respect to enhancing access of Native students, boosting Native degree attainment, and increasing Native visibility. It may, for instance, help student success personnel rethink assimilative normative notions of educational success and formulate counter-hegemonic points-of-view of success. It can equip teachers, professors, and administrators alike with the knowledge and empathy to build support structures and weaponry that enable all students to succeed, weaponry in the shape of culturally-sustaining and responsive pedagogies, curricula, policies, and practices that impede the inclination of schooling toward the social reproduction of racial and class inequalities.

REFERENCES

Mignolo, W. D. (2018). What does it mean to decolonize? In W. D. Mignolo & C. E. Walsh (Eds.), *On decoloniality: Concepts, analytics, praxis* (pp. 105–134). Duke University Press.

paperson, la. (2017). *A third university is possible.* University of Minnesota Press.

Tuck, E. (2009). Suspending damage: A letter to communities. *Harvard Educational Review, 79*(3), pp. 409–427.

Author Bio

BHAVIKA SICKA is an international student from India pursuing a PhD in Higher Education at Old Dominion University, USA. She holds a BA in English from Lady Shri Ram College, Delhi University and an MFA from Old Dominion University. She has previously worked as an Adjunct Professor of English, a Writing Specialist for TRiO Student Support Services, and an Account Planner for Google. She speaks Hindi, Bengali, and English. She is interested in advancing diversity, equity, and inclusion in higher education, both in the US and her home country of India. sickabhavika@gmail.com

© *Journal of International Students*
Volume 12, Issue 4 (2022), pp. 1052-1054
ISSN: 2162-3104 (Print), 2166-3750 (Online)
ojed.org/jis

Student Migrants and Contemporary Educational Mobilities

Waters, J & Brooks, R. (2021). *Student Migrants and Contemporary Educational Mobilities*, Palgrave Macmillan. ISBN 978-3-030-78295-5 (eBook). 264 pp., $109.

Reviewed by
Ling Gao LeBeau, Syracuse University (USA)

Student Migrants and Contemporary Educational Mobilities offers a timely, holistic, and engaging contribution to the field of international higher education with focus on the status and trend of international student mobility (ISM) and various issues related to international students in the global context. International educators who work with international students closely as well as scholars with a research focus on international student wellbeing and success will find this book extremely informative and insightful.

This book reflects the profound geographic changes of ISM as well as its social-economic diversification in the past decade. Waters and Brooks argue that the ISM flow has shifted from students pursuing education in the traditional regions (i.e., countries and institutions in the Global North) to the Global South led by Asia: China, Hong Kong, Malaysia, and Singapore. Students from middle-class families have increased substantially as a proportion of this group as compared to the conventional ISM model (i.e., students from privileged and wealthy families). These fundamental changes have brought many new perspectives to the field of ISM and internationalization of higher education, such as: 1) implications of international student diversification; 2) social characteristics of international student learning; and 3) ethics in relations to ISM.

Waters and Brooks argue that the conventional trend of students uniformly seeking education in the "Anglophone West" with the predefined conceptual framework has diverged in the past decade. The depictions of ISM as a Global South to Global North or East to West phenomenon cannot capture the nature and complexity of ISM anymore. Waters and Brooks utilize China as an example and illustrate China as a newly emerged destination for international students, with over a 400 percent increase from 1999 to 2008 and continuous increase after that point. Most international students who study in China are from less affluent backgrounds and show little interest in permanent relocation as traditionally framed in ISM literature a decade ago. They study in China, the authors argue, because of scholarships offered by the Chinese government, though that government lacks interest in financial gain as many conventional international student destinations do. For the Chinese government, the current motivation of attracting international students lies in the expansion of soft power. Another example Waters and Brooks discuss is the Erasmus program, which increases the prevalence of middle-class students pursuing education across national borders in popular EU destination countries.

The socio-economic diversification of international students implies a potential change in the role ISM plays in "state-building" (via the granting of residency and citizenship), emergence of new education system stratification, and the differential value of international education. For example, China's soft-power competitive strategies to award scholarships to international students; tension between international students and locals in Singapore; international students as considered by immigration policy and Brexit debate in U.K.; and the education abroad opportunities pursued by less economically privileged students. Waters and Brooks then continue to discuss two new perspectives in ISM related to international students' academic learning and ethical concerns that ISM may bring. They argue that divisions between domestic and international students still exist in many education abroad destinations. Cultural hegemony continues to prevail, and the notion of engaged and inclusive pedagogy remains minimumally explored. International students are more exposed to racism and discrimination compared to domestic students. For example, international students with strong accents in English or less proficient English may be perceived as less intelligent.

Waters and Brooks present a timely critical review of the mobility flow changes and its implications for society, politics, and economy, three major rationales of international education. The analysis in chapter 2 to 5 is holistic and comprehensive with both cases and data. Chapter 6,

Learning and Classroom Experiences, stands out among existing ISM literatures for its unique and insightful perspective on international student learning: this is an area that has been overlooked by the existing international education literature but is essential to student success. Chapter 7, Ethics and Student Mobility is comparatively less convincing. It would have been helpful to narrow down its discussion topics and focus on one to two issues.

In Chapter 2, Waters and Brooks articulate the emerging and different ISM patterns, for example, multiplied and decentred destinations and non-traditional students. What is most interesting in this chapter is that Water and Brooks clarify cities' role in ISM. For example, a university located in rural area may establish a site in an urban area to attract international students. What is missing in this chapter is that some universities from the Global North are establishing education sites in the Global South to offer education mostly to local learners. In Chapter 6, Waters and Brooks raise a critical topic related to international students' learning. The existing scholarly work and initiatives in international education rarely discuss how to support the academic success of international students. This is an area overlooked by many higher education institutions and professional organizations in the world. As Waters and Brooks point out, a large body of relevant literature focus on students from East Asian countries studying in Anglophone nations of the Global North, while ignoring the new geographies of student mobility. The authors spearhead a study that needs to examine how international students (other than the traditional student population being studied) learn in their respective destinations, for example, how American students study in Europe, how African students study in China, and others.

Overall, this book offers a timely and unique analysis of international student mobility and issues related to international students from the global lenses. It allows international educators and international education researchers to have a deeper understanding of strategies and initiatives associated with international students.

Author Bio

LING GAO LEBEAU is Associate Director of International Student Success at Syracuse University. LeBeau is a scholar practitioner in the field of international higher education with years of experiences in teaching, research, and administration. LeBeau holds a PhD in Higher Education and MS in Language Education from Indiana University Bloomington. E-mail: lglebeau@syr.edu

www.ingramcontent.com/pod-product-compliance
Lightning Source LLC
Chambersburg PA
CBHW051553030726
47592CB00001B/267